TILL ONE DAY THE SUN SHALL SHINE
MORE BRIGHTLY

UNDER DISCUSSION
Marilyn Hacker and Kazim Ali, General Editors
Donald Hall, Founding Editor

Volumes in the Under Discussion series collect reviews and essays about individual poets. The series is concerned with contemporary American and English poets about whom the consensus has not yet been formed and the final vote has not been taken. Titles in the series include:

Till One Day the Sun Shall Shine More Brightly

The Poetry and Prose of Donald Revell

Derek Pollard, Editor

UNIVERSITY OF MICHIGAN PRESS

Ann Arbor

Published in the United States of America by
the University of Michigan Press
Manufactured in the United States of America
Printed on acid-free paper

First published January 2020

A CIP catalog record for this book is available from the British Library.
ISBN 978-0-472-03769-8 (paper : alk. paper)
ISBN 978-0-472-12658-3 (ebook)

Contents

Part 2: Reviews, Interviews, and Online Texts

Digital materials related to this title can be found on the Fulcrum platform
via the following citable URL: https://doi.org/10.3998/mpub.11449954

Acknowledgments

I would like to thank the editors, Kazim Ali, Susan Cronin, and Marcia LaBrenz especially, and the production staff at the University of Michigan Press for helping to bring this book into print. I am grateful for the trust everyone placed in the project and the careful stewardship it received. I would also like to thank each of the contributors for providing such thoughtful, provocative insights into Donald Revell's writing, which continues to attend to the world so compellingly and with such compassion. I would be remiss were I not to mention the role that Peter Covino in particular played, as he and I began discussing this project while we were still in graduate school together at the University of Utah—just a few years back now. And, of course, my sincerest thanks go to my family, old and new, as well as to the many friends and colleagues who had wanted to contribute to this anthology but who were unable to do so. I look forward to reading your essays when they come into print.

Portions of two chapters have been previously published and appear here in substantially revised form. Permission to reprint is gratefully acknowledged.

"'The Real Sun No One's Ever Seen': New Blakean Gnosticism in the Poetry of Donald Revell" by Geoffrey Babbitt was originally published in *The California Journal of Poetics*, issue 2 (2016).

"On Donald Revell" by Dan Beachy-Quick was originally published as a blog post on the Alice James Books website as part of their month-long celebration of Donald Revell's work in September 2015.

"Reclamations of the Marvelous" by Bruce Bond was originally published in *Kenyon Review*, vol. 39, issue 3 (May/June 2017).

"Donald Revell: 'The Northeast Corridor'" by Stephanie Burt appears on the Poetry Foundation website as part of their Learning Lab program: https://www.poetryfoundation.org/resources/learning/core-poems/detail/49685#guide

"Recuperating the Brilliant Picture: Language as Transubstantiation in Donald Revell's Later Poems" by Kathryn Cowles was originally published in *Interim: A Journal of Poetry & Poetics,* vol. 34, issue 2 (2017).

"The ply of spirits on bodies": Diaspora and Metamorphosis in Donald Revell's "Short Fantasia" by Mark Irwin was originally published in *Interim: A Journal of Poetry & Poetics,* vol. 34 issue 3 (2017).

"Songs without Words by Paul Verlaine, Translated by Donald Revell" by Dan Disney was originally published on the *Verse* website on June 21, 2014.

"Tantivy by Donald Revell" by Andrew Haley was originally published on the *Sugar House Review* website on December 26, 2013.

"'At My Soul's Edge': Donald Revell's *My Mojave"* by Nathan Hauke was originally published in *Electronic Poetry Review,* issue 7 (2005).

"'Shadows of Leaves': Donald Revell" by Richie Hofmann was originally published as a blog post on the Alice James Books website as part of their month-long celebration of Donald Revell's work in September 2015.

"Donald Revell: An Interview by Tod Marshall" by Tod Marshall was originally published in *American Poetry Review,* vol. 25, issue 4 (July/August 1996).

"Review: Forrest Gander's *Science and Steepleflower* and Donald Revell's *There Are Three"* by Tod Marshall was originally published on the *Boston Review* website on February 1, 1999.

"Celebrating Presence: Recasting the Poetry of Loss" by Tod Marshall was originally published on the *Boston Review* website on February 1, 2003.

"*Alcools: Poems by Guillaume Apollinaire,* Translated by Donald Revell" by Marjorie Perloff was originally published in *Boston Review,* vol. 21, issue 1 (February/March 1996).

"Houses of Poetry after Ashbery: The Poetry of Ann Lauterbach and Donald Revell" by Susan M. Schultz was originally published in *Virginia Quarterly Review,* vol. 67, issue 2 (Spring 1991).

"An Interview with Poet Donald Revell" by Nick Twemlow was originally published on the *Poets & Writers* website on April 5, 2002.

"*The Illuminations* by Arthur Rimbaud, Translated by Donald Revell" by Eric Weinstein was originally published in *Prick of the Spindle,* vol. 3, issue 3 (2009).

DEREK POLLARD

Introduction

As a writer who himself subscribes to Donald Revell's poetics of radical attention, I find—increasingly among the chaos of our daily lives—that each of us is writing toward a silence. For some, as with Laozi, Mina Loy, John Cage, Henry David Thoreau at his wildest, which is to say at his best, that silence is both the goal and the goal's accomplishment—Arcady, to recall the title of one of Revell's collections of poems. As the following essays, interviews, and reviews attest, Revell belongs among that company of writers who have pursued silence in their writing as an act of faith and who have given courage to the rest of us to write and to read with similar grace, urgency, and tenderness. My sincere hope is that the texts gathered here—which, out of a sense of deference, I choose to let speak for themselves—invite an even broader, more wide-ranging conversation about the significance of his poetry, translations, and criticism on "the poetic tradition" in all its contemporary forms.

Palm Beach Gardens, FL
2019

PART I

Essays

MARY ANN SAMYN

Gladness
On the Poetry of Donald Revell

In times of trouble, poetry proves its beauty *is* its practicality. That's when I've turned to Donald Revell's work for sustenance and renewal. Revell's is a striking spiritual vision, and a beautiful one at that, leaving out, it seems, the suffering. Eliding it. The focus, rather, is on redemption: a true Easter story, rare in our culture and in our poetry. But needed, sorely, to bring us to our senses.

How we got here is the focus of much poetry, beginning as it often does with Problems. Commonly ending there, too. In Revell's poems, however, the focus is on the *here*, and on the *here and now*: that is, the kingdom of heaven within. Why wait?

So, joy and wonder are the landscape we're in—*look*—the speaker having finally caught up to the truth: "I have a soul, and it's no problem / To feel it slipping away from me . . . Heaven's handy. . . ."[1]

What sorrow there is is beautiful, too, and Revell expresses compassion for it: there's nothing wrong, but it is sweetly human to think otherwise:

Overhead, a long-legged bird
Circles my sweet house. I feel
He is waiting for me to join him,
To find real wings and rise out of my own mind
Into his air.
What would I find there?
Portals and invisible heavy traffic . . .
My mother as a baby, my father a cowboy,
My sister, finally, after so much heartbreak,
A girl.
The body travels inside the soul.
The body's a passenger.
This has nothing to do with Jesus
Though he is right here beside me.
He is unhurt.[2]

A mature spiritual vision is hard to come by. A mature poetry also. In Revell's work, both are present and disarmingly direct: "Birds . . . / Are physicians to us."[3] All scaffolding—reliance on story or subject matter, persona, inherited verse forms, arcane diction—has been taken down and put away. Knowledge is worn lightly and lit from within. Milton, Shelley, Tennyson, O'Hara; father and mother and sister; and "my Jesus" and Christ are among Revell's companions back into childhood, and earlier, and onward to the afterlife, available just now.

Indeed, "The Afterlife" is one aptly named section of *Tantivy*. "Here is a happiness with nothing underneath,"[4] Revell writes, that light, again, come to bear:

> I did not think the end would fall in the middle way
> But I am happy now
> That now is the hour
> Even burrowing animals become creatures of the air[5]

There is a good humor here, a rare willingness. These poems, unlike so many, are not propelled by fear or dismay, but by faith, and are not set at a safely ironic distance from experience but up close and in love with it.

In *Invisible Green: Selected Prose*, Revell notes that "I write poems because I love the sounds of poems. My faith rests there . . . . In poetry, the particular is good health to me, and saneness."[6] Indeed, what draws me to Revell's poems is their deep sanity. Gladness is the true order of things, a natural poetics: "I believe in Heaven / Simply because there must be someone at one / O'clock in the morning who answers the phone."[7]

Part of the particular beauty of poetry is its lineation—this one thing said this one way—and, by extension, its faith in lineation: that is, in the power of the line to deliver. Lineation and syntax are challenging to discuss; they are the movement of a mind. We may follow only so far. Into the origins of thought, we are not admitted, the trail extending off the page, into the air. Or, rather, arriving from there, right on time. Timeliness—and timelessness—that's the feeling of authority: seemingly effortless. Such is the case in Revell's work. Moves that might register as affectation in another poet's writing—punctuation or the lack thereof, for instance, or syntactical speed mixed with moments of leisurely consideration—simply don't here. These things come and go, as needed; we're being talked to directly. There's no cause for fuss, and thus, no fuss. Nothing gets in the way. Indeed, Revell's work is about *not getting in the way*. I was taken aback—

—and now I go and come back. That's how it is, isn't it, with strong work? The intensity on the page requires the same intensity off, and time away feels essential. Very often, I read a poem and jump up; I want to experience for myself what Revell has just pointed toward: "Vision runs up a hill called Vision."[7] Yes! That's what's happening, now I see, in my yard: sparrows in the pussy willow, a neighbor cat among the fallen branches of the sassafras. There's tea in those leaves. A whole history, or future, by which I mean my present. I've got to go. Now. Revell will, I know, understand.

Notes

1. Donald Revell, "Tools," *The Bitter Withy*, 3.
2. Revell, "Long-legged Bird," *The Bitter Withy*, 57–58.
3. Revell, "Birds small enough . . . ," *Tantivy*, 37.
4. Revell, "Made Mention," *Tantivy*, 57.
5. Revell, "Last Man," *Tantivy*, 69.
6. Revell, *Invisible Green*, 114.
7. Revell, "The Library," *Drought-Adapted Vine*, 33.
8. Revell, "Foxglove," *Drought-Adapted Vine*, 75.

Works Cited

Revell, Donald. *The Bitter Withy.* Alice James, 2009.
Revell, Donald. *Invisible Green: Selected Prose.* Omnidawn, 2005.
Revell, Donald. *Tantivy.* Alice James, 2012.

NORMAN FINKELSTEIN

With Donald Revell in Binghamton, 1973–75

Lawrence

We met in a class on D. H. Lawrence. Don sat a row or two to my right, closer to the front, and he made his presence known in every respect. His engagement with the subject was obvious. Lawrence's romantic vision of modernity; his iconoclasm; the churning, contradictory passions on the surface of his language; the dark mysticism of its depths—all of it was reflected in Don's responses to the prof's questions. He spoke up frequently, and what he had to say was thoughtful, witty, and invested with a sense of urgency, a sense that these works counted. As a matter of fact, he spoke about as often, and with as palpable a feeling of commitment, as I did. *Who is this guy?* I wondered, not without a touch of edgy competition. By then, English was at the center of my life, and nothing meant more to me than the discovery, author by author, of what I would eventually be taught to call the canon. Demonstrating how serious I was about it to my teachers and fellow English majors meant a lot, too, which is to say I was rather full of myself. Lawrence loomed large. I wanted, at age nineteen, to take him in. And so, apparently, did this somewhat intimidating person to my right, who was eyeballing me every bit as much as I was eyeballing him.

In the fall semester of 1973, Donald George Revell stood out on the campus of SUNY-Binghamton. Broad shouldered, well over six feet tall, he had straight brown hair about halfway down his back and a scruffy beard growing on a broad face that was still just passing out of adolescence. His smile was a bit wolfish, and it appeared often, though it had a guarded quality and would sometimes fade into an expression of dissatisfied determination that signified rebellious intellectual challenge. It was an expression with which I became very familiar. He dressed in the jeans and plaid flannel shirts that were more or less the undergraduate uniform, looking a bit like Neil Young (Don was a fan). On cold Binghamton days, he wore an old postman's coat of light blue wool, and he carried a very worn messenger bag, in which could be found his notebook and any of a number of random volumes of poetry, which, if you were to open them, were marked in his rather florid script. When it came to the arts—because what, after all, was more important?—he was indeed a messenger, assertive, even aggressively evangelical, come to set you straight.

In the Lawrence class, it took us a few weeks to start a conversation. Not accidentally, it was dissatisfaction that finally got us talking—dissatisfaction with the prof, whose view of Lawrence was perhaps a little too "hallucinogenic" for our shared tastes. I wish I could recall the text under discussion on the day that we turned to each other to express our mutual disgruntlement. Perhaps it was *The Man Who Died*, but that would be all too symbolic—death, resurrection, the union of old and new mythoi, the renewal, both erotic and cosmic, of the imagination. It was Lawrence and writers like him whom we felt were opening a path for us, fraught with risk and impossible promises of vision. Think of "Song of a Man Who Has Come Through": "Not I, not I, but the wind that blows through me! / A fine wind is blowing the new direction of Time."[1]

Reading

How long did it take for us to admit that we wrote poetry? I think we must have intuited it from the start. Soon we started exchanging poems. We sat in the snack bar of the Student Center, reading each other's work. Don had an apartment farther from campus, in the rundown suburb of Endicott. I went to dinner at his place; he served Cornish hens stuffed with rice. He was a good cook, proud of what he could do. The talk was almost always of poetry. Even when we were discussing music, film, or painting, we were ultimately seeking to find common ground, an aesthetic understanding, a shared poetic.

Don's youthful work was rhapsodic. He loved rhyme, strong but loose rhythms (lots of dactyls and anapests), the direct power of a refrain. His Christianity was always there, troubling my Jewish skepticism; one felt it even when it was not overt—a desire to adore. Women were worshipful. Girlfriends past and present floated through the poems, and Eros cast a dark, ambiguous veil over his imagery. The shadowed rooftops of the Bronx figured frequently.

Car radios crooned broken prayers. Unlike me, he sought to transfigure common life. My work was more abstract; history and myth provided graspable moments, but there was an awful lot of cosmic blur. Don had his share, too.

Ironically, I was starting to read in a modernist tradition that warned against this in no uncertain terms. When I was a high school senior, I had won a citywide poetry prize. I took my Brentano's gift certificate and bought Pound's *Personae*. My freshman year at Binghamton, I won the alumni prize in the same competition. Off to Brentano's I went again to purchase *The Cantos*. I had already read Eliot, or at least "Prufrock," in high school. But Pound was the poet from whom I wanted to learn, even if I wasn't quite getting the lessons right. Yeats, too, whose crucial transformation into a more hardened modernist didn't fully register on me either. I was too dreamy, too much a Romantic. Poetry equated to prophetic trance, and though later I would understand its shamanic roots, at this early stage, my poems were altogether too subjective, too full of yearning for the patent sublimation of the absolute. Don, who had a taste for the absolute, too, was immensely supportive. We were not critical readers of each other's work. We felt we needed a loyal ally, and that is what we became for each other.

I don't think that Don had shared his poems with many other people before we met. In high school, he had been in a band, to which he devoted a great deal of his creative energy; I had worked on the literary magazine, edited the yearbook, and wrote lyrics for the competitive class musicals with my friend Lewis, a talented pianist and composer. It was one of my English teachers who had submitted my poems to that contest, completely unbeknownst to me. At Binghamton, there were a number of tracks in the English major; one could concentrate on literature or creative writing. Don opted only for literature; I did both, which meant a series of workshops in which my work was discussed regularly. I got used to the critical give-and-take of the workshop method. Ironically, it was Don who would teach mainly in various creative writing programs, while I, through my long career at Xavier University, would teach mostly literature courses, with only the occasional poetry workshop.

My instructor in the first of the workshops at Binghamton, which I took as a sophomore, was Henry Weinfield. Six years older than me, Henry was an MA student, brilliant and opinionated. His work had appeared in *Poetry*, and he had already published a beautiful chapbook, *The Carnival Cantata*. He looked at my early efforts and, despite all the warts, dramatically declared me to be a real poet. After a good deal of turmoil and ferment, Henry would eventually finish his doctorate at the CUNY Graduate Center under Allen Mandelbaum and go on to an extraordinary career as a poet, scholar, and translator, teaching in the Program of Liberal Studies at Notre Dame.

In those days, if Don was my brother in poetry, Henry was a youthful but stern mentor. Grounded in the English poetic tradition, Henry also was a serious reader of philosophy. Soon after we met, he immersed himself in Hegel and Marxist theory and became involved with the Labor Committee, from which, fortunately, he would disentangle himself, finish his doctorate, and secure his position at Notre Dame. Though much of his work has been on canonical English poets, throughout the years he has remained a keen, sometimes impatient critic of contemporary poetry, reading the avant-garde decisively against the grain. He encouraged me to study George Oppen and William Bronk, both of whom he knew personally, and would eventually take me to meet Bronk at his big old house in Hudson Falls. Through all the vicissitudes in our lives, Henry and I kept up an intense correspondence, seeing each other when we could, gradually becoming very close friends. And like Don, Henry and I remain close friends to this day.[2]

In the workshop I took with Henry, he assigned Donald Allen's *The New American Poetry*, and as for so many other poets of my generation, it proved to be a book that changed my life. It was in that anthology that I learned of the Black Mountain poets, the San Francisco Renaissance, the New York School, and the Beats. The section on poetics was a revelation. In Don's generous introduction to my volume of essays *Lyrical Interference* (the title comes from Olson's essay "Projective Verse"), he writes how he read to me from Lowell's *Lord Weary's Castle* and I responded with Olson's "The Distances." True enough. Indeed, Don then produced a number of poems structured similarly to some of Olson's medium length, ode-like poems. In retrospect, however, I think Hart Crane, to whom he first introduced me, and Dylan Thomas, with whom I was already familiar, were Don's strongest early influences, filtered, as it were, through what was then a Beat sensibility. Rimbaud was crucial, too, and it came as no surprise to me, many years later, when Don told me he was translating him. Before long, he was reading Ashbery (he gave me *The Double Dream of Spring* for my birthday) and was absorbing Ashbery's complicated understanding of temporal and linguistic flux. He came to understand how in Ashbery, syntax can also open the individual moment, affectively and perceptually, in response to particular psychic pressures. Learning about the power of the momentary—concrete, specific, but still open to visionary insight—was crucial to Don's early development. It got refined, I think, through his deep reading of William Carlos Williams, and then Williams's great disciple, Robert Creeley, who would become Don's teacher and friend in Buffalo.

This was still ahead. Yet, I think many of the seeds were already planted as we lounged in my room, in the apartment I shared with three science majors (two pre-meds, one chemistry), pulling books off the shelf and saying, in effect, "wait, listen to *this*." And as the evening grew late, there was always that moment when we put the old Caedmon LP on the turntable, and in utter, reverential stillness, listened to Pound reading "Exile's Letter": "What is the use of talking, and there is no end of talking, / There is no end of things in the heart."[3] How many birthday gifts and Christmas cards I would receive from him over the years, with those lines inscribed?

Foosball

We would meet most days for lunch at the campus pub. Theorists of gender would call the Harpur College pub at lunchtime a homosocial space, but I certainly had no awareness of such phenomena back then. Don was already a regular when I met him; he hung out with a group of guys (David Litwak, David Blaiwas, Eric Solomon, Myron DeWitt), drinking beer (Molson or Labatt usually), eating chicken wings, and playing foosball on a worn but solid table in the center of the room. It was a competitive, testosterone-charged atmosphere, and though Don ruled, everyone wanted a piece of him. Blaiwas would challenge him repeatedly, and it could get ugly. They were both very aggressive, almost always keeping the left hand on the goalie while moving the right rapidly among the other three rows of men. We played singles or doubles for beers or quarters. I was not a talented player. When Don and I teamed up, I usually played defense. "Just be a block of wood" he growled, as my goalie let another shot through. But sometimes, the tables would turn. Even the goalie can be played offensively, and there was nothing more satisfying than the moment when the goalie blocked a shot and slammed the ball across the whole length of the table for a score. The thunk of the ball going at top speed and hitting the goal was always a rush. Considering that none of us, as far as I know, did anything very athletic, foosball was probably the most exercise, other than walking across campus, that any of us ever got.

It was also a necessary release. We were highly motivated students, but if you were an English major, or in any of the other humanities, you didn't let it show. Don and I would talk about writing papers for our courses. Most of them did not require much research, and I hardly spent any time in the library. Don would formulate a thesis, and that, of course, was the most difficult aspect of the work. He called writing the rest of the paper—that is, proving the thesis, providing examples, analyzing the text—"taking out the trash." It was a coarse expression, but I think it indicated a certain *sprezzatura* in the face of conventional critical formulations—despite the fact that as undergraduates we were only just learning how those formulations were meant to work. For Don, it was like setting up a shot in foosball. The idea would be dribbled, passed between the lines, then and only then shot forward toward its conclusion. When I think of how his prose has developed in works like *Invisible Green*, *The Art of Attention*, and most recently, *Essay*, I realize how artfully oblique his writing about poetry can be. He bends literary concepts, demonstrating a verbal dexterity equivalent to the sudden flip of the wrist, the unexpected spin. And scores.

William Bysshe Stein

In the fall semester of 1974, at the start of our senior year, Don took a nineteenth-century American literature course with Professor William Bysshe Stein. I can say with confidence that Don's meeting and studying with Professor Stein had a profound, lifelong effect upon him. It shaped his thinking about literature and language, it matured his understanding of critical discourse and the power of philological scholarship, and it enriched his affinities to a range of major authors centered in the canon of the American transcendentalists but extending historically back to the English Renaissance and forward into modernism. Stein was the author of numerous magisterial essays on Melville and Thoreau, but he wrote with equal authority on figures from a number of other periods—Ben Jonson, Laurence Sterne, Henry James, Samuel Beckett. But just as importantly, Stein gave Don an advocate, a mentor, and a literary father-figure at a crucial time in his personal development. In the academic world that Don was about to enter, Stein proved generous and protective. He was, inevitably, a foil to Don's own father, who was, as Don so lovingly and frankly reveals in his amazing essay "The Moving Sidewalk," an illiterate small-time criminal in The Bronx enclave where the Revell family lived.[4] Yet Stein, to whom Don dedicated *From the Abandoned Cities*, had a kind of boldness and aggressiveness, if not the brute power, of an intellectual outsider who had little patience for gentility, academic or otherwise.

I sensed Stein's importance to Don quickly, because Don's response to the class he was taking with him was completely unprecedented. In other instances, Don would speak about both the instructor and the material, however much he might have liked them, with an attitude that amounted to "sure, of course." Not so now. Now it was "What Melville is doing in *The Confidence Man* is . . ." or "In *Walden*, when Thoreau says that he. . . ." Stein's teaching was a provocation, and as Don's guide to the American Renaissance, to Thoreau in particular, Stein deepened Don's understanding of literature's spiritual capacities, while at the same time demonstrating to him the elusive, even deceptive, powers of language when one engages in metaphysical speculation. For years, Stein had been studying and writing about the Hindu, specifically the Yogic, sources of Thoreau's work. For Stein, I believe, language, when used skillfully, enters into the endless weaving and unweaving of Maya. The writer lacking such skill is unmade by illusion, but the great authors, such as Melville and Thoreau, become the ultimate confidence men; and their literary snares can charm and enlighten us, though they may endlessly perplex us as well.

I had the honor of learning all this myself when Don and I took Stein's senior seminar the following semester. The course consisted of only two works: *Tristram Shandy* and *Moby-Dick*. I had actually not seen Stein up until the moment he walked into the classroom, and I was wondering what to expect. (Don had imitated his sardonic, whiplash speech but had given me no indication of his appearance.) The elderly man who walked into the classroom had a bright, sanguine complexion. He was bald, with a fringe of white hair, slightly stooped, with big glasses that enlarged his eyes, which would dart about the room or settle into one of the many texts he would lay before him or have piled up nearby. These texts were carried dutifully by Stein's graduate assistant, Mr. Pinker, who also lit the professor's Pall Malls (I have a memory of him using a cigarette holder, but maybe that's a fantasy). Stein had no problem putting students on the spot. He interrogated us constantly, and when dissatisfied with a shallow response, he would open one of the two huge volumes of Farmer's and Henley's *Historical Dictionary of Slang*, which Mr. Pinker would schlep to every class session. "Do you know what that word *really* means?" Stein would ask his chosen victim—and proceed to prove yet again how Sterne's use of slang not only resulted in filthy word play but demonstrated the endlessly polysemous nature of literary genius, which in turn unveiled the illusory nature of reality, the false binaries through which we vainly seek to structure and stabilize our inescapably limited worldviews.

By the time I was in graduate school and studying literary theory, it occurred to me how similar Stein's understanding of language was to that of Derrida and deconstruction—the linguistic indeterminacy; the sliding along chains of signifiers; the play and polysemy that underpins and undercuts any set discourse; and above all else, the incipient collapse of any binary opposition due to the inherently unstable nature of words. I'm not aware of whether Stein was reading French theory or its American derivatives, but I suspect not. He displayed something of an allergy to any forms of abstract discourse, and anything that smacked of academic trendiness would probably have evoked his disdain. Rather, I think that Stein came to his own critical vision following the implications of his primary sources, and if that vision was in some respects congruent to that of deconstruction, given its literary and philosophical roots, this should come as no surprise.

Consider the episode in *Moby-Dick* when the heads of a sperm whale and a right whale are lashed to either side of the *Pequod*, an episode to which Don often referred. The deceptive power of binary thinking has rarely been presented with greater subtly. Here is Ishmael:

Can you catch the expression of the Sperm Whale's there? It is the same he died with, only some of the longer wrinkles in the forehead seem now faded away. I think his broad brow to be full of a prairie-like placidity, born of a speculative indifference as to death. But mark the other head's expression. See that amazing lower lip, pressed by accident against the vessel's side, so as firmly to embrace the jaw. Does not this whole head seem to speak of an enormous practical resolution in facing death? This Right

Whale I take to have been a Stoic; the Sperm Whale, a Platonian, who might have taken up Spinoza in his later years.[5]

Shortly thereafter, when Tashtego falls into the sperm whale's head while drawing forth the spermaceti and must be rescued by Queequeg, who pulls him out of the head like a midwife, in a bizarre parody of birth, Ishmael observes:

> Now, had Tashtego perished in that head, it had been a very precious perishing; smothered in the very whitest and daintiest of fragrant spermaceti; coffined, hearsed, and tombed in the secret inner chamber and sanctum sanctorum of the whale. Only one sweeter end can readily be recalled—the delicious death of an Ohio honey-hunter, who seeking honey in the crotch of a hollow tree, found such exceeding store of it, that leaning too far over, it sucked him in, so that he died embalmed. How many, think ye, have likewise fallen into Plato's honey head, and sweetly perished there?[6]

Drawing on Melville, this was one of Stein's most important lessons. Do not be caught between two "heads," two contrasting philosophies (the Stoic, the Platonian); and do not seek to delve into any head's sanctum sanctorum, lest you sweetly perish.

This is one source of Don's rejection of "imagination," in the coda of *Invisible Green*: "And so, clearly, there's no need for imagination. It would be a downright hindrance. The poem is entirely of its real place and moment. Nothing is missing which the imagination might supply. Write where you are. Our art is simply one form of attention, a going out to meet the world that comes so freely, so effortlessly to us and to our senses."[7] This statement emerges from a consideration of Dickinson and William Carlos Williams, but I detect Stein's good teaching of Melville here, too. Stuck in a "honey head," even that of one's own imagination, one fails to pay attention. Stein taught Don what such risks entail and how the writer may avoid them.

Stein wanted both Don and me to remain at Binghamton after we finished our undergraduate studies. Knowing that we both planned to go to graduate school in English, he was arranging fellowships for both of us. Don accepted his offer; he took his MA at Binghamton and continued to take courses with Stein every semester he was there. Then, he went on to Buffalo for his doctorate. I declined the professor's offer. My girlfriend and I had decided to get married after graduation (she was at Oberlin, and we had maintained an on-again off-again long-distance relationship for four years). She wanted to go to library school, and so we spent a long time coordinating graduate applications, looking at universities that had good English departments and graduate programs in librarianship. We ended up at Emory, where I was offered a full first-year fellowship. The die was cast, and I had to tell Stein.

Don had already informed him that he would stay at Binghamton. I walked nervously into his office and told him of my decision. He was disappointed. He had dismantled my final paper, praising all my ideas but telling me that my prose was a mess: no matter how brilliant and subversive my insights, they had to be couched in proper academic discourse; and I still had a lot to learn. Yet, he had given me an A. Now I was leaving. And when I told him I was going to Atlanta, he warned me, knowing full well who and what I was, to be careful of anti-Semitism. I was shocked. I had never experienced anti-Semitism, and the idea that I was going somewhere where I might be unwelcome, or at least regarded suspiciously, because I was Jewish, had never crossed my mind. As it turns out, I never had to deal with it in the five years I spent in the South. Yet, Stein had wanted me to take care. I thanked him for everything and said goodbye. I never saw him again. He died in 1983.

The Broken Juke and Antiphony

I would never have gone to Emory—I had never even heard of it—if I had not become friends, during my last two years at Binghamton, with Patricia and Jack Wilcox, who came from Georgia and had studied at Emory many years earlier. Jack was a professor in the Philosophy Department at Binghamton; his area of expertise was Nietzsche. Pat was a poet and novelist. Boisterous, extravagant, generous, a passionate reader of Jane Austen and Byron, a terrific cook, and a wonderful hostess, she was a member of a writing group that I was invited to join by Donald Weiss, a colleague of Jack's with whom I had studied. I was the only undergraduate in the group (another member was the poet Molly Peacock, who had finished her BA at Binghamton some years before). At some point, I introduced Don to the Wilcoxes, and they immediately hit it off. Pat had always wanted to start a small press. She was enchanted by Don's poetry, and so it was decided that the first book to be published by the Iris Press would be Don's *The Broken Juke*. It came out in 1975, preceding Don's "official" first book, the National Poetry Series winner *From the Abandoned Cities*, by eight years.

Still available online from rare book sites for rather princely sums, *The Broken Juke* is, as the biography at the back puts it, "a young man's book." Its purpose, as the biography goes on to note, "can be found in Revell's hope always to see the whole thing as one, the real as a reason to build, to 'bridge' rather than to despair."[8] The hero-precursors invoked are Hart Crane, LeRoi Jones, and Jack Kerouac, and it includes a charming poem called "me and rimbaud go to the movies" (the poems, and most the rest of the volume, are all in lower-case). The prosody of the poems is decidedly jazzy, but the line breaks sometimes work against the rhythms, partly due to the way Pat edited the text. I first heard many of the poems when Don read them to me right out of his notebook, and after more than forty years, there are lines that still bop about in my head, coming into consciousness at the oddest moments. Their music endures for me, though Don has never reprinted any of the poems.

Between *The Broken Juke* and *From the Abandoned Cities*, Don's style changed dramatically, and he adopted a sort of formalism, which he has since renounced. To quote once more from "The Moving Sidewalk," "I know that many of the poems in my first book, *From the Abandoned Cities*, adopted traditional forms out of an impulse to feign a distance I did not feel and a manner I merely envied. . . . Form gave me the illusion of control and escape."[9] As I read Don's poetic development, it is not until his third book, *New Dark Ages* (1990), that he truly comes into his own. In that volume, still one of my favorites of all his collections, he brings together the passion for (and ambivalence toward) urban experience that he first expresses in *The Broken Juke* with the formal rigor (but not what he decries as feigned distance) of *From the Abandoned Cities*. Additionally—and this is a mark of his maturity—his understanding of the urban agon is immensely deepened by a serious engagement with political history. Consider the opening stanza of "Wartime":

> All the more beautiful in the concert hall
> with people in their fine clothes and yourself
> in the same place as the original music.
> The rest, I imagine, must be like the sound

of a radio orchestra in the nineteen-forties,
Europe fiddling beneath the darkness,
and those abandoned in the capital cities
leaning into the sound as it becomes noise.[10]

Reading this poem, and many more like it, I realized just how rich, provocative, and intelligent was the "matter" of Don's poetry from the very beginning. Time, hard work, and deep study were bringing it to fruition. And as the work has unfolded over the years, I continue to be regularly dazzled.

While *The Broken Juke* was coming into being, Don and I were collaborating on a poetry magazine. *Antiphony* lasted exactly one issue, appearing not long before we graduated in the spring of 1975, and I can guarantee that no rare book sites will have any copies available. Don provided the title; it comes, of course, from Crane's "Atlantis": "Whispers antiphonal in azure swing."[11] The funding came from various units of Harpur College, plus donations from family and friends. It was, even by seventies standards, a very low-tech production. The text was produced on an IBM Selectric in that immediately recognizable and decidedly ugly sans-serif type. There were pen and ink drawings by the artist Melanie Ruben (whom I don't believe I ever met). The entire book was black and white—we couldn't afford a bit of color—but it was perfect-bound, and my copy, a little yellowed, still holds up today.

As for the poetry itself, I feel that a surprising amount of it holds up as well. Don and I worked hard, sorting, arguing, bargaining over the submissions we had received, almost all of which were solicited from undergraduate friends in creative writing and the members of the writing group to which I still belonged. We began the issue with a manifesto, because isn't that what young visionary editors are supposed to present when their journal first appears? The tone and message were portentous, to say the least:

American poetry stands at a crossroads. On the one hand is a path that may only be described as amoral. A path which leads not to the illumination of the language, but to that of the self. To continue down such a path could lead nowhere but to a static, and hence, self-indulgent poetic. This is a path heavily traveled of late. Despite the plaudits of a once proud literary establishment, those poets who have elected to move in this direction have served only to delay a process which is, by its very nature, selfpropagative. . . . That other path, that other direction, though regrettably unexplored, is rich in promise—a promise foretold to us by those voices of the past century that have truly counted. Equipped with the tools those voices have provided, we must now venture past the marches into this realm, into the new.[12]

What exactly were Don and I referring to in all of this? I recall that we disliked confessional poetry; thus, the reference to a static, self-indulgent poetic. The New American poets were of great importance to us—think of how Don had turned from Lowell to Olson and Ashbery, and the degree to which a more open, process-oriented poetry would free up his imagination. We thought that a poetry that dwelled too much on the self would prove to be a dead end, so I would venture to guess that we were also setting ourselves in opposition to a workshop model that emphasized writing from a standpoint of the personal, the old idea of writing what you know. Ours was not a particularly sophisticated stance, but behind it, at least, was a growing awareness of the necessity for careful critical evaluation, an awareness that had led us to start a magazine in the first place.

In our manifesto, we also emphasized a concern with language. "To understand the language," we declared, "to release the energy that is stored therein, is to reaffirm the essential humanity which must underlie all viable creative endeavor. Such a poetic is not of necessity a single-minded one. Rather, it entails a variety of form, texture, and emotion, bonded together solely by a clear and outright reverence for the language."[13] From a distance of over forty years, it seems to me that however jejune we may have appeared, and however vague our terms may have sounded, we were attempting to mediate between a view of language as an autonomous power and a view that language was subordinate to and in the service of a sort of prophetic humanism. Impossibly volatile and inchoate, the concepts we were attempting to articulate (or toward which we were gesturing) would surface within a decade in the debates around language poetry, deconstruction, postmodernism, and the legacy of the New American poets. Meanwhile, two brash, smart, and talented friends had accomplished what they had set out to do and were preparing to graduate and to go their separate ways.

We did a public reading to celebrate. I remember that there was a big turnout. By then, we had quite a few friends. Our initiative had made an impression, and we were pleased with the attention.

Don and I read each other's poems in addition to our own. The atmosphere was festive but unquestionably valedictory. I don't recall even seeing him at commencement, and by then, I was deep into plans for my life after Binghamton, which is to say marriage and graduate school in Atlanta. Don was invited to the wedding, which was held in Pittsburgh, my girlfriend's hometown, but he did not attend. We headed south, where, as I was to discover, a new literary community awaited me. Don and I corresponded and soon became intensely critical of each other's new poems. I distrusted the formalism creeping into his work. He was even writing sonnets! We argued, made up, would correspond again, and then would often fall into long periods of silence. Yet, our friendship never truly gave way. In 1980, I completed my doctorate and was hired that spring by Xavier University in Cincinnati. By then, I had a one-year-old daughter, and I was thrilled to have a tenure-track job in a good-sized city within driving distance of my wife's family in Pittsburgh and mine in New York. After Don finished his PhD at Buffalo (he wrote a dissertation on Ashbery), he would hold a number of positions over the years—Tennessee, Ripon, Denver, Utah, and finally University of Nevada, Las Vegas.

Not too long after I moved to Cincinnati, Don came to Xavier to read. Our friendship returned to an even keel, and over the years we have continued to support each other's work, reading it deeply, occasionally writing about it, respecting our differences but knowing deep down that we share a founding vision. When I opened *The Art of Attention* and saw that Don had dedicated it to me, I felt that that vision had flowered. We see each other rarely, and yet, I cannot escape the sense that we may still be each other's best readers. "Belief turns teachers into friends," Don writes at the end of *The Art of Attention*.[14] But belief turns friends into teachers, too. We continue to teach each other.

Notes

1. D. H. Lawrence, "Song of a Man Who Has Come Through" *Selected Poems*, 74.

2. Weinfield has recently published his own memoir of his early days, including those in Binghamton, in relation to his friendship with George Oppen. See "With Oppen."

3. Ezra Pound, "Exile's Letter," *Personae*, 136.

4. I only met Don's family once, when I visited him at home in The

Bronx. There was tension between him and his rather overbearing mother, and Binghamton had enabled him to escape from her, as was the case with my mother and me. I recall his father as huge, quiet, and sad. In "The Moving Sidewalk," Don writes that "As I matured, I learned that my father was literally a nobody outside the narrow circuit of his thefts and that he was as confined by that circuit as by a cell" (*Invisible Green,* 177). This was indeed the man I briefly met. Don met my parents on a number of occasions. He got along well with my father, who managed a lumber yard in Hoboken and dealt regularly with roughnecks like Revell *père.* As for my mother, an elementary school teacher, she thought Don was a wise guy and cordially detested him, referring to him as "Svengali" because she thought he was a bad influence on me.

5. Herman Melville, *Moby-Dick,* chap. 75.

6. Melville, *Moby-Dick,* chap. 78.

7. Donald Revell, *Invisible Green,* 186.

8. Revell, *The Broken Juke,* 53.

9. Revell, *Invisible Green,* 179.

10. Revell, "Wartime," *From the Abandoned Cities,* 47.

11. Hart Crane, "Atlantis," *The Complete Poems and Selected Letters and Prose of Hart Crane,* 117.

12. Finkelstein and Revell, 1.

13. Ibid., 1–2.

14. Revell, *The Art of Attention,* 166.

Works Cited

Crane, Hart. *The Complete Poems and Selected Letters and Prose.* Edited by Brom Weber. Doubleday, 1966.

Finkelstein, Norman, and Donald Revell. "The Antiphony Manifesto." *Antiphony,* vol. 1, no. 1, 1974, pp. 1–2.

Lawrence, D. H. *Selected Poems.* Edited by Kenneth Rexroth. Viking, 1959.

Melville, Herman. *Moby-Dick; or, The Whale.* Project Gutenberg, https://www.gutenberg.org/files/2701/2701-h/2701-h.htm

Pound, Ezra. *Personae: The Collected Shorter Poems.* New Directions, 1971.

Revell, Donald. *The Art of Attention: A Poet's Eye.* Graywolf, 2007.

Revell, Donald. *The Broken Juke.* Iris Press, 1975.

Revell, Donald. *Invisible Green: Selected Poems.* Omnidawn, 2005.

Revell, Donald. *New Dark Ages.* Wesleyan University Press, 1990.

Weinfield, Henry. "With Oppen." *The Oppens Remembered: Poetry, Politics, and Friendship.* Edited by Rachel Blau DuPlessis. University of New Mexico Press, 2015, pp. 111–26.

SUSAN M. SCHULTZ

Houses of Poetry after Ashbery
The Poetry of Ann Lauterbach and Donald Revell

Critics have written much about John Ashbery's relation to the poets who precede him but little about his influence on poets who follow him. I will argue here that two of the finest of the poets who have gone to school to Ashbery, namely Ann Lauterbach and Donald Revell, are now revising his vision to fit a more social context. I am especially interested in their use of houses as metaphors for poetry and for community. Where Ashbery abdicates the traditional metaphor of the house (associated as it is with community) as a location for poetic creation, Revell and Lauterbach in different ways reclaim the trope as the site for their poetry. Where Ashbery elides the problematic tension between confinement and freedom, form and the drive toward transcendence, Revell and Lauterbach both reinstall the problem and fail—or refuse—to go around it. Revell investigates the site of marriage and marries Ashbery's distrust of language's instability with a more earnest desire for the confinements of poetic form. Lauterbach considers the house as the home of female creativity and wants the comfort of that tradition even as she means to get past its tyranny.

A sense of place is not what we have come to expect from John Ashbery, although the desire for one sometimes shows through. When asked by an interviewer if "homesickness [would be] an underlying sentiment in your poetry," Ashbery replied, characteristically having it both ways: "I guess, but I grew up in Sodus, a small farm town in western New York State near Lake Ontario, and I certainly wouldn't want to live there."[1] Ashbery's poetic response to the problem of place is no less complicated; in one of his most extended meditations on the subject, "Houseboat Days," he evades the problem through a kind of collage that places an image for confinement on top of an image for freedom, rather than next to it. I am thinking in particular of Elizabeth Bishop's fantasy of the house by the sea as a place of retirement, freedom in "The End of March," from her last book, *Geography III*. In that poem she discovers that her "proto-dream-house, / . . . crypto-dream-house," set on pilings, is boarded up, an impossible refuge.[2] Ashbery's extended meditation on place, "Houseboat Days," the title poem to his 1977 collection, instead proposes a conflation of liminality with place; his is a house *on* the water:

> The mind
> Is so hospitable, taking in everything
> Like boarders, and you don't see until
> It's all over how little there was to learn
> Once the stench of knowledge has dissipated, and the trouvailles
> Of every one of the senses fallen back.[3]

In "The Freedom of the House" from *Shadow Train,* an opera house gives the poet access to the solitary nature of happiness; the metaphor is again oceanic, as if he attended a floating opera. The house becomes a metaphor not for communion with other concertgoers but for solitude:

> A few more might have survived the fall
> To read the afternoon away, navigating
> In sullen peace, a finger at the lips,
> From the beginning of one surf point to the end,
> And again, and may have wondered why being alone
> Is the condition of happiness, the substance
> Of the golden hints, articulation in the hall outside,
> And the condition as well of using that knowledge
>
> To pleasure, always in confinement?[4]

Ashbery presses the house metaphor further in "Houseboat Days," however, by extending it into the political realm, equating the fall of government with the dissolution of its house of parliament:

> Pinpricks of rain fall again,
> And from across the quite wide median with its
> Little white flowers, a reply is broadcast:
> "Dissolve parliament. Hold new elections."[5]

Yet the further he goes, the more need there is for retrenchment, for a conservatism at once literary and political to counteract anarchy; hence, the poem's final image is one of bland domesticity. Here is Ashbery's latter-day aesthetic refuge, his palace of art:

> As the rain gathers and protects
> Its own darkness, the place in the slipcover is noticed
> For the first and last time, fading like the spine
> Of an adventure novel behind glass, behind the teacups.[6]

The poem's trajectory diminishes steadily, then, as if one looked at transcendentalism through the wrong end of a telescope, seeing Blake's grain of sand in the world rather than the other way around. In the world of Ashbery's poetry, one might feel claustrophobia in an empty airport. For here, absolute freedom resembles absolute tyranny; the hospitable mind is, after all, empty. Emptiness, as we know from "And *Ut Pictura Poesis* Is Her Name," is for Ashbery a kind of muse:

> Something
> Ought to be written about how this affects
> You when you write poetry:
> The extreme austerity of an almost empty mind
> Colliding with the lush, Rousseau-like foliage of its desire to
>   communicate[7]

Has Ashbery dissolved the tension between confinement and freedom, or has he only created a new problem? For Revell and Lauterbach, Ashbery's dissolution of the tension cannot work; this conflict is at the heart of both their poetic projects. Life is various, but the self in Ashbery's work is ever solitary; the social fabric behind his work seems at times much too thin. Only in solitude, perhaps, can the poet dissolve these tensions. Revell and Lauterbach both write about their relationships with other people: Revell finding solace in confinement not just as a literary principle but also as a personal one; Lauterbach refusing to emancipate herself from the liminal spaces she investigates, including the erotic sites that Ashbery also tends to elide.

As readers of contemporary poetry and criticism are aware, a battle currently rages over Ashbery's place in literary history; he has more places than I can mention here. His many ancestors descend in a paradoxical line through his lines; he is at once Romantic and postmodern, conversational and abstract, often within the same poem. According to his major promoter, Harold Bloom, Ashbery is

Wallace Stevens's best ephebe; he is (again) the last Romantic— alongside Bloom. Lauterbach's work comes out of Ashbery's Stevens line, and her interrogations of tradition direct themselves at both poets.

But Ashbery himself has noted the influence of W. H. Auden. "One thing Bloom has ignored," he told an interviewer, "although I've told him, is that I feel that Auden has been more of an influence than Stevens. Auden was the first poet to really speak to me. . . . At first I was really put off by the fact that he used ordinary everyday speech as the language of the poetry. And little by little I began to see the beauty of that."[8] I see Revell's work coming out of Ashbery's Auden side rather than his Stevens side.

There are more differences than those of vocabulary between Auden and Stevens, of course. There is also the matter of the poet's constructions of place and of form, the internalization of place into poetry. Stevens's project is late transcendentalist; mind supplants place in his poetry as it cannot do in Auden. Form there is in his work, but mainly in the engine of iambic pentameter that drives his blank verse forward. Auden is in that sense more modern and more postmodern, for his landscapes contain abandoned relics of the modern world, not to be looked away with a Stevensian whoosh of a verb. Places refuse to mirror the poet's subjectivity:

> This land, cut off, will not communicate,
> Be no accessory content to one
> Aimless for faces rather there than here.
> Beams from your car may cross a bedroom wall,
> They wake no sleeper; you may hear the wind
> Arriving driven from the ignorant sea
> To hurt itself on pane, on bark of elm
> Where sap unbaffled rises, being spring;
> But seldom this. Near you, taller than grass,
> Ears poise before decision, scenting danger.[9]

Auden's frequent use of repetition (he often uses the sestina and the villanelle forms) serves to highlight the way in which language writes through the poet. Form, more than content, or form as content, is for Auden the engine that recirculates tradition. Auden's nostalgia for a Romantic landscape-mirror, paradoxically greater than Stevens's, is masked by his use of form. For form, as Auden and Revell know, can be used to frame the opposite of form; it can signify the formless and obsessional state of someone who grieves for something lost. In that sense, the greatest disorder expresses itself as order.

But let me begin with a point of contact between Revell and Lauterbach, two instances of their use of the house-metaphor to represent time, which is insubstantial. In "Psyche's Dream," from her book *Before Recollection*, Lauterbach writes, and I quote at length:

> If dreams could dream, free from the damp crypt
> And from the bridge where she went
> To watch the spill and the tree
> Standing on its head, huge and rootless
> (Of which the wasp is a cruel illustration
>
> Although its sting is not), the decay
> Now spread into the gardens, their beds
> Tethered to weeds and to all other intrusions;
> Then the perishing house, lost from view
> So she must, and you, look out to see
> Not it but an image of it, would be
>
> Nowhere and would not resemble, but would languish
> On the other side of place[10]

This last phrase echoes Stevens's lines about the nothing that is not there and the nothing that is, although her literalization of the passing time/perishing house analogy is more radical than Stevens's use of the snowman, whose melting we are not privy to. What we gain, as well, are the two pronouns—not just "you must have a mind of winter," but "she must, and you, look to see" it. Here is Revell, from "St. Lucy's Day":

> History is laughing all the time,
> shaking the little bridge between itself
> and islands of freedom, the remote tribes there
> talking themselves into a frenzy, forgetting
> the one history lesson that matters.
> The present is easy. It hangs there
> like a rough pendant in the shape of a house.[11]

The house in this passage already is an image, hanging "like a rough pendant" around the neck of history, which is annexed to "islands of freedom" by a "little bridge." Yet Revell's house, like Lauterbach's, while it partakes of what Lauterbach terms "the other side of place," is also a place—a place where he is holding a party:

> You press a door. Everything inside is too small
> to hurt you, easy to walk around
> in ideal floor plans—tract house, cloister,
> brownstone. Even easier to stand
> at the sink and to consider your options.[12]

Here, Revell situates the metaphorical next to the literal, translating from his situation to ideas about his own place:

> As the yard fades, is it too late for me
> to stagger through the window towards the dark house
> at the fenceline, which is to say the past,
> those uneasy rooms? Or better to fall
> backwards into the deep end of the night ahead?[13]

"So," he writes, "my lifetime gutters between two real lives";[14] so, too, does his image gutter between essence and idea, between house and Home, "which I shall never reach . . . / dark, slow, and filling with days that will not get longer."[15]

Yet, although Revell uses the house as a metaphor for memory, which can be at once comforting and terrifying (see his brilliant poem "Charleston," among others), he feels a nostalgia for houses, rooms—just as his use of form seems at times "older" than the content of his poems. In "The Next Marriage," he writes that he has "taken a room," and tries to imagine a life at once various and confined, wondering: "Is it so wrong to want as many lives // as even a room has?"[16] And this may be why he turns to Dickinson, describing her mirror in Amherst:

> Looking into it head on,
> I feel contained and ready to understand
> the short lines' skewed New England syntax mouthed
> into so strict a frame.[17]

This, we should note, defines Dickinson's confinement more than her freedom. Revell's second book, *The Gaza of Winter,* begins from dispersal and chronicles his attempt, more anxious than Lauterbach's, to be secure within a house. His sense of dispersal is disturbingly literal, like a shaman's. In "Why History Imitates God," he describes the parts of torsos that he collects:

> For my own comfort, I press my face against them.
> It makes the bronze strange and that eases
> the occult poverty of the hour,
> a body smaller than mine. I'm poor. My house
> has no hands or legs and the near silence
> of the statues dies away as I move closer.[18]

This metaphor of his house of broken statues is a literalized metaphor of the self as a house, like the perishing house that Lauterbach describes. But freedom from the house is merely the freedom to be in another house or in another room of the house, as Revell knows, which is really no freedom at all:

> It is safer elsewhere with limbs, in other houses.
> I want to be set free in the next room
> to press my face against the strange heat
> of bronze whose silence could not love me less.[19]

The poet's loss of his marriage, a metaphorical place, leaves him "Balkanized": like Auden in "The Secret Agent," he knows how to use the Cold War as an objective correlative for personal loss. His Gaza is exile, liminal as any shore, but also a place of political displacement. If a marriage is Gaza, it is also a place of repetitions, themes, and variations. Revell uses forms of repetition, such as villanelles and sestinas, or variations on them, to show how obsessions are the mind's own places and the way that loss can be strangely refigured as poetic gain, as in the self-reconstructing phrase, "I have lost." There is deeply ironic nostalgia in his desire for an occupied city, not a free one. He writes in "Prague," a poem that is characteristically "closed" in its form, and where phrases are repeated in different contexts, as if better to close the possibilities of meaning:

> I once lost everything
> who was the one person I loved in a free city.
>
> In the Balkans I can free her again.[20]

Yet, Revell's use of form bespeaks his desire to break it; he means to break form, to get things wrong, and so to misname the world.

He writes in form, it seems, only so that he can subvert it. In "Descriptive Quality," he writes:

> Spite the wind. Describe it wrong, knowing
> each partisan inaccuracy to be
> a blow against the treaty of air that bends
> solid, helpless things into stick figures
> and then mistakes the little sticks for words.[21]

Like Hart Crane in "A Name for All," Revell believes that names mutilate the objects they pin down:

> Malice is the country home of names
> and of the isolations they describe.
> All the sad mishaps unfold out there
> In every room of the huge house, in weak light.
> The shadows lunge into silence. Everyone
>
> except a vacant-eyed young man drifts off
> into the twilit, deep garden. He lifts
> a china bowl with both hands and calls it *flower,*
> *shattered, twilit leaf,* or any other
> solid, helpless thing that he has seen.[22]

To alter the language is, of course, to alter the self and to risk the very vacancy that afflicts this new Adam in his lonely attempt to rename the world. Poets more radical than Revell could well criticize him for not performing this act himself but instead rendering it as parable not fact. But what Revell does is attempt to reshape the words we do have, even as he acknowledges their desire to steer him elsewhere. His poems are dramatic in the conflict they present between language-as-self and the self as a user of language. He revels in the strictures of language only because he sees words as the only way out; he is in that sense more conservative than the Language poets, who aim to burn the house down. But Revell shows us, better than the Language poets do, how we can write poetry that, even as it knows itself dictated by language, still tries to use that language instrumentally, employing it as an instrument of desire, not desiring only what it offers us. His obsessive desire to keep the self whole may seem to some nostalgic, but I suspect that it is, ultimately, a nostalgia worth having.

Lauterbach's use of the house is complicated by her gender, for limitations—and poems—have been historically male constructions:

> Garden, hedge, pool,
> Planned to guard the old line, define
> And compose the imagination's brown capacity.
> Our extent is more than memory
> Or the text of a poem willed to the wall
> Although our tenacious forebears whisper
> Collections, passed from father to son to son
> While mother prunes.[23]

That the "old line" is poetic as well as social is especially worrisome for a female poet; that the poem, like the "will," enforces limits means that her poems must resist those same kinds of limitation. "It is not the dark that scares me, but the limit / which places the house in the field, the horse in its stall."[24] Hers will not be the "garden, hedge, pool"—the Eden of social memory—but the house itself. For Lauterbach, to be at home is both a blessing and a curse, for it metaphorically represents a feminine line of creation at the same time as it closes her out of Whitman's open road. She attempts to get past this by opening her house to infinitude, as Dickinson did. In "Naming the House," she posits the conflict between a "longing for dispersal" and the "joy of naming it this, and this is mine":

> And I think also of how women, toward evening,
> Watch as the buoyant dim slowly depletes
> Terrain, and frees the illuminated house
> So we begin to move about, reaching for potholders
> And lids, while all the while noting
> That the metaphor of the house is ours to keep
> And the dark exterior only another room
> Waiting for its literature.[25]

This poem is an apt response to Dickinson's poem about the differences between prose and poetry, confinement and freedom, which is built on the metaphor of a house:

> I dwell in Possibility—
> A fairer House than Prose—
> More numerous of Windows—
> Superior—for Doors—[26]

where it becomes clear that Dickinson is describing a house not circumscribed by walls but by the sky:

Of Chambers as the Cedars—
Impregnable of eye—
And for an everlasting Roof
The Gambrels of the Sky—[27]

Just so Lauterbach sees the outside as "only another room" and the poet as someone who "dallies now in plots / But feels a longing for dispersal."[28] We can read "plots" as plots of ground, as grave plots, or as the prose that represents for Dickinson the genre of confinement, the woman's genre. The word "household" tells the story nicely.

Where Ashbery seems content to evade the question, posed so incessantly by Stevens, of the relation between reality and imagination, between place and the thoughts we have about it, Lauterbach is not: she personifies this dualism as "Bishop" and "Beckett" in "Saint Lucia." "Elizabeth Bishop" she uses to mean a reverence for the place itself; "Samuel Beckett" to mean the allegorization of place. The dualism does not, of course, bear too much scrutiny, something that Lauterbach doubtless knows well enough as she places herself between them:

The sea, solitary or not,
Implies the confines of a dream.
I'm between Beckett and Bishop,
The one entirely in, the other there
Civilizing Brazil, clarity to clarity.[29]

Lauterbach's conversation with Stevens is ongoing but nowhere so compelling as in "Carousel," where she takes on Stevens's "The Idea of Order at Key West" and Ashbery's early poem "The Painter" from *Some Trees*. This poem, like so many of Revell's, works by repetitions of key images, the working of language apart from human agency. Stevens's woman/artist, we recall, ordered the sea through her song:

She sang beyond the genius of the sea.
The water never formed to mind or voice,
Like a body wholly body, fluttering
Its empty sleeves[30]

Where Stevens gives us an image of a woman walking beside the sea, Ashbery in his sestina "The Painter" gives us an image of the artist *as* the sea—an image that he comes to acknowledge is dangerous. The mechanical working of the poem reflects the inhuman machinations of the painter's scene:

> Imagine a painter crucified by his subject!
> . . .
> Others declared it a self-portrait.
> Finally all indications of a subject
> Began to fade, leaving the canvas
> Perfectly white. He put down the brush.
> At once a howl, that was also a prayer,
> Arose from the overcrowded buildings.[31]

Both the painter and his painting are thrown off the tallest building and are devoured by the sea, which had been his subject.

Lauterbach presents herself as both the agent of order and as someone who distrusts order. It is she, seemingly, who sets Ashbery's painter right in "Carousel," where she wears the sea's sleeves:

> I like masks, deeper in shades of blue,
> How it concludes black.
> A swimmer is adorned with one arm
> Rising out of the blue.
> A man in the sea.
> A painting of a man in the sea.
> I like the way it comes out of the blue.
> The horse rises and falls; my sleeves are waving.
> It is not dark that scares me, but the limit
> Which places the house in the field, the horse in its stall.[32]

The man in the sea is again the same as a painting of the man in the sea but without the chaos portended in Ashbery's poem. Instead, what frightens this poet is precisely the opposite: the limits that Ashbery had so blithely erased in his poem. The image with which she ends the poem preserves the contrast between limit and limitlessness:

> Over her shoulder, the painting depicts will.
> Staring at the view, she has a sense of place
> And of omission. The ways in which we live
> Are earmarked for letting go, and so
> She makes her descent, plucks it, rises into the blue.[33]

Lauterbach's resolution of the problem, then, is its revaluation; the poet's job is to trace "[t]he syntax of solitude . . . / To witness versions that clock and petal, / Enfolding instances."[34] This clocking (mechanical) and petaling (organic) are the edges of the liminal space in which Lauterbach operates; it is a house, but one that perishes before her eyes. "[T]he soul's haphazard sanctuary" is more like Stevens's dump than like Dickinson's house, but the final chamber promises, even if it does not deliver, revelation:

> We might think of this as a blessing
> As we thrash in the nocturnal waste:
> Rubble of doors, fat layers of fiber
> Drooping under eaves, weeds
> Leaning in lassitude after heavy rain
> Has surged from a whitened sky.
> Thunder blooms unevenly in unknowable places
> Breaking distance into startling new chambers
> We cannot enter; potentially, a revelation.[35]

This comes from the first poem in the book, "Still." The last poem, "Sacred Weather," describes a "gathered dispersal."[36] This is an elegy for her father, "[w]hose sleeve was last seen bound to a wing," in that liminal space he shares with Stevens's last philosopher in Rome.[37] The moment of transcendence she describes as a place, a landscape:

> Nevertheless a balance forms, its crest
> The start of radiance like that grassy limit
> Of shore. Certain early episodes rub,
> Curiously nearby, poised to ensue.
> A pale linearity hangs a new surface in the air
> Like a mute plow stretching the light.[38]

In the poem's final section, Lauterbach uses puns (pine and pain is one) to show how language itself becomes "a new surface in the air." But more telling is her use of the word "refrain" in what follows, the final lines of *Beyond Recollection:*

> May have ceased to pine.
> Stasis is an attribute, domain of the lily.
> Even the sky gives color up,
> An ecstasy too slight, less than free.
> I myself long to refrain

But would bleed and bless
Robe opening on slowly mounted stair.[39]

That she longs to refrain bespeaks a double, and contradictory, desire; to read the word as a verb indicates a desire to cease, even to die. Yet, poetic refrains are precisely those passages that repeat themselves, and the poetic act is itself one of repetition. Her final image, likewise, speaks both of death and of eroticism, of enclosure and of opening.

Are Revell and Lauterbach, then, mere backpedalers in the literary history now creating itself around us? Have they quailed at the radicalism of Ashbery's project, which seems in so many ways both late Romantic and postmodernist? This is perhaps not for any of us to say—yet. But, if Ashbery seems the darling of deconstructionists, his poems (like "Houseboat Days") undoing themselves as purposefully as Penelope's tapestry, then Lauterbach and Revell will surely appeal more to critics wanting to stop the gaps in deconstruction's logic. Certainly they will not be the darlings of New Historicists— they are too Ashberyan for that—but they may show us how Ashbery's model can be revised to include social, even political, contexts. For, even if Revell and Lauterbach trade more in metaphor than in fact [Revell's Gaza is *not* that of the Palestine Liberation Organization (PLO), to one reviewer's chagrin], their metaphors are grounded more consistently in the social and political realm than are his. If these two poets do not give us the radical wealth we are accustomed to in Ashbery, they at least give us hope that we can, still, make coherent selves for ourselves.

Notes

1. John Ashbery, interview by Mark Hillringhouse, *Joe Soap's Canoe*.
2. Elizabeth Bishop, "The End of March," *Geography III*, 43.
3. John Ashbery, "Houseboat Days," *Houseboat Days*, 515. Note that this and all subsequent excerpts from Ashbery poems are from *John Ashbery: Collected Poems 1956–1987*.
4. Ashbery, "The Freedom of the House," *Shadow Train*, 701.
5. Ashbery, "Houseboat Days," *Houseboat Days*, 516.
6. Ibid.
7. Ashbery, "And *Ut Pictura Poesis* Is Her Name," *Houseboat Days*, 519.
8. John Ashbery, interview by Mark Hillringhouse, *Joe Soap's Canoe*.
9. W. H. Auden, "The Watershed," *Collected Poems*, 33.
10. Ann Lauterbach, "Psyche's Dream," *Before Recollection*, 43.

11. Donald Revell, "St. Lucy's Day," *New Dark Ages*, 38.

12. Ibid.

13. Ibid.

14. Ibid., 39

15. Ibid., 40.

16. Revell, "The Next Marriage," *The Gaza of Winter*, 53.

17. Revell, "Emily Dickinson's Mirror, Amherst," *The Gaza of Winter*, 62.

18. Revell, "Why History Imitates God," *The Gaza of Winter*, 35.

19. Ibid., 36.

20. Revell, "Prague," *The Gaza of Winter*, 42.

21. Revell, "Descriptive Quality," *The Gaza of Winter*, 64.

22. Ibid., 65.

23. Lauterbach, "Bridgehampton, 1950, 1980," *Before Recollection*, 4.

24. Lauterbach, "Carousel," *Before Recollection*, 41.

25. Lauterbach, "Naming the House," *Before Recollection*, 13.

26. Emily Dickinson, "I dwell in Possibility," *The Poems of Emily Dickinson*, 215.

27. Ibid.

28. Lauterbach, "Naming the House," *Before Recollection*, 13.

29. Lauterbach, "Saint Lucia," *Before Recollection*, 18.

30. Wallace Stevens, "The Idea of Order at Key West," *The Collected Poems of Wallace Stevens*, 128.

31. Ashbery, "The Painter," *Some Trees*, 28.

32. Lauterbach, "Carousel," *Before Recollection*, 41.

33. Ibid., 42.

34. Lauterbach, "Saint Lucia," *Before Recollection*, 20.

35. Lauterbach, "Still," *Before Recollection*, 3.

36. Lauterbach, "Sacred Weather," *Before Recollection*, 68.

37. Ibid.

38. Ibid., 71.

39. Ibid., 72.

Works Cited

Ashbery, John. *Houseboat Days. John Ashbury: Collected Poems: 1956–1987.* Edited by Mark Ford. Library of America, 2008, pp. 489–550.

Ashbery, John. Interview by Mark Hillringhouse. *Joe Soap's Canoe*, no. 13, 1990.

Ashbery, John. *Shadow Train. John Ashbury: Collected Poems: 1956–1987.* Edited by Mark Ford. Library of America, 2008, pp. 695–729.

Ashbery, John. *Some Trees. John Ashbury: Collected Poems: 1956–1987.* Edited by Mark Ford. Library of America, 2008, pp. 1–39.

Auden, W. H. *Collected Poems.* Edited by Edward Mendelson. The Modern Library, 2007.

Bishop, Elizabeth. "The End of March." *Geography III.* Farrar, Straus, and Giroux, 1976, pp. 42–45.

Dickinson, Emily. *The Poems of Emily Dickinson.* Edited by R. W. Franklin. Harvard University Press, 1999.

Lauterbach, Ann. *Before Recollection.* Princeton University Press, 1987.

Revell, Donald. *The Gaza of Winter.* University of Georgia Press, 1988.

Revell, Donald. *New Dark Ages.* Wesleyan University Press, 1990.

Stevens, Wallace. "The Idea of Order at Key West." *The Collected Poems of Wallace Stevens.* 1923. Knopf, 1967, pp. 128–30.

ERYN GREEN

There to Here
Donald Revell's Westward Migration as Map of Poetic Evolution

Regarding Maps

The numerous radical acts of departure in Donald Revell's poetry throughout his multi-decade career offer poignant insight into the evolution of the poet's attention. From the classical concerns and proto-formalist investigations of *From the Abandoned Cities, The Gaza of Winter, New Dark Ages,* and *Erasures,* which orient and explore the situation of the individual in isolated spaces of cosmopolitan modernity, to the mystical meditations and prayerful desert companionships that characterize the middle and latter portions of the poet's work—especially *Arcady, My Mojave, Thief of Strings, The Bitter Withy,* and *Drought-Adapted Vine*—few writers have pivoted so decisively and with such great emotional force in their writing lives as Revell.

One way of charting the change visible in Revell's published oeuvre is to chart the geography of his concerns: that is, to survey the literal landscapes of his poems. Beginning his life and writing in New York (first in The Bronx, then in Binghamton, then in Buffalo), subsequently decamping to Missouri, then Denver, then Utah, and finally Nevada, Revell's westward migration serves as a cartography not only of physical transport but also of his critical poetics (as one of Revell's teachers, Charles Olson, iterates, "There is a limit / to what a car / will do"[1]—or as Revell himself writes, "We must not mistake the transport for delightful transportation").[2]

Put neatly, Revell's work has grown more expansive—wilder and more generous—as his vantages have. As one explores the relationship between the codified urban/urbane spaces of the poet's first four books and the free-range environment of his latter volumes, a kind of codex reveals itself. For his part, Revell echoes this recognition and allows for such a topographical reading of his career, as he writes in *Invisible Green*:

The outside is unprecedented, and poetry has no word for it. But *in* the delightful moment, it finds a new word which is nothing less than itself, suddenly atoned. This kind of thing can happen. There are records: poems.[3]

Wild Work

Such career-spanning considerations as these compel a reader to begin at the beginning. The early terrain traversed by Revell in his 1983 National Poetry Series award-winning debut, *From the Abandoned Cities*, differs significantly from the landscapes inhabited in his later work and in meaningful ways. Poet and critic Stephanie Burt, in her 2003 essay "The Revell Variations," published in *The Nation*, exploring the ways in which Revell's early postmillennial works (*Arcady* and *My Mojave*) feel almost "like the work of an entirely different man" when compared to his first collections, remarks how, unlike Revell's later collections, "[*From the Abandoned Cities*] evoked bleak cityscapes . . . 'where sadness clings to the ground / like fog.'"[4] This differential quality is true not only of the landmarks that populate the writing—a ghostly vision of Central Park, worn-out New York City skylines and Belfast streets, various interior rooms buried like organs within the carapaces of buildings, as opposed to the sublime natural order (desert valley vistas, rocky mountain-hewn alcoves, etc.) everywhere evident in the later work—but also of its formal preoccupations. As Burt notes, in much the same way that sadness clings, the poems in Revell's first books often cleave anxiously to canonical poetic structures, rarely finding rapture in the relation. Placed alongside the landscapes, impulses, and concerns of his most recent poems, the difference is striking.

Otherwise phrased—as Burt keenly points out—in Revell's earliest work there is a mechanical emphasis not found in his later writing that includes the controlled parameters of the sestina, the rigid definitions of the villanelle, the virtual property lines of the sonnet, and the boundaries of terza rima—historical demonstrations of prosody that conform to a classically conditioned aesthetic, much like modern cities conform to notions/models of urbanity and civilization originated ages ago. These forms are odd bedfellows indeed alongside Revell's later oeuvre, especially for those initiated into his more oft-recognized postmillennial works, which orient themselves frequently around unbounded poetic statements and movements such as "Faith is meant for bursting forth," and "The work of poetry is trust"—yet the variation here is central to understanding the poet's development.[5] The constraints of classical form are demonstrably mirrored in the organizations of urban spaces in Revell's earliest collection, *From the Abandoned Cities,* as we see in the poem "Belfast":

> where girls chant
> over a piece of wood called "Doll-Who's-Dead"
> and where the streets you walk are a dead giant
> who won't rise. Here, History is the unfed
> beast past scaring who comes down from the hills
> in daylight. It kills anything, in broad
>
> daylight, then is itself stalked until
> the men corner it in some back street. They save
> the town for the next beast the granite hills
>
> won't hold.[6]

Whereas, above, the world and its history are monstrous ("the unfed beast past scaring . . . / the next beast the granite hills") and the city a sarcophagus, both dead and waiting for us to die, in one of Revell's recent volumes, the aptly titled *Drought-Adapted Vine,* the visage of the world is verdant and robust, full-throated in its vitality and openness, overflowing with "no traffic at all, for hours," bursting with "ripe berries any soul can find," echoing a concord of "sound in the shape of cellos."[7] The landscapes we see in the first book are in general quite a bit paler, more toned in cinder, where "nothing has changed along [the] street,"[8] and some of the most optimistic contemplations pertain to the modest potential for the slowing of inevitable demise:

> If you could wrap your mind
> around the park, the way these walls do, you
> would rot a little more slowly. Maybe if
> you dreamed the way a building dreams
> you might even heal.[9]

Such melancholic tone is obviously different from the ecstatic (often linguistically so) abundance presented by Revell in *Drought-Adapted Vine,* where "the wasp unfolds. Flowers sing for joy, /

'One at least! One at least!'Tatterdemalion my."[10] But astute read-
ers will notice that the tonal differences—the differences beheld
in words—are deeply wedded to stark contrasts of world; unlike
his ecstatic desert (the post-pastoral home inhabited by Revell
today), where nature's work and other "such perfections make the
sun to rise," the urban world witnessed in his earlier collections is
decidedly less organic, made of forms inherently more rigid and
fallible because explicitly human (buildings, constructed parks,
corporations, numbered avenues).[11] Burt also noticed the chro-
matic difference, in the beginning "all gray, and restrained-blue
gray," as opposed to the verdure of the later writing.[12] The palettes
and landscapes don't alter considerably in Revell's second, third,
and fourth books, *The Gaza of Winter, New Dark Ages,* and *Erasures,*
respectively. In each of those volumes, as their titles suggest, the
world is conspicuously muted, weighted and evaporated by aware-
ness of historical suffering and sadness, the domination of hubris-
tic architectures—our modern circumstance. In "Birthplace," for
instance, from *Gaza:*

> Looking for one hand waving out of the shadowbox
> of streets, the staggered cars and railings,
> lights hesitating between the shifts of wind,
>
> I do not find it. Designed for no one,
> no effect in mind, these fronts and disappearing
> corners are as dour as they are plainly habitable.[13]

Or from "Survey," in *New Dark Ages:*

> I am so lonely for the twentieth century,
> for the deeply felt, obscene graffiti
> of armed men and the beautiful bridges
> that make them so small and carry them
> into the hearts of cities written like words
> across nothing[14]

Revell echoes a similarly achromatized sentiment in "Muse,"
where "The truth of those black messages is cold. / The imagina-
tion has no power over life."[15] If there is any doubt about a tonal
and geographical distinction between early and late periods of
Revell's poetry, the juxtaposition of another poem from *From the
Abandoned Cities* alongside one from *My Mojave,* Revell's 2003

paean to the sacred desert, helps make the distinction crystal clear. In "Here to There," from 1983, Revell writes:

> The biggest part of any story is rooms
> and the things inside them. Everything else is too
> vague, too uncertain in the way it happens,
> changes or recites the lines it was
> created to recite to live on its own.[16]

Here, the invocation of "rooms" is pertinent because rooms, like stanzas in classical formalism, are rigidly defined, pecuniary, capable of being counted, enumerated, translated into the commerce of capital and therefore controllable (generally, tragically)—and as such a remarkable difference from the more unbounded writing of Revell's recent career. An audience knows what a room is—we have a predisposed anticipation awaiting confirmation, quite unlike the space an original poem ideally occupies and represents. Such control, and its inherent focus on margin, not unlike the lines delineated (often tyrannically, economically) between neighborhoods in a city, is explicitly rejected by present-day Revell as anti-poetic—for example in "Mechanics" from *My Mojave*:

> What neighborhood? Only death and trees, or one
> Tree. Someone once explained to me the difference
> East from West is the imagination
> Of a single tree as against a forest.
>   . . .
> At Big Sur, there are too many sounds to count one.
> The forest is countless. A tree is almost none.
> This is the house that Jack built East to West.
> He was smiling, and his teeth were planted in rows.[17]

It's not every day that we are given, as readers, the opportunity to synthesize the poetic lessons of a lifetime, filtered through one mind, as it grows and redacts and evolves and becalms—but the changes we can see in Revell's catalogue provide just such a boon. Above, we have the outline for the transit of Revell's entire career— from East to West, from controlled formalism to boundless imagination, from countable rooms to innumerable trees.

It should not escape notice either that the poet invoked in "Mechanics," Jack Spicer, was himself outspokenly pro-West in his poetical thinking and writing style (he once lamented during his residence in Manhattan that "there is no violence of the mind or heart . . . no one screams in the elevator"), favoring the messy, unrestrained line over the neat and tidy—the shore over the city street.[18] Spicer is the poet who so disarmed himself as to invite Martians to write his poems, and who said of his preferred compositional style, "If this is dictation, it is driving / Me wild."[19] Revell writes about Spicer in *Invisible Green* in detail, and taking his cue in *Arcady*—the text which perhaps best signals the distinction between his earlier style and his later interests—"Wild work / Needs wilderness."[20] So, the poet moved on, from the abandoned cities and erasures of his childhood and early writing life, into larger, greener, rockier pastures. The significance of the movement doesn't escape Revell's attention. Writing in *Invisible Green*, he observes that "[w]hen value is worldly, poetry goes to the world," and "It is good to be going. I mean, it is Good to be going. Some poems show the way."[21]

Which is simply to say, once Revell was gone, he was gone. For Good.

Moves Around

"Poetry, the soul of poems, does not reside in them. It goes. We follow. We read to go where poetry has gone and to preserve the possibility of a delightful contact," Revell elaborates in *Invisible Green*.[22] As his career evolved, Revell followed the way West shown by his poems, and the result was an ever-increasing awareness that "there must be a place / In the soul for perfection / I think it moves around."[23] In his oeuvre after *Beautiful Shirt,* the claustrophobic, spaceless confines of the ancient-modern city are replaced by the borderless expanses of rough country, and new poetic forms follow. Instead of commercial spaces, enumerated, gridlocked, and formal, the mind at work in Revell's later body of poetry becomes uncountable, unaccountable, unfixed, as-yet-defined—an agent of vision actualized by environs that correspond to the poet's wildest imaginings, his sense of hope (what Revell articulates as a feeling of being "[u]ncontrollably newborn").[24] This innocence represents quite a departure from the speaker who once described his weariness in worn-out urbanity as "living in one city, dying in another."[25]

Notably, Revell's migratory pattern harkens back to Henry David Thoreau, who incomparably decamped Concord for Walden

Pond, and, given Revell's noted affinity with the Massachusetts saunterer, as much ought not be surprising. Thoreau leaves Concord to get out of the city—to break from what he viewed as the diminishing agreements of an organized, pre-planned, carriage'd social space, to know beans. Revell moves similarly. I think neither writer's abandonment of the city is necessarily a jab at cities, which both knew well (Revell, New York; Thoreau, Boston), but rather at the diminishment of *any* manufactured horizon that "builds the sepulchers of the fathers," forgetting the inherent, animistic, prevailing cosmological context Emerson once described as "an occult relation between man and the vegetable."[26] This issue bears upon the land, certainly, but it is also perspectival. Thoreau writes in "Walking," "Of course, it is of no use to direct our steps to the woods, if they do not carry us thither. I am alarmed when it happens that I have walked a mile into the woods bodily, without getting there in spirit . . . The thought of some work runs in my head and I am not where my body is . . . In my walks, I would fain return to my senses. What business have I in the woods, if I am thinking of something out of the woods?"[27] For comparison, Revell similarly rebukes what he views as the mistaken notion that wild landscapes are necessarily shrieking encampments of fallen nature, in *Arcady*:

Wilderness does not howl
It is the imagination of
The traveler that howls

And the mind in which
The valley and apples
Have failed cries out[28]

Gone here are the anxieties and limited color pallets of urbanity from Revell's first four books. In *My Mojave,* for instance—the book which formally initiates the poet's residence in the regularly forsaken desert outside Las Vegas—Revell's world is heavenly, chock-full of the busted-up and redolent chroma of unconfined, undelegated spaces and agents. There is just so much that is *green* now, Revell constantly reminds us, even in the desert where none is expected (as he writes elsewhere in "Against Creation":"What men call Extinction, / I call Home").[29] This new world, and the new life the poet lives inside of it, in his poems, is sacred, often ecstatic, and it is a far cry from the cities of the earlier period.

For visualization of the migration from inside to outside, look at the first poem in *My Mojave*, "Arcady Again," a lush meditation leading the reader past the boundaries of the *polis*, the known terrain, into deserted harmony:

> Beside the house a path
> Green leaves as low
> As my eyes and a low
> Gate into the rainy yard
> Opens and even the little
> Grass is very wide[30]

This is not the same cultured space in which the writer used to reside. Here, the parks are not walled off, the gates are always open, and the smallest glimpse of a thing, a single blade of greensward (Whitman's "leaves" here becoming "little grass") excites expansion. Revell writes of the way his spirit is increased by such prospects ("west into the stars") in his beautiful "Kentucky," from *The Bitter Withy*:

> Ground-dwelling birds reply to thunder.
> It is sunrise somewhere over there, while here
> Stars shine still, and the secret doors inside the pines
> Remain wide open. Which way to go?
> When I walk into the sun, my children
> Hurry beside me. I hear footsteps and machines.
> When I go west into the stars, I see
> Nothing I could show you: ghosts
> Who are not ghosts at all, hearts
> On their sleeves, eyes like melted diamonds.
> I truly believe that someone loved me once.
> A bird alighted on a bee alighting
> On a green stem, and I heard thunder. God's favorites
> Are the little stars He drops into the sun.[31]

Or perhaps more clearly, from "Little Bees," in the same collection: "What I win / Is the Earth translated, / All its green things passing into blue.[32]

Do you remember the greyscale of the earlier works? Neither does Revell. As previously noted, sestinas, villanelles, sonnets, and other corpuses culled from classicism are present in the first four city books. The physical shape of the poems beginning most apparently in *Arcady* are often the antithesis of such work. The writing becomes increasingly shattered, entropic (another word for this behavior is *ecstatic*), and everywhere resistant to inherited patterns of decorum. It is almost as if, upon heading West, the poems and poet are gifted a whole new vocabulary, a new gait, befitting the topology. Look, for instance, at one of the first true paragons of Revell's poetic *vita nova*, "Light Lily Lily Light Light Lily Light," from *Arcady*, here in its entirety:

Light lily lily light light lily light

Imagically
Lightli ly

Outline stones for the wind

All creatures come
To mind to oneness

Where I am formless   When I go back into
My breaking through   The ground the deep
Will be far greater   In me whence I came[33]

This poem, rooted in sudden flowers, escapes itself by becoming unattached to itself, literally—the stanzas' doors are flung wide open, a channel forms at the end of the poem, words are disrupted from their own meaning, given new life. Disabused of old ways of moving, finding subject and subjective experience in a world beyond the one the poet thought he knew, the poem surprises. This is "formless"; this is "breaking through"; this is "far greater;" and it is notably different from any formalism of Revell's earlier works. The difference is everything: here, the poem isn't what was planned; in fact, it is the result of taking a new way to work, of heading out of the house differently than yesterday, and finding astonishment in the undiscovered path. In a city, too often we think we know where the gardens are to be found—in Denver, for instance, from whence this poem comes to us, one knows that the Botanical Garden abuts Cheeseman Park, between the neighborhoods of Congress Park and Capitol Hill—and yet, here, the most notable living shoots are not found within the parameters of the garden. The poetry they evince is not cultivated by any docent; they are untended but by the sun. The experience they compel as a reader is equally indicative of wild work—the words Revell employs arrive split, open-faced as the flowers themselves, broken up by sidewalk, lineated by wall and warp, rather than convention or conventional wisdom. Further evidence of this evolution can be found in the eponymous poem "My Mojave," which opens:

Sha-
Dow,
As of
A Meteor
At mid-
Day: it goes
From there.

A perfect circle falls
Onto white imperfections.
(Consider the black road,
How it seems white the entire
Length of a sunshine day.)

Or I could say
Shadows and mirage
Compensate the world,
Completing its changes
With no change.[34]

Here, we witness Revell finding solace in the shapes of the world itself even as it is stripped bare, in the interior substance of words themselves, rather than prim constructions. And, basking in the plentitude of natural forms, even desiccated or meteoric ones, no addition is necessary in Revell's eyes to complete the perfection ready at hand. No finish need be applied by the poet's mind to reconcile some perceived or anticipated deficiency. There is no need to "compensate" the world. At this point in Revell's poetic evolution, he seems suddenly recuperated, vitalized by a newness of residence, the fresh façade of a second (or third, or fourth) home, one which constantly moves, as he writes in "Moving Day," the poem that precedes "My Mojave" in the collection:

We're not home yet.
And I'm still new
To my callings:
Teacher, drunkard, absent minister.

I was in Carcassonne once.
I saw two horses there
And God who invented them.[35]

So, what did Revell gain in his westward expansion? Expansion. Largess. A working knowledge that, invention being already done, there is little need for our constructions, our hubristic imaginings, when we have horses to fawn over, to teach our poems gallop. When in "My Trip" he asks the question, "Does anything remain of home at home?" the incredibly hopeful answer he arrives at— "Plenty remains"—is the obvious result of moving onward, paradoxically, away from the old idea of home:

Next day is no way of knowing,
And the day after is my favorite,
A small museum really perfect
And a good meal in the middle of it.
As I'm leaving,
I notice a donkey on a vase
Biting the arm of a young girl,
And outside on the steps
A silver fish head glistens beside a bottlecap.
Plenty remains.

The work of poetry is trust,
And under the aegis of trust
Nothing could be more effortless.
Hotels show movies.
Walking around even tired
I find my eyes find
Numberless good things
And my ears hear plenty of words
Offered for nothing over the traffic noise
As sharp as sparrows.

A day and a day, more rivers crossing me.
It really feels that way, I mean
I have changed places with geography
            . . .
Catching a glimpse of eternity, even a poor one, says it all.[36]

It is clear here that the landscape—the geography Revell trades places with—constitutes (or at least provides access to) the "glimpse of eternity," of forms made and remade and ever ongoing in cosmological recycle, in stark contrast to the impermanent stateliness of manmade shapes. And it is here that Revell finds his true abode. Plenty remains.

There to Here

What I mean to say, then, is that the poet we—many of us—have come to know and to hold dear, is the very byproduct of migration, evolution, rupture; his work is a true record of peregrination, demonstrative finally of heavenly receipt. The signature, hallmark characteristics of his mature work are the exact result of his lifelong travails and travels west. Did it have to be west? For Revell, not for everyone. The point seems to be that moving onward into new spaces (of terrain, of emotion, of heart) shatters the parameters of what we had previously imagined. Another way of saying this is that perhaps Eden—Revell's true residence in the later work, after all, wherever he finds himself—enters in through the cracks and apertures in his poetry. Perforation, exposure, break—in poems, these are all overtures to powers beyond us, not our own standards of excellence but the universe's, and viewed from above, they are the hallmark characteristic of Revell's life's work. At this point in his career, if Revell maintains a fidelity any longer to form, it is the forms of eternity—as he writes in *Arcady,* "Conforming to the fashions of eternity / I feel no conflict only one with prosperity."[37] The Revell we as a reading public know today has moved; his poems ever moving. Without the movement, he wouldn't be here. Simple as that. The fundament of Revell's later career, which grew out of his first four books, is his ability to find heavenly fullness in deserted spaces, spaces rendered devoid of history and its reified attachments, and to recognize the abundance that everywhere appears when we move *outward*—as he writes at the very end of *My Mojave*:

> Disappearance equals increase, and emptiness
> Rises or falls according to no pattern
>
> Because there isn't any pattern yet.
> Etc. Etc. Bring out the mustangs now,
> And memory, and terror. A birth
> Yesterday so near, today seems far.

Should old acquaintance be forgot, sing
Another. And Jesus Christ is the next thing.[38]

The next thing redeems Revell, again and again—like the next
horizon in one's migration, and the next, and the next. Thus, Revell's movement through his life and career serves as a map of his
poetic evolution; thus, does he make of the trip the whole story.
And we—those of us who read his poems, who follow his
trajectory—are granted the truest gift poetry can offer: a road map
for our own onward, whatever direction we are compelled to take,
and an awareness that, as he concludes in "Foxglove," the final poem
in *Drought-Adapted Vine*, no matter what we depart from, so long as
we keep moving, our true home awaits: "We can breathe. We have
time. We have plenty of it."[39]

Notes

1. Charles Olson, "Letter 22," *Maximus Poems*, 102.
2. Donald Revell, *Invisible Green*, 29.
3. Ibid., 28.
4. Stephanie Burt, "The Revell Variations," *The Nation*, https://www.
thenation.com/article/revell-variations/
5. Revell, "My Trip," *My Mojave*, 9.
6. Revell, "Belfast," *Pennyweight Windows: New & Selected Poems*, 5.
7. Revell, "Chorister," *The Drought-Adapted Vine*, 3.
8. Revell, "Central Park South," *Pennyweight Windows: New & Selected
Poems*, 3.
9. Ibid.
10. Revell, "In Paradise Alone," *Drought-Adapted Vine*, 10.
11. Revell, "Beyond Disappointment," *Drought-Adapted Vine*, 8.
12. Burt, "The Revell Variations," *The Nation*, https://www.thenation.
com/article/revell-variations/
13. Revell, "Birthplace," *The Gaza of Winter*, 5.
14. Revell, "Survey," *New Dark Ages*, Kindle edition.
15. Revell, "Muse," *Pennyweight Windows: New & Selected Poems*, 63.
16. Revell, "Here to There," *Pennyweight Windows: New & Selected Poems*,
15.
17. Revell, "Mechanics," *My Mojave*, 7.
18. Jack Spicer, "Letter to Allen Joyce," *My Vocabulary Did This to Me*, xvi.
19. Spicer, "From Ten Poems for *Downbeat*," *My Vocabulary Did This To Me*
423.
20. Revell, "Conforming to the Fashions of Eternity," *Arcady*, 14.
21. Revell, *Invisible Green*, 28–29.
22. Ibid., 28.

23. Revell, "The Stars Their Perfection," *Arcady*, 33.
24. Revell, *Invisible Green*, 36.
25. Revell, "The Northeast Corridor," *New Dark Ages*, Kindle edition.
26. Ralph Waldo Emerson, "Nature," *Nature and Selected Essays*, 39.
27. Henry David Thoreau, "Walking," *Essays*, 243.
28. Revell, "Anaximander," *Arcady*, 45.
29. Revell, "Against Creation," *The Bitter Withy*, 44.
30. Revell, "Arcady Again," *My Mojave*, 1.
31. Revell, "Kentucky," *The Bitter Withy* 35.
32. Revell, "Little Bees," *The Bitter Withy*, 50.
33. Revell, "Light Lily Lily Light Light Lily Light," *Arcady*, 13.
34. Revell, "My Mojave," *My Mojave*, 13.
35. Revell, "Moving Day," *My Mojave*, 12.
36. Revell, "My Trip," *My Mojave*, 8–9.
37. Revell, "Conforming to the Fashions of Eternity," *Arcady*, 14.
38. Revell, "New Year," *My Mojave*, 67.
39. Revell, "Foxglove," *Drought-Adapted Vine*, 75.

Works Cited

Burt, Stephanie. "The Revell Variations," *The Nation*, April 24, 2003, https://www.thenation.com/article/revell-variations/

Emerson, Ralph Waldo. *Nature and Selected Essays*. Penguin Classics, 2003.

Olson, Charles. *The Maximus Poems*. Edited by George F. Butternick. University of California Press, 1985.

Revell, Donald. *Arcady*. Wesleyan University Press, 2002.

Revell, Donald. *The Bitter Withy*. Alice James, 2009.

Revell, Donald. *Drought-Adapted Vine*. Alice James, 2015.

Revell, Donald. *The Gaza of Winter*. University of Georgia Press, 1988.

Revell, Donald. *Invisible Green*. Omnidawn, 2005.

Revell, Donald. *My Mojave*. Alice James, 2003.

Revell, Donald. *New Dark Ages*. Wesleyan University Press, 1990. Kindle edition.

Revell, Donald. *Pennyweight Windows: New & Selected Poems*. Alice James, 2005.

Spicer, Jack. *My Vocabulary Did This to Me: The Collected Poetry of Jack Spicer*. Edited by Peter Gizzi and Kevin Killian. Wesleyan University Press, 2008.

Thoreau, Henry David. *Essays: A Fully Annotated Edition*. Edited by Jeffrey S. Cramer. Yale University Press, 2013.

MARK IRWIN

"The ply of spirits on bodies"
Diaspora and Metamorphosis in Donald Revell's
"Short Fantasia"

The fantasia, a musical composition in free form and often in an improvisatory style, becomes a model for many of Donald Revell's later poems. Since his first collection, *From the Abandoned Cities,* Revell has addressed matters of body and spirit, but it is in his later, more transparent forms that he achieves a transcendence less possible in his earlier, more formal work. Although long influenced by Thoreau and Emerson, Revell achieves a marked openness in his work after moving to the southwestern edge of the Las Vegas Valley.

"The poet either is nature or he will seek it. The former constitutes the 'naïve,' the latter the 'sentimental' poet."[1] Friedrich von Schiller argues that the naïve poet is a part of nature and is able to represent it without imposing any of his or her own personality or nostalgia. The sentimental poet is often one who feels exiled and finds nature more in the imagination than at first hand. Schiller does not use either term in a pejorative sense, and he goes on to mention that genius is "naïve." The works of Hölderlin, Keats, Rimbaud, and Dickinson come to mind immediately as examples of just such genius as this, which requires that the poet sustain an unmediated vision over time, a rare feat even among those writers capable of the naiveté Schiller theorizes. Like many poets, Revell begins in the sentimental mode, but in numerous later poems, he achieves that more difficult mode that is one with the natural world and with creation. "Survey," for instance, from the 1990 collection *New Dark Ages,* is predicated on the very nostalgia that marks the "sentimental" poet according to Schiller, as we see in the poem's opening lines:

> I am so lonely for the twentieth century,
> for the deeply felt, obscene graffiti
> of armed men and the beautiful bridges[2]

Compare this to the more calligraphic and at-one-with-nature vision of these lines from "No Difference I Know They Are," from the 1998 collection *There Are Three:*

> this day
> there is no paint like the air
> this day
> is a godsend to the wasps[3]

I am not suggesting that Revell must leave form completely to attain this way of writing about nature from the inside—here, for example, the poem finds a syllabic 2/7 form with its last four lines—but what I am suggesting is that Revell's work moves in a diasporic manner toward the world of spirit where a more recognizable authenticity is attained, one where forms dissolve and recombine with greater energy. Here, in full, is Revell's "Short Fantasia," a variation on the sonnet that appears in his 2003 collection *My Mojave:*

> The plane descending from an empty sky
> Onto numberless real stars
> Makes a change in Heaven, a new
> Pattern for the ply of spirits on bodies.
> We are here. Sounds press our bones down.
> Someone standing recognizes someone else.
> We have no insides. All the books
> Are written on the steel beams of bridges.
> Seeing the stars at my feet, I tie my shoes
> With a brown leaf. I stand, and I read again
> The story of Aeneas escaping the fires
> And his wife's ghost. We shall meet again
> At a tree outside the city. We shall make
> New sounds and leave our throats in that place.[4]

Although the narrative of this poem is somewhat straightforward, the forms and locations within it, especially those representing heaven/earth, often change or become interchangeable. Here, passengers landing in an airport struggle with the new landscape they have not yet caught up to, a struggle that appears to be precipitated by a conflation between sky and earth, for we are told that the descending plane "Makes a change in Heaven, a new / Pattern for the ply of spirits on bodies." Our perspective, which we share with the passengers, is wonderfully altered through slippage, for where we expect to encounter the real beneath the inspirited, we actually encounter a simultaneity of the real and the spiritual in a time-worn transitional moment—passengers at the end of a flight arriving to an airport and beginning to de-plane—made unfamiliar through Revell's use of what we might call the "language-of-jet," a transportational syntax that reinforces the concept of contemporary diaspora: "We are here. Sounds press our bones down. / Someone standing recognizes someone else."

The phrase "Sounds press our bones down" suggests the non-fixity of this new existence as it prefigures the "New sounds" at poem's end, but it first becomes the signal and catalyst for rapid transformation: "We have no insides. All the books / Are written on the steel beams of bridges." Revell's two-fold "Fantasia" is not only improvisational through language but also through resonant metaphor. Are we on the tarmac, a bit disoriented, jostled, and jet-lagged; or, have we actually been transformed in some fantasy Heaven on the way back to earth? The phrase "We have no insides" oddly recalls the pupal stage of the insect, in which the larva dissolves to a liquid before reforming into an adult insect with wings—a biological form of transformation, a kind of pre-Heaven, as Revell's canvas grows larger and language becomes a city-text: "All the books / Are written on the steel beams of bridges." The transformation here is marvelous, for language moves us from a reflective to a utilitarian state: to cross from one space, from one moment, to another, we must read the book of the bridge across which we are journeying.

Relentless in its dislocations, "Short Fantasia" provides nothing less than a kind of transfiguration for the reader who struggles with new coordinates and joins in the speaker's conflation of sky and earth: "Seeing the stars at my feet, I tie my shoes / With a brown leaf." The vulnerability of this new existence seems joyously imperiled, for how does one tie a shoe "[w]ith a brown leaf"? Perhaps nothing less than a ritual by which to pass into a new world, Revell's poem recalls a theme by another poet, William Blake, who also defies dimensions:

> To see a World in a Grain of Sand
> And a Heaven in a Wild Flower[5]

"Short Fantasia" culminates in a recasting of Aeneas's classic flight. It is a re-visioning that propels us, even in our bewildered disorientation, toward yet another new place and, possibly, yet another transfiguration:

> and I read again
> The story of Aeneas escaping the fires
> And his wife's ghost. We shall meet again
> At a tree outside the city. We shall make
> New sounds and leave our throats in that place.[6]

The reference here, of course, is to Book II of *The Aeneid*, where Aeneas recounts the fall of Troy and the death of his wife Creusa, who follows behind and is lost as Aeneas carries his father Anchises on his back while his son Ascanius follows. The speaker in Revell's poem could be reading the classic text as the plane lands—and what better epic of place to read than Virgil's to contrast Revell's boundless voyage? Ascanius (also called Iullus, prefiguring Julius Caesar) will continue the lineage in Italy and become the ancestor of Augustus, to whom Virgil dedicates his poem.

Revell ends "Short Fantasia" with another compelling diasporic, metamorphic gesture: "We shall make / New sounds and leave our throats in that place." How beautiful and boldly reconceived is the throat when we consider it a column of speech. But then, what is poetry if it doesn't change us, or make the familiar unfamiliar, as Frost suggests? What better assurance that this is so than a poem such as Revell's that reminds us that the body is itself a transformation and a journeying?

Notes

1. Friedrich von Schiller, *Naïve and Sentimental Poetry & On the Sublime*, 110.

2. Donald Revell, "Survey," *Pennyweight Windows: New & Selected Poems*, 35.

3. Revell, "No Difference I Know They Are," *Pennyweight Windows: New & Selected Poems*, 131.

4. Revell, "Short Fantasia," *Pennyweight Windows: New & Selected Poems*, 159.

5. William Blake, "Auguries of Innocence," *Selected Poetry and Prose of Blake*, 90.

6. Revell, "Short Fantasia," *Pennyweight Windows: New & Selected Poems*, 159.

Works Cited

Blake, William. *Selected Poetry and Prose of Blake*. Edited by Northrop Frye, Random House, 1953.

Revell, Donald. *Pennyweight Windows: New & Selected Poems*. Alice James, 2005.

Schiller, Friedrich von. *Naïve and Sentimental Poetry & On the Sublime*. Ungar, 1979.

PETER COVINO

Faith and Faithlessness in *A Thief of Strings*
Donald Revell's Epic Vision

Introduction

Devotion versus loyalty. Fidelity versus frustration. Spiritual endur-
ance versus psychic dissolution. Let's set these difficult abstractions
and sometimes paradoxical concepts into play and move toward
outlining a parameter for Donald Revell's developing epic vision.
During the first decade of the new millennium, Revell's protean
work was confronting long-enduring moral and spiritual questions
related to his legacy, his growing family responsibility, and his own
complicated health concerns as a result of a diagnosis of multiple
sclerosis, even while his singular vision and poetic confidence were
soaring, all against the backdrop of the Iraq War and the troubling
American political scene in the wake of the September 11 terror
attacks. Lesser critics might be tempted to write off his work from
this period as the result of a mid-life crisis or the fear of dying—
there is a fair dose of self-rumination and visionary ranting in the
desert—but so unrelenting, precise, and farsighted are his poetic
explorations that only John Ashbery, Tomaz Salamun, and Louise
Glück come to mind as comparable contemporary exemplars. Revel-
ell's facility with language and the various poetic modes and regis-
ters he employs make his poetry, for me, closest to Salamun's—by
turns quizzically inspired by the Dadaists and Cubists, conversa-
tional, quick-moving and disjunctive, but also filled with childlike
wonder, sophisticated erudition, and a meditative world-weariness
that is amplified and elaborated through his essay collections and
translation projects.

In attempting to chart the trajectory of Revell's work with the
epic, this essay draws from the consistent metaphorical richness of his
poetry collections, the titles of which announce themselves as com-
plex sites of rigorous psychological and spiritual interrogation: thus,
we are offered images of contested boundaries *(From the Abandoned*

Cities, The Gaza of Winter) and ideas of historical re-inscription (*New Dark Ages, Erasure*), while also welcoming visions of ephemerality, obliquity, the reordered (*Pennyweight Windows*), and the fast-moving (*Tantivy*). Revell also sets the spiritually tenuous and transformative against issues of natural perseverance in more recent collections (*A Thief of Strings, The Bitter Withy,* and *Drought-Adapted Vine*), not to mention that we also encounter a revitalized objectivist ideal (*Beautiful Shirt*) and an idyllic pastoral (*Arcady, My Mojave*) that together become semiotic terms ordaining a complex network of signifiers for a poetic aesthetic of a distinctly philosophical dimension.

The central metaphors that emerge even from this brief list, consisting of a handful of titles from Revell's twenty books published over four decades—which have of late become increasingly spare, religious, even mystical—represent confident gestures, or incisive sections, that build toward a complex epic worldview of and for the twenty-first century. During the aughts, Revell published two important essay collections, *Invisible Green: Selected Prose* (2005) and *The Art of Attention: A Poet's Eye* (2007), where he continued to theorize and locate his own poetics. Central to my argument in this essay is an acknowledgement of the intertextual relationship between these various genres on the poet's growing oeuvre. The level of production in that fertile, urgent decade is rather astounding when we consider that during those same years Revell also published prizewinning translations of Apollinaire (*The Self-Dismembered Man: Selected Later Poems* in 2004) and Rimbaud (*A Season in Hell* in 2007), which underscores the fact that from 2002 to 2009, over the course of just seven years, he published nine books: five poetry collections, two collections of essays, and two books of translations.

A Thief of Strings (2007) and *The Bitter Withy* (2009) were written mostly during my years as a PhD student studying with Revell at the University of Utah, during which time I regularly saw and talked to him about the poems he was writing and other, related work. This was a particularly intense and trying time in Revell's life, as he battled the ever-debilitating effects of multiple sclerosis (MS) and endured prolonged absences from his family in Las Vegas while he taught in Salt Lake City, more than four hundred miles away. Revell's own professor-mentor of many years, Robert Creeley—Revell earned his PhD at the University of Buffalo, where Creeley taught for many years—died on March 30, 2005, and the second section of *A Thief of Strings* features a sonnet crown in Creeley's honor.

It is impassioned, mythical, and timeless writing of measured lamentation and remarkable poetic restraint, full of personal detail and the appreciation of the "things" of Revell's own life against the aforementioned backdrop of war, familial tension and loss, and the fear of more imminent catastrophe. Revell's sister and mother also died during that decade, while he was left to grapple with his own advancing sense of physical deterioration and psychic dislocation—not dissimilar to the struggles endured by William Carlos Williams later in his life—amid the larger and increasingly violent din of war, unchecked capitalism, and environmental catastrophe. Every time I read Revell's poems in this knowledge, I marvel at their self-possessed experimentation and their willingness and ability to articulate a more accommodating, a more generous and tender vision.

"An Ocean Made of Paper"

A Thief of Strings, the third of the poetry collections published by Alice James Books, is the collection where I see his work becoming the most idiosyncratic and visionary. *A Thief of Strings*—notice the communal, universalizing use of the indefinite article in the title—is dedicated to his children: Lucie, at the time recently adopted from China, and Benjamin, not yet then quite a teen. The significance of the dedication can be considered Virgilian, as Revell, faced with the recent loss of several loved ones, contemplates his legacy, his responsibility to his own children, and by extension, his readership. In this context, Revell is the Anchises father figure, who miraculously hopes "his son approach(es) across the green valley floor of Elysium."[1] Elysium is famously described in detail in Book VI of Virgil's epic the *Aeneid,* where Aeneas travels to the underworld to be reunited temporarily with his deceased father, Anchises, and where he receives the prophecies for the founding and history of Rome. Back-to-back poems, "Sibylline" and "After Williams," the twelfth and thirteenth in the sonnet crown of section "II—14 for Robert Creeley," recall figures that further illustrate Revell's growing consciousness of the epic form. The first alludes to the priestess at Cumae who leads Aeneas's journey into Hell, while the second, appropriately, recalls in its concise objectivist style the poetry of William Carlos Williams. Williams's much-revered *Spring and All* comes to mind in this instance because of the way it weaves together verse and prose commentary, a hybridization that Williams later uses to such mesmerizing effect in his own epic, *Paterson.*

In Revell's spare and intimate poetic idiom, both of these poems, "Sibylline" and "After Williams," combine impressive erudition with an appealing domestic focus, while somehow maintaining a wild, undomesticated, and mysterious intensity. In "Sibylline," against the backdrop of recent deaths, the speaker notices that one of his "trees has gone yellow in the East"; readers will recall that Aeneas was required to pluck a golden bough or "Argicida," as Revell writes, in order to enter Hell.[2] Yet, the speaker seems likewise inspired to abandon this arduous metaphysical task in favor of the simple—yes, according to Revell, it is always simple—task of following the poem toward its articulation:

> And later at night in the deep chair
> When the movie is black & white,
> It finds one Deborah Kerr
> In tears on the beach in furs,
> Connecticut, not Elysium,
> And the moon rising from an ocean made of paper.[3]

"An ocean made of paper" seizes our attention above all and suggests the writerly qualities and playful vastness of Revell's work, along with his growing belief in the need thoroughly to document his poetic experiences during these years. Revell's style and images are clever postmodern innovations, likely written with Book Four of *Paterson*—where Williams meditates on Thalassa, the Sea Goddess mother of Venus, and the persona's own nostalgic return to "the blood dark sea"—in mind.[4]

In "After Williams," Revell wakes to see his wife Claudia washing the remains of a dead sparrow fallen out of their garden umbrella, and the poet asks, "What is a good place / To break down to die / To ask such a question / Is one heaven."[5] These familiar figures—wife, sparrow—take on a typically charged, emblematic quality that invites us to consider with greater immediacy this most unforgiving of questions, as well as the others it engenders: Can we converse with the dead? Can the poet, through her or his skillful art, ever be one with Heaven? By tuning our attention so, the poem invites not only this type of ontological speculation but also a greater appreciation for what lies before us and what surrounds us: the earthly mundane of our everyday lives, animals, insects, and flowers—bees, rabbits, dogs, and hummingbirds are ubiquitous in *A Thief of Strings*. "I find myself praying, / Yes, for bees one hundred years dead [. . .] The bees / Strike into the sunlight, / Giving it a sound. / The echo is flowers," Revell writes in the third poem of this middle sonnet sequence, aptly titled "On My Fiftieth Birthday."[6] Revell also meditates upon his own faith, mortality, and, by extension, his connection to a genealogy of poetry making that is, as he confides in his essays from this period, founded on the writings of Whitman and Thoreau.

While Virgil, along with Whitman and other key transcendentalist thinkers, are frequently invoked throughout Revell's work, in *A Thief of Strings,* he mentions in the second, somewhat apocalyptic poem that he has been "[r]eading Ovid today on Ovid's birthday."[7] Ovid's epic *Metamorphoses,* and its more quickly paced narrative, transforming moods, characters, and landscapes, speaks directly of a lapsarian world where amorous and religious conflict, the despoliation of natural resources, the loss of innocence exacerbated by war, and ongoing sociopolitical injustice can, perhaps, if not be redeemed by the poet-singer at least be sung to posterity in the hope of greater wisdom and compassion in the future.

In the first section of *A Thief of Strings,* we seem to be fully immersed within Ovid's fallen Iron Age of man:

> whose base vein
> Let loose all evil: modesty and truth
> And righteousness fled earth, and in their place
> Came trickery and slyness, plotting, swindling,
> Violence and the damned desire of having.[8]

In the opening poem of the collection, "Landscape: A Delirium," which immediately follows the dedication to his children, Revell seems also to invoke Ovid, along with Rimbaud, when he writes, "The enemy is maniacs. And we, Poem, are with the other side, / The savages. / [. . .] War *on* terror? War *is* terror . . . only ask / The Great Wall falling to pieces / Or Li Po."[9] Presumably, the writers and readers of poetry have the power to conceptualize poetic time as discontinuous, ever-present, and unified, regardless of attempts at destruction. It is not clear, for example, if the Great Wall here refers to the Great Wall of China, to the Berlin Wall, or to those walls being ruined in Iraq and other countries as the result of warfare, but the oblique reference to his daughter, Lucie, adopted from China as I mentioned earlier, and the desperate need to keep humanity intact against its own destructive impulses, strikes me as especially poignant, even more so considering that this is the first poem we encounter.

Similarly, the poet-speaker of *A Thief of Strings* sees himself besieged, as was the eighth-century Chinese poet Li Po, whose pastoral, contemplative lyrics changed dramatically after the peaceful Tang Dynasty was ravaged by the An Lushan Rebellion.[10] For Revell, the poet and the innocent children invoked in the poem—"Jack and Annie / And a bear & a baby"—are stand-ins for his own children and others, and the collection begins *in medias res* with "a too-rough lullaby, / A paradise too early. / Swarming with golden bugs / And wishful thinking."[11] Instead of a direct invocation to God, poetry and the "poem" seem to be part of the epic convention of a statement of theme and writing itself a potentially redemptive act.

As mentioned, two of the four dystopian, "delirious landscape" poems that open this collection reference Ovid directly. The second was written in the spring of 2003, when Revell served as a visiting professor at the University of Alabama. "Landscape with Warhol and the Coming of Spring 2003" speaks to Revell's mastery of imagistic conflation, sonic punning (war-haul), and his profound, multilayered epic vision. Once again, exact meaning is difficult to pin down in these multifaceted, Cubist-inspired poems, but the wide prismatic range of signification in this one is particularly fascinating and provocative, as when we learn that the speaker of the poem stops reading Ovid when he gets to the awful story of five-year-old "Itys / Hacked to pieces by his mother and poor Philomela, / Cooked and served up hot to the king his father."[12] The intertextual allusions and psychological intensity here are remarkable for the way they call to mind the unbearable cruelty of humanity—recall that Revell is writing here at the outset of the second Iraq war—as well as the poet's own precarious state of mind while living away from his wife and family without lingering on images of gratuitous violence.

Turning to Ovid, readers will recall that Procne killed her son by Tereus, Itys, after learning that her husband had brutally raped her virgin sister, Philomela, and then cut out her tongue. Philomela, in an apparent partial updating of the Homeric Penelope story, was able to weave a tapestry for her sister Procne that told of this horrific crime, and then they both escaped their tormentor by turning into birds (nightingales, in some versions). At the end of "Landscape with Warhol and the Coming of Spring 2003," the realities of the poet's temporary house in Alabama and the TV news program featuring the vast landscapes of bombed Iraqi cities intermingle and once again conflate without facile resolution or a fixed perspective, as the persona notices "In Baghdad / The Morning is a desert pastel with no wind, / And birds are singing even as the blue jays sleep, I guess, / Around my house."[13] The timing and uncertainty of the phrase "I guess" is particularly affecting and convincing, as the birds of Warhol's real or imagined wall print and the blue jays around the poet-persona's temporary home are all stilled by the poet's imagistic conjuring of the windless allure of a pastel desert.

"A Complex of Addictions"

My partner, a medical doctor and an avid reader of poetry, and now also a friend of Donald Revell's, is fond of arguing with me about the poet's prolificacy, likening his writing to "semen spread across the world." I try to argue for less graphic "seeds," but he proposes that Revell's work is much messier, more ecstatic, more human and humane as it fearlessly and uncontainably spills over into the meta-physical ineffable, with every ounce of a man's unpredictable and limited lifeblood.

> Manhood is escape, a complex of addictions,
>   . . . a wine made in Italy
> Meant to taste like grasses in bright sunlight.
> The grass on hillsides is, I think,
> As helpless as God, and as addictive. Yesterday
> I was drinking in my garden, looking toward the hills.
> I saw a white linen floating in the sky.
> An angel[14]

We must be as "helpless as God, and as addictive" to be able to care for and nurture the world while mitigating destruction, against in-credible odds. Revell seems to argue for prayer above all and a vi-sionary way of being in the world heightened by an uncompromis-ing way of seeing and feeling. Of course, "addiction" is a strong, potentially harmful term, as it also refers to compulsive behavior and works at a psychological interstice between the functional and the corruptible, but Revell is not afraid to insist on a quietism equal in measure to that found in the writings of Emily Dickinson. Here, we also have Whitman's grass, and the very tangible and utilitarian "handkerchief of the lord" presented in *Song of Myself*, re-inscribed.[15] By extension, we cannot help but think as well of Whitman's insistent reordering, editing, expanding, and juxtaposing of his one book, the epic and relentlessly, startlingly beautiful *Leaves of Grass*.

The "seeds" of Revell's epic conversations start to take an even firmer hold when we consider this poem. As an Italian-born immigrant to this country, "a wine made in Italy" speaks to me directly, and perhaps speaks to the carefree stereotype many people share about contemporary Italian culture, as well as about the high quality of Italian wine. The palpable litany of addictions, pitched at a higher octave earlier in "O Rare," also reverberate: "The birds are Addiction, a skin to break through, / a prayer already prayed and answered in Eden."[16] The Eden also becomes Revell's enclosed garden in his not-so-idyllic idyllic Mojave, in his desert, where prophet-like and Saint Jerome-like he prays and prays and rebukes and stammers out his credo in quick flashes of revelation. "God is flat on the ground. I lie beside him. / Together we can hear the tender, / Unvarying trill of sunlight in the dirt."[17]

Prostrate, given over to his vision and the Noah-esque drunkenness of his powerful art, the speaker of "O Rare" is suddenly accosted: "Birds in the invisible trees / Called to me. They came and clad me for death . . . Nearer than you suppose, / A skin of a kind and then the skins of every kind / Broke. The sun was born where it is buried, / Here in my bosom and at home."[18] I don't know if there's a recording to track down of Revell reading this powerful, far-seeing poem, but there should be. I hear and feel these insistent, transformative images at their lightning-quick speed pierce right through me. These were not easy years for him, when his MS became chronic and ever more debilitating, to the point of affecting his heart function. In fact, sobriety and references to drinking are mentioned on a few significant occasions and serve as an important leitmotif, no doubt related to the fear and pain, both psychic and physical, he was experiencing during these unsettling days of failing health.

Of this, Revell makes gorgeously messy, embattled, and startling art of the utmost quality and candor without becoming reductively autobiographical. "You asked for my autobiography" he writes in "Election Year," another of the experimental sonnets in the sonnet crown for Creeley in the second section—"Imagine the greeny clicking sound / Of hummingbirds in dry wood."[19] The birds of addiction Revell alights on in "O Rare" come full circle in a holy communion of sorts in this image invoked later in the collection, of the hummingbird that also functions as a delicate and wondrous avatar for the poet himself. In *The Art of Attention*, Revell reasserts this dictum, this recurring epic theme further, in what may at first seem more prosaic language that is actually no less poetic and challenging to parse: "Wit is always impious and aggressive, too. Peace and piety comprise the actual circumstance of love poetry and no argument. Where effort yields to inarguable attachment—eyebeam and heartstring—love is all."[20] Thus, these first two sections of *A Thief of Strings* share a common epic directive that could be summed up in Revell's words as "Love lives in the eye; it is quick there. It furthers the eye in the direction of its inarguable innocence."[21]

The "Delirium" poems in the first section of *A Thief of Strings* attain their crescendo in "O Rare." The hazier and more aggressive, impressionistic landscapes of Revell's Ovid-inspired mythologies, where Pentheus and Acteon figure in "Landscape Near Biloxi, Mississippi" or the hacked-apart Itys appears in "Landscape with Warhol and the Coming of Spring 2003," become flatly and devastatingly broken. The initial "lost threads" of conversation in "The Plow That Broke the Plains" give way to a "soundtrack swell" where gradually even "Horses disappear in every direction,"[22] or, as in "Storks," one adult stork starves out the sharp cries of his young birds once his mate dies. Revell's own children and childlike reveries (let us not forget that "revell" means "dream" in French) are also juxtaposed against more unsettling images of death, war, abandonment, and dismemberment in the first two parts of this collection. From the middle sonnet sequence to Creeley, specifically in "Hallowe'en, Blue Diamond, Nevada," Revell writes, "As up ahead of me our children / (Three of them: Death, / A Fairy, and towheaded Starvation) / Go from door to door to get their candy."[23] Yet, in "Storks" (from the first section), he seems already to have answered his fears by suggesting that the innocence and carefree sprit of children must be anterior and be valued above all else: "The children's song is human / But unconcerned with the affairs of men."[24]

Apollinaire and his Cubo-Futurist and Dada-inspired freewheeling lyricism are clear and consistent inspirations throughout this collection, even as Revell puzzles over, rhapsodizes on, folds-in, and collapses contrasting themes from religion; mythology; film; and unraveling issues of faith, faithfulness, and fidelity. "Jules and Jim," also from the first section, is a poem that directly precedes "O Rare" and is yet another complex and interesting exemplum, as it creates the occasion for Revell to directly reference Apollinaire while watching the famous Francois Truffaut film from 1962 about a ménage-à-trois set against World War I and its immediate aftermath. Fittingly, "Jules and Jim" is also visually engaging, as some lines are indented and others are not, thus creating a bifurcated field where various narratives compete. Of course, the film *Jules and Jim* ends tragically when the Jeanne Moreau character, also mentioned in the Revell poem, drives off a bridge with her lover, Jim, leaving her husband, Jules, to attend to the tragedy. In Revell's quick-moving, suggestive poem, a letter arrives from a former lover (similar to the film), some thirty years later with "a photograph too sad, too vacant to describe."[25] The poet-narrator instead finds consolation: "Because of a great movie / I have lived this far this long, / My worlds by worlds destroyed, / But never the sky, which is a lover."[26] This subtle juxtaposition and artful sequencing strike me as particularly effective in the way they suggest that art—the movie, as well as Revell's own poems—have served as artistic balms against the larger destruction of the wars he contemplates throughout the poems of the collection's first section.

Revell seems to fully possess the worlds he describes; he doesn't remain comfortably outside them. But, by using the personal pronoun "my," he acknowledges his complicit role in the narrative of a complex and imperfect life, where seduction and attraction are forces that can potentially threaten stability and a sense of emotional intactness. In fact, it seems Revell's faith and his constant exploration and visualization of his relationship to a larger, less containable power—the sky in this particular poem—anchors him verbally at least to a transformed "hieratic face" or a priest-like or religious poetic tradition.[27]

To my imagination, "Jules and Jim" especially, along with other poems in the collection, including the John Frederick Peto painting on the cover of the book, *Old Time Letter Rack,* have the collaged, sculpted, and free associative feel of much of William Carlos Williams's groundbreaking *Paterson*, which readers will recall included excerpts from letters written to Williams by the writers and poets Edward Dahlberg, Marcia Nardi, Allen Ginsberg, and Gilbert Sorrentino.[28] Revell's Mojave desert is the shimmering, corruptible desert that we also encounter in collections such as *My Mojave,* contrasted against the more idealized landscapes of *Arcady,* also from this especially fecund decade. Peto's evocative oil painting is an especially apt visual representation of the poet's (dis)continuous relationship with both the physical and psychic realities of his life. Set against a dark background, the painting creates a provocative trompe l'oeil effect, painted as it is as if rendered on wood paneling, but has the aspect of a collaged wallboard where objects seem to float enigmatically in three-dimensional space. Strong geometric shapes converge to form a large "X" or quasi-bulls-eye in the middle of the painting, which is set against painted "imaginary" postcards and/or ticket stubs, calling cards, and letters with postage markings, as well as bits of newspaper clippings tacked onto the canvas where the postcards seem once to have been. This strong yet solemn and haunting visual play within the painting is further heightened by a small photograph of President Lincoln slightly off kilter just to the middle of the "X" at its center. There is also a suggestive piece of coiled string in the lower left corner, which adds to the eerie, disembodied feeling one gets from the cover, even as it serves as an understated primer for how to read the collection and its assembled sections.

"Six Guitar Strings"

Section III of *A Thief of Strings* begins with an ominous epigraph from the tortured, dissolute, yet sublimely talented poet Jack Spicer: "This is where my love, somehow stops."[29] Revell's tone is somewhat more reproachful and unsettling in this section, which starts with three poems that juxtapose and rebuke fixed, non-animistic views proffered, he asserts, by Christians, Jews, and Muslims alike. In "To the Christians," "[A] robin's nest / In the scrawny pines" becomes "[b]abies open bright throats to the sun."[30] "To the Jews" begins with another idealized female figure from Ovid, the beautiful, swift-footed (and androgynous) warrior-maiden of the Arcadian woodlands, "Atalanta, / From inside a drop of dew / Comes the speed to outspeed you." Revell, the poet-narrator continues: "Is my dog a god because he kills a rabbit / I lay my head beside the broken animal. / Our eyes meet. The world belongs to him."[31] Again, there is a strong sense of prismatic conflation in this fable-like imagery between the ongoing fighting in Israel and throughout the Middle East, as Atalanta is ultimately a doomed character in the *Metamorphoses;* she, too, fails to thank and praise the goddess Venus for the love of her young suitor, Hippomones, and both are turned to lions.[32]

These are figures that are startlingly similar to the "broken animal(s)" that Revell bemoans in this poem and many others throughout his work, figures capable of thought and reflection that require more peaceful effort but who act out of primal instinct alone. These ideas are reprised in Revell's poem "The Birth of Venus," when he mystically contends, "I went *inside* the mountains / Gods to the left / The low / The lion / The grasshopper curved green-gray / And there were no gates anymore."[33] I love Revell's unpretentious line breaks throughout this collection and his moments of hard-won directness and clarity—the *ideas* in his poetics matter above all—and he seems to be insisting with an Objectivist intensity that poetry invites us to see and to experience the world at its most minute levels, especially with regard to the earth's "lowest" creatures. Of course, there also seems to be something of Saint Francis's mysticism adhering to these poems—poetry as meditative and revelatory process—and why *not* bless and revere all animals, as St. Francis did?

In "To the Muslims" Revell asserts, "I hear what a pagan would have made: / The higher sound is bees; / The lower, a dove alone . . . All together it is one God, who never made a desert / And whose circus we are, all clowns swimming."[34] The circus image is familiar from Apollinaire, and Revell exhorts us to leave our violence and limiting belief systems aside for something potentially more complex, which is also entertaining, playful, and forgiving. Essentially, he invites us to put our fears aside and notice the power poetry has to blend images and ideas in order to create boundless, richer, more fascinating worlds.

"The Last Guitar" and "Thief of Strings" are two longer poems in the last of the three sections of *A Thief of Strings*; they are both rapturous and breathless tours de force that reward careful attention, each differently inspired by Rimbaud, whom Revell was also translating at the time. "The Last Guitar" begins:

> *Le printemps, c'est l'automne*
> > the last guitar alive;
> *De l'aube claire,*
> > the last guitar alive.
>
> Or is it the golden dog
> I always see at home
> Running against the sky?
> We call him *Roof Dog.*

I cannot imagine my life
If I had never seen him.
I'd know no peace.

Which foreign movies do you like?
All of them.
Coming out of the fog—dogs and words.
And the magic is—they never die,
Not so long as one guitar's alive.

Between French and death
The houses sail like baseballs.
. . .
It is October
This is the World Series
We sail on baseballs made of Gold.[35]

The speaker appears to delight in welcoming all of the important
facets of his creative existence and his life's daily work. In this epic
digression or cataloguing of sorts, Revell praises the song of the
guitar and, by extension, modern day troubadours and poet-singers
everywhere. He likewise praises the French language, French films,
the night sky, and skygazing—the autumn constellations feature
both Canis Major and Canis Minor, and they are especially visible
from Revell's desert home in Las Vegas.

Three of the four sections of this longer poem are decidedly
more despairing, as when the poet-narrator muses that "life on
earth is only / Possible anymore as snow, as something very close /
To melting all its life."[36] "Cybele (Venus or love) will not return"
becomes his wailful refrain in this "*saison brumeuse,*" or hazy sea-
son,[37] and this catalogue of difficult realizations takes on the solem-
nity of the epic funeral games common in classical literature by
both acknowledging loss and striving to carry on.[38] In a direct nod
to Rimbaud's work and that poet's "A Drunken Boat," Revell fur-
ther muses, "Memory / Rides in paper boats on mysteries / Too fast
to freeze. *Le printemps, c'est l'automne* . . . / The climate, thinking
with its knees, / Knows nothing, thank God. / The last guitar is but
the first of many."[39]

In "Thief of Strings," the last poem in the collection, we seem
to be in the company of only a single thief, and the despairing
tone of some of the earlier poems turns to outright dejection and
humiliation:

My life's gone out of mind.
Let us see, Sky, but not me.
I'm no company anymore.

The poor thief running out of the guitar shop
Was stopped and searched and humiliated
Not ten feet from me as I waited
For the train. Down on his knees he gave up
A pocketful of strings, and I couldn't see any more.
. . .
Gone. Whatever I'd thought to do was gone
. . .
My whole life, from the end of childhood
To this very moment of the sassafras
Wound in shoals, had disappeared.[40]

In the second of the poem's thirteen parts, Revell reflects on
scenes from his childhood and, associatively, on his relationship with
his own son, the bearer of his legacy. Not surprisingly, the image of
the metaphorical ball, a talisman of a youthful past and an unknown
future, once again resurfaces: "Much later, my son is in the hotel park-
ing lot / Waiting to catch a ball I've thrown too high into the air. It's
/ unbearable."[41] In "Elegy for the Word Dusk," the third part of this
long poem, the poet recalls writing, "'I want to go to the Garden of
Eden to die.'"[42] Poetry threatens to fail the poet, yet Rimbaud and
French poetic forms, including several experimental sestina-like parts
that hinge on a series of six evocative words and fragmented re-
sponses, continue to provide inspiration and solace—Part Four, for
instance, includes the following list: "Evergreen / Burr-marigold /
Gentleman / Dogwood / Anybody / Eerelong,"[43] while the untitled
Part Ten features brief meditations on botanical species, among them
eglantine, briar-rose, goldenrod, daisy, azalea, and honeysuckle, "which
you cannot kill," his friend the poet Alice Notley claims.[44] In Part
Eleven, the hummingbird reappears when the poet asks, "What use
to a man is Man? / We cannot even hear the hummingbirds. / We
steal guitar strings."[45] In Part Thirteen, he answers these complex
philosophical and ontological queries, when he says through poetry
"[t]hese metaphors mix themselves, / And I say hurray for helpless-
ness! / . . . / From the end of childhood / Until this very moment /
Is one bird nowhere. / Not forgotten. Free."[46]

If we turn once again to *The Art of Attention,* we can begin to parse
Revell's prose commentary, in which he offers a detailed reading of

many of his best poems up until *My Mojave,* and where he details a unique ars poetica that more clearly defines his objective and literary goals. Inspired by Rimbaud's concept of "derangement," the poet sees by "degrading the I. So doing, he exalts the eye set free from its false sovereign, Self. A deranged eye sees fine. The light enters it effortlessly and unimpeded. The optic nerves speed the news."[47]

In preparing *Pennyweight Windows: New & Selected Poems,* it makes perfect sense that Revell would begin a rigorous self-assessment and poetic reckoning process that also defines the later *The Art of Attention. A Thief of Strings* stands as an even more unpredictable reenactment of and testament to these poetic processes put to the test at a time of great personal suffering. Fortunately for us, Revell's sense of dire urgency and the sheer depth of his formidable poetic skill flourished during the decade in which these books were written, providing further strength to the foundation he had previously laid and upon which he continues so splendidly and so searchingly to build.

Notes

1. Donald Revell, *The Art of Attention,* 46.
2. Revell, "Sibylline," *A Thief of Strings,* 34.
3. Ibid.
4. William Carlos Williams, *Paterson,* 201. Williams also offers: "You will come to it, the blood dark sea / of praise. You must come to it. Seed / of Venus, you will return to / a girl standing upon a tilted shell, rose / pink," 200.
5. Revell, "After Williams," *A Thief of Strings,* 35.
6. Revell, "On My Fiftieth Birthday," *A Thief of Strings,* 25.
7. Revell, "Reading Ovid on Ovid's Birthday," *A Thief of Strings,* 5.
8. Ovid, *Ovid's Metamorphoses.* Trans. Rolfe Humphries. Bloomington: Indiana University Press, 1995, 7.
9. Revell, "Landscape: A Delirium," *A Thief of Strings,* 3–4.
10. *An Online Resource for Asian History and Culture.*
11. Revell, "Landscape: A Delirium," *A Thief of Strings,* 4.
12. Revell, "Landscape with Warhol and the Coming of Spring 2003," *A Thief of Strings,* 5.
13. Ibid.
14. Revell, "O Rare," *A Thief of Strings,* 17.
15. Walt Whitman, "Song of Myself," *Leaves of Grass,* 33.
16. Revell, "O Rare," *A Thief of Strings,* 16.
17. Ibid., 18.
18. Ibid., 19.

19. Revell, "Election Year," *A Thief of Strings*, 29.

20. Revell, *The Art of Attention*, 51.

21. Ibid., 52.

22. Revell, "The Plow That Broke the Plains," *A Thief of Strings*, 9.

23. Revell, "Hallowe'en, Blue Diamond, Nevada," *A Thief of Strings*, 28.

24. Revell, "Storks," *A Thief of Strings*, 11.

25. Revell, "Jules and Jim," *A Thief of Strings*, 15.

26. Ibid.

27. Ibid.

28. William Carlos Williams, *Paterson* 45, 48, 64, 76, 87–90, 172–74, 210–11, 212.

29. Quoted in Revell, *A Thief of Strings*, 37.

30. Revell, "To the Christians," *A Thief of Strings*, 39.

31. Revell, "To the Jews," *A Thief of Strings*, 40.

32. Ovid, *Metamorphoses*, 252–57.

33. Revell, "The Birth of Venus," *A Thief of Strings*, 48.

34. Revell, "To the Muslims," *A Thief of Strings*, 41.

35. Revell, "The Last Guitar," *A Thief of Strings*, 43.

36. Ibid., 45.

37. Ibid.

38. Part Six of "Thief of Strings" includes two lines in all caps that forebodingly announce: "Thoughts That Blot Out the Earth Are Best. / I Come From the Funeral of Mankind," 58.

39. Revell, "The Last Guitar," *A Thief of Strings*, 46.

40. Revell, "Thief of Strings," *A Thief of Strings*, 52.

41. Ibid., 53.

42. Ibid., 54.

43. Ibid., 56.

44. Ibid., 64.

45. Ibid., 65.

46. Ibid., 68.

47. Revell, *The Art of Attention*, 126.

Works Cited

An Online Resource for Asian History and Culture, Columbia University, October 2, 2016, achttp://afe.easia.columbia.edu/at/libo/lb01.html

Ovid. *Metamorphoses*. Translated by Rolfe Humphries. Indiana University Press, 1995.

Revell, Donald. *The Art of Attention: A Poet's Eye*. Graywolf, 2007.

Revell, Donald. *A Thief of Strings*, Alice James, 2007.

Whitman, Walt. "Song of Myself," *Leaves of Grass*, 1891–92 ed. David McKay, pp. 29–79. *The Walt Whitman Archive*, edited by Kenneth M. Price and Ed Folsom, University of Nebraska-Lincoln, https://whitmanarchive.org/published/LG/1891/whole.html

Williams, William Carlos. *Paterson*. New Directions, 1992.

ANDREW S. NICHOLSON

"Eyesight Is Prophetic Instantly"
Phenomenology in the Poetics of Donald Revell

"My poetic is neither method nor craft: it is my way of being in the world."
—DONALD REVELL[1]

Introduction

In his critical work *The Art of Attention*, Donald Revell outlines a poetics of attending to the world around him. The poetics he outlines sets the writing of the poem as an act of observation as opposed to traditional notions of craft where the phenomenal facts of the world are sculpted into meaning. This concept of attention that Revell details has a kinship with the existential phenomenology of Martin Heidegger. As in existential phenomenology, the Revellian poem begins with an attention aimed at things in the world rather than beginning with a claim or a predetermined form. As with Heideggerian uncovering, the poem discovers unseen truths through its focus on the phenomenal world rather than using the phenomenal world to illustrate predetermined truths.

Revell and Heidegger differ, though, on the ultimate aim of their respective activities. While Heidegger hopes to move his existential phenomenology into a structured, cultural project, Revell hopes each poem will be a renewed attention. By emphasizing the method of composition and avoiding a structured philosophical project, Revell presents a post-Heideggerian ontology attuned to the fluid epistemology of poetic writing over philosophical claims.

Heidegger's Existential Phenomenology

Heidegger gives the fullest account of his existential phenomenology in the section of *Being and Time* entitled "The Phenomenological Method of Investigation." Heidegger is interested in a philosophy that returns to things themselves and defines his concept of examining phenomena in contrast to everyday concepts of observing the world. Working with the Greek root of phenomena, Heidegger gives the meaning of φαίνεσθαι as "to bring to light, to put in the light."[2] Phenomena, for Heidegger, are not obvious facts but truth brought to light.

Heidegger's definition recasts phenomena as actions whereby the unseen becomes seen. His definition veers from a casual notion of phenomena as what is already seen or what seems self-evident to an observer. The casual notion is, in Heideggerian terms, "'appearance,' or still less a 'mere appearance.'"[3] The distinction between "mere appearance" and "phenomena" aims to solve a potential epistemological issue within phenomenology. Humans witness a variety of sense data whose appearance does not correspond to the facts they imply. Optical illusion, hallucination, mistaken beliefs, and human error all involve misleading sense data. If phenomenology claims access to truth by observing the phenomenal world, it could run into the error of claiming this misleading sense data as truth.

Science has an analogous problem, and Heidegger's distinction between "mere appearance" and "phenomena" solves phenomenology's problem in an analogous manner to science's. Like phenomenology, science grounds its claims to truth in an observation of the world. Like phenomenology, science needs to distinguish between accurate sense data and misleading sense data in order to maintain this claim. David Hume gives one famous version of this distinction when discussing appearance and truth in observing the act of moving away from a table:

> The table, which we see, seems to diminish, as we remove farther from it: but the real table, which exists independent of us, suffers no alteration: It was, therefore, nothing but its image, which was present to the mind. These are the obvious dictates of reason; and no man, who reflects, ever doubted, that the existences, which we consider, when we say, this house and that tree, are nothing but perceptions in the mind, and fleeting copies or representations of other existences, which remain uniform and independent.[4]

When we move away from a table, the table appears to get smaller. We do not, though, mistake this mere appearance as a truth about the table's size. Science may ground its claims in the observable world, but epistemologies like Hume's claim science's aim as a truth over and above the representations of sense data. Likewise, Heidegger's distinction admits the "mere appearances" of the observable world but claims as phenomenology's aim a truth that is not identical to the representation of mere appearance.

Heidegger aims at a notion of truth he identifies as aletheia. Truth is not mere appearance or merely how something appears but "[t]he true is what corresponds to the real, and the real is what is in truth."[5] With aletheia, Heidegger claims access to the existence of truth: "Truth means the nature of the true. We think this nature in recollecting the Greek work aletheia, the unconcealedness of beings."[6] The real exists prior to the observing subject. The real can be obscured or uncovered but not created. Heidegger's aletheia frames truth as action, as the interaction between the subject and the real. Where the subject and the real stand face-to-face—on equal terms, the one observing and the other self-disclosing—the human stands in true relation with "things themselves."[7]

Heidegger's existential phenomenology differs from most scientific accounts of epistemology in its claim of truth as interaction and relationship. While for Heidegger the real exists prior to the subject observing it, anything that could be called "meaning" or "truth" appears in the phenomenological act itself. Phenomenology is the subject's worldview; its truth insists on the observer's face-to-face encounter with the observed. Heidegger, in fact, would reject the scientific view of a subject-object position in the act of observation. In Heidegger's writing, the human regularly loses its position as a subject dominating the objects of the world: "Man speaks" becomes "Language speaks" becomes "Man speaks only as he responds to language."[8] Heidegger's interrogation of language breaks down the traditional subject-object position of humanity and language until it becomes a relationship where humanity and language are intertwined with each other.

The consequence of phenomenology as the subject's worldview could be truth as pure subjectivity, but Heidegger denies a purely subjective truth. His regular breakdown of traditional subject-object positions denies the subject as a maker of truth. Even language is no longer a human invention. Aletheia is truth born out of the relationship between the human and existence. Aletheia is not truth invented by an ego projecting its subjectivity outward.

The work of art is an activity that allows unconcealedness to occur, and the work of art is a phenomenological act that reflects the maker's worldview: "The work sets up a world."[9] Heidegger is after something broader than the collection of loosely held beliefs that might be implied by "worldview." What is unconcealed is the world that the maker has always inhabited: the culture, forms of life, and beliefs that have always immersed the maker:

> The world is not the mere collection of the countable or un-countable, familiar and unfamiliar things that are just there. But neither is it a merely imagined framework added by our repre-sentation to the sum of such given things. The world worlds and is more fully in being than the tangible and perceptible realm in which we believe ourselves to be at home. World is never an ob-ject that stands before us and can be seen. World is the ever-nonobjective to which we are subject as long as the paths of birth and death, blessing and curse keep us transported to Being.[10]

As was the case in his thinking about language, in Heidegger's de-scription of the world, what is being observed by the subject stops being a passive object. Heidegger represents it as an active partici-pant in the relationship between observer and observed: "The world worlds."[11] Heidegger looks to swerve away from subjective truth, and the result of that swerve is to reimagine art not as a statement of personal belief but as an uncovering and active participation in the cultural world in which the artist is born.

Revell's Visionary Phenomenology

In 2007, Donald Revell published *The Art of Attention* as part of the *Art of* series edited by Charles Baxter for Graywolf Press. Baxter was curating "a new line of books [to reinvigorate] the practice of craft and criticism. Each book will be a brief, witty, and useful explora-tion of fiction, nonfiction, or poetry by a writer impassioned by a singular craft issue."[12] James Longenbach's *The Art of the Poetic Line* explores the issue of the line in poetry. Charles Baxter's *The Art of Subtext: Beyond Plot* opens the craft of narrative by examining how subtext offers narrative possibilities beyond conventional plotting. Revell's entry, though, was not a book about a singular craft issue but about an entire poetics. His was a book claiming the epistemo-logical and ontological value of attention as a poetic method.

Calling for poetry to attend to the world broadly rhymes with

Heidegger's early call "To the things themselves!"[13] And, as Heidegger insisted in his existential phenomenology, Revell insists on a distinction between his own notion of attention and the limits of mere appearance. In the first paragraph of *The Art of Attention*, Revell breaks past those limits: "I see that poetry is a form of attention, itself the consequence of attention. And, too, I believe that poems are presences, events as may be called, in Dame Julien of Norwich's word, 'showings.'"[14] Revell brings in Norwich on the very first page, in the very first paragraph of the book. The first writer Revell claims an affinity with is a mystic visionary, a woman whose notion of the observable world expands beyond the quotidian facts of that world.

Julien of Norwich is the first in a series of writers throughout *The Art of Attention* whose notion of observation is broader than the surface appearance of the world. Revell reads through passages of these writers, developing attention as an active, expansive manner of existing in the world. Early in the book, he quotes from William Blake's famous account of seeing the sun, an account where observation moves far past surface appearance into the mystical:

> "What," it will be questioned, "when the sun rises do you not see a round disk of fire somewhat like a guinea?" Oh no, no! I see an innumerable company of the heavenly host crying, "Holy, holy, holy is the Lord God Almighty!" I question not my corporeal or vegetative eye any more than I would question a window concerning a sight. I look through it and not with it.[15]

Blake's account of the sun could mistakenly be simplified as a hallucination. Yet, while Blake experienced the type of vision Saint Augustine defined as a corporeal or bodily vision, he regularly discounted the need for an experience that could be termed hallucinatory. In *The Marriage of Heaven and Hell*, Blake has the prophet Isaiah claim, "I saw no God, nor heard any, in a finite organical perception; but my senses discover'd the infinite in every thing, and as I was then persuaded, & remain confirm'd; that the voice of honest indignation is the voice of God, I cared not for consequences but wrote."[16] Blake's Isaiah did not see or hear God with his literal "organic" eye or ear. Blake's Isaiah claims his authority to know God, prophesize, and write as an authority granted by his senses moving beyond surface appearance. In Blake's account of the sun, his corporeal eye is a window to "look through . . . and not with."

Revell insists that Blake's introduction of the heavenly host is not a willful invention. Blake opposes his experience of the sun to an experience that sees the sun as an object "somewhat like a guinea." The rejected experience is one that uses simile, that sees the sun with the corporeal eye and deploys the strategy of comparison to relate the object to its audience. But Blake's vision is revealed when he looks *through* the corporeal eye; it is not something created alongside corporeal sight. Isaiah's vision is revealed when his senses discover the infinite by moving beyond the organic, which is not an infinite invented for effect. Revell insists that Blake's imagination and eye do not take part in separate poetic acts but perform a single, continuous act:

> The art of poetry is not the acquisition of wiles or the deployment of strategies. Beginning in the senses, imagination senses farther, senses more . . . [Blake's] imagination is the capacity of his eye. The art of poetry, then, involves the sustained and sustaining increase of just this capacity . . . The capacity of his eye is the direct consequence of his faith: not faith in dogma or superstition or simple wish, but faith *in* his eye.[17]

Association, memory, cosmic implication, and the syncretic are all a part of attention. Handling "Song 3" from *The Maximus Poems,* Revell highlights Charles Olson's close observation of a leaky faucet and how close observation expands observable fact: "the leaky faucet, if you listen closely, accomplishes a cosmic transformation: a broken sink becomes time."[18] Attention is expansion but not symbolic abstraction. Blake does not choose the sun to stand in as a symbol for the heavenly host. Blake looks at the sun, and in the act of looking, the divine presents itself. Olson does not choose the faucet to stand in as a symbol for time. Olson is present with the faucet, and while he is present, the faucet marks time and the marking of time draws him to time past, to memory.

To return to Heideggerian terminology, Blake's account of looking at the sun is pure phenomenology. Blake's worldview differs from a quotidian worldview or the worldview of a scientist for whom only the facts of mere appearance are admitted into observation. Blake has faith that the divine is ever-present, and he experiences his belief as he exists in the world. When he looks, he does not see only with his corporeal eye. He also "sees" his experience of the world. Sun and the heavenly host are linked together; they call to each other. Attend to one, and the other appears as a part of that attention. In Blake's experience, the phenomenon of sun includes both "sun" and "heavenly host." Or as Revell phrases it: "Eyesight is prophetic instantly."[19]

What in Heidegger is a broadened definition of phenomena is in Revell a broadened definition of attention. Blake's description of the sun uncovers meaning, but it does not create meaning; it does not conceive of the observable sun as meaningless quotidian fact needing to be crafted into meaning. For Revell and his exemplars, the world before art is not essentially meaningless: it has meaning—always already—and as attention stretches, more meaning is uncovered, more meaning becomes accessible. The poem of attention is "a poem that entrusts its form and literally every one of its words not primarily to what the poet does, but to what is already accomplished."[20] The poet does not invent the poem through craft; the poet attends to the poem that already exists in the world.

Revell's attention is similar to Heidegger's phenomenology, but Revell shows none of Heidegger's anxiety about his method dissolving into subjective truth. While Heidegger steps away from the individuality of phenomenological experience, Revell embraces it. The latter explores the embrace of particularity in experience while looking at a poem by Larry Eigner:

> trees green the quiet sun
>   shed metal truck in the next street
>   passing the white house you listen
>   onwards
>   you heard
>   the dog
>   through   per
>   formed circles
>   the roads near the beach
>   rectangular
>   rough lines of the woods
>   tall growth echoing
>   local water[21]

No great feat of imagination occurs in Eigner's poem, and no exotic association enters in. Eigner states his observations. Revell insists that Eigner is as much a part of the poem as Blake or Olson. Eigner is active due to his position as observer in a particular place at a particular moment in time: "Eigner is not passive here; he is unaggressive. The activated eye (light is stimulus after all) accepts each thing in its particularity and in the order of its arrival. This is a method, a technique if you will, practical as well as ideal. Imposing no order, the poet finds one, the coherence already there *in place.*"[22] Revell's valuation of Eigner radically departs from Heidegger's poetics. An eccentric association or imaginative image can be rehabilitated in Heideggerian poetics by being a part of the poet's cultural world. A poem made as an arrangement of things in the haphazard order of their arrival has no place. A poem like Eigner's is purely the experience of the individual. It stands apart from a Heideggerian notion of art as a cultural project.

Emersonian Anti-Fascist Poetics

Heidegger's relationship with fascism is too broad a topic to cover in this essay. Heidegger's notion of art, though, was collective. The Greek artists Heidegger valorized did not have an eccentric experience of landscape but a cultural experience, a Greek experience. The "world" of Greek architecture is not the world of a single architect—it is the world of society, the "volk." For Heidegger, as for the progenitors he acknowledges, the ideal art is national, syndical.

Revell takes as his primary guides eccentrics like Julian of Norwich and William Blake. The visionaries he valorizes are witnesses to their own experiences, not prophets of new religions or founders of new nations. Attention is an act—it happens in the present, in time. Instead of an ossified cultural monument, the poetry of attention locates itself in an individual's experience. The aim in poetry, according to Revell, is to attend and to continue to attend: "On my deathbed, I shall want a longer not a more elaborate life. I shall want an extension, not a revision."[23]

In contrast to Heidegger's hope for an art that solidifies the ontological world of the "volk," Revell defines poetry as an anti-systematic activity, as we see when he quotes from Henry David Thoreau's journals, "The poet is a man who lives at last by watching his moods."[24] In his preference for an active life over and against systematic activity, Revell's use of attention sets him in kinship with Thoreau's transcendentalism, and in addition to Thoreau, writers influenced by transcendentalists including Emerson, Whitman, Ronald Johnson, and John Cage.

Emerson gives one of the clearest accounts of a transcendentalist anti-systematic approach to ontology in his essay "Circles." This essay describes a universe constantly in motion, continually a discovery, a universe where art could arise as "a form of attention," an art that records and makes present the universe showing the universe: "There are no fixtures in nature. The universe is fluid and volatile. Permanence is but a word of degrees. Our globe seen by God is a transparent law, not a mass of facts. The law dissolves the fact and holds it fluid."[25] Against the backdrop of unfixed nature and law as the fluid dissolution of scientific fact, Revell's holding up of Eigner's poem comes into focus. The poem functions with an Emersonian view in which it is enough to accept "each thing in its particularity and in the order of its arrival" because law and divinity is demonstrated through its fluidity, through what a systematic thinker would view as disorder.[26] While Heidegger's fear of subjectivity moves him toward a nationalist cultural project, Revell and the poets he keeps company with write from an anti-fascist poetics—no system needs to be fixed to create meaning, no order needs to be imposed: "Imposing no order, the poet finds one, the coherence already there *in place.*"[27]

Notes

1. Donald Revell, *The Art of Attention*, 62.
2. Martin Heidegger, *Being and Time*, 51.
3. Ibid.
4. David Hume, *An Enquiry Concerning Human Understanding*, 104–5.
5. Heidegger, *Poetry, Language, Thought*, 49.
6. Ibid.
7. Heidegger, *Being and Time*, 50.
8. Heidegger, *Poetry, Language, Thought*, 187, 188, 207.
9. Ibid., 44.
10. Ibid., 43.
11. Heidegger, *Poetry, Language, Thought*, 43.
12. Charles Baxter, front matter to *The Art of Attention*.
13. Heidegger, *Being and Time*, 50.
14. Revell, *The Art of Attention*, 5.
15. William Blake, *The Marriage of Heaven and Hell: The Complete Poetry & Prose of William Blake*, 12.
16. Ibid., 38.
17. Revell, *The Art of Attention*, 12–13.
18. Ibid., 17.
19. Ibid., 101.
20. Revell, *The Art of Attention*, 31.
21. Quoted in Revell, *The Art of Attention*, 36.

22. Ibid., 38.
23. Ibid., 21.
24. Quoted in Revell, *The Art of Attention,* 21.
25. Ralph Waldo Emerson, "Circles," *Essays and English Traits,* 149.
26. Revell, *The Art of Attention,* 38.
27. Ibid.

Works Cited

Baxter, Charles. Front matter in *The Art of Attention: A Poet's Eye,* by Donald Revell. Graywolf, 2007.

Blake, William. *The Marriage of Heaven and Hell: The Complete Poetry & Prose of William Blake.* Rev. ed. Edited by David V. Erdman. Anchor, pp. 33–45.

Emerson, Ralph Waldo. "Circles." *Essays and English Traits.* P. F. Collier & Son, 1937, pp. 149–60.

Heidegger, Martin. *Being and Time.* Translated by John Macquarrie and Edward Robinson. Harper, 1962.

Heidegger, Martin. *Poetry, Language, Thought.* Translated by Albert Hofstadter. Harper Collins, 2001.

Hume, David. *An Enquiry Concerning Human Understanding with "A Letter from a Gentleman to His Friend" and "Hume's Abstract of a Treatise of Human Nature."* 2nd ed. Edited by Eric Steinberg. Hackett, 1977.

Revell, Donald. *The Art of Attention: A Poet's Eye.* Graywolf, 2007.

GEOFFREY BABBITT

"The Real Sun No One's Ever Seen"
New Blakean Gnosticism in the Poetry of Donald Revell

> *"Jesus said, 'I shall give you what no eye has seen, what no ear has heard, what no hand has touched, what has not arisen in the human heart.'"*
> —THE GOSPEL OF THOMAS

Strange circumstances surround the most major discovery of gnostic texts. In 1945, Egyptian farmer Muhammad Ali Samman and his brother were digging for fertilizer when their mattocks happened upon a terra cotta urn, which they smashed open, revealing thirteen leather-bound codices. And so began one of the great archeological finds of the twentieth century. The brothers, however, had recently avenged their father's death by cutting off the limbs and devouring the heart of their father's murderer. Since they were under investigation and feared attracting further police attention, Samman stashed the contraband papyrus manuscripts with a priest, who in turn sold some and gave one to a historian—all of which triggered a complicated investigation that eventually led to the manuscripts' recovery. Now known as the Nag Hammadi Library, the thirteen codices contain a total of fifty-two surviving texts—most of which are gnostic. Some of the texts—Samman has said—were, unfortunately, burnt by his mother, who loaded papyrus and straw into the family's blazing fire.

I've begun with the story of the Nag Hammadi discovery for two reasons. First, its elements of secrecy, illegality, and discovery befit an introduction to gnosticism, whose allure can partly be attributed to its clandestine, heterodox, and revelatory nature. Second, and perhaps more importantly, the image of the brothers smashing the clay vessel to find sacred gnostic texts formally mirrors the movement of gnosis itself, which I will explain shortly.

First, though—what is gnosticism? In the aptly titled *What Is Gnosticism?*, Karen L. King proves that adequately answering that question requires an entire book. For convenience, let's simplify. Gnosticism is a renegade strain of early Christianity, an offshoot that rejects key tenets held by the mainstream. It is also considered heresy. As such, it has functioned historically as a construct, a category that the mainstream has strategically used as a dumping ground for characteristics that it wanted to push away from. That is, mainstream Christianity has helped define itself by painting gnosticism as its heretical antithesis.

Before the Nag Hammadi discovery, there were far fewer gnostic sources, so religious historians had little choice but to listen to mainstream thinkers, i.e., critics of gnosticism. Therefore, much of what we first knew about gnosticism came from those who despised it. And since misinformation naturally abounds when you try to understand a group by talking with their enemies, it is tricky defining their beliefs.

Gnosticism is complex and multitudinous. So, saying "gnosticism" is, in one sense, misleading. That is, the term is more of a banner under which we can herd together several similar syncretic variants of early Christianity. As such, gnosticism has multiple sources, a complicated history, and divergent traditions and beliefs. In a strict sense, it is not homogenous or monolithic, and it does not have a single essence.

Before we sketch William Blake's specific brand of gnosticism, we should identify two core gnostic principles alive in Blake's work: gnosis and dualism. Gnostics reject the resurrection as a literal event and understand it symbolically, believing that salvation comes through *gnosis* instead. In *The Gnostic Gospels*—still the most popular introduction to gnosticism—Elaine Pagels stresses that the goal for gnostics, rather than to emphasize a historical event, is to "experience [Jesus's] continuing presence."[1] Gnosis, or "knowledge," is not doctrinal or directly transmittable through teaching; rather, as Pagels and other scholars have observed, it is similar to Buddhist enlightenment. Or we might compare gnosis with Jewish mysticism, whose Kabbalists read the Torah for the "secret life which streams and pulsates below the crust of its literal meaning," as Gershom Scholem has written.[2]

In any case, Hans Jonas tells us in *The Gnostic Religion*, "'Knowledge' is by itself a purely formal term and does not specify what is to be known; neither does it specify the psychological manner and subjective significance of possessing knowledge or the way in which it is acquired."[3] In fact, knowing often happens *via negativa*—by way of what we do not or cannot know. Jonas goes on to stress that gnosis's nature is religious, so we should associate it with a form of faith rather than reason. He says, therefore, that gnostic knowledge "is closely bound up with revelatory experience, so that *reception* of the truth either through sacred or secret lore or through inner illumination replaces rational argument and theory."[4] In achieving that knowledge, one fundamentally changes. In knowing God, "the soul transforms the knower himself by making him a partaker of the divine existence."[5] The individual merges with the divine.

Gnosticism is also characterized by radical dualism. The material world that we perceive with our senses is the lesser, fallen world of darkness. But there is also "the divine realm of light, self-contained and remote," as Jonas phrases it.[6] The world of light is foreign in nature, absolutely *beyond* the entire cosmos and everything we are capable of perceiving sensually. The Demiurge who created the earth is lesser than the Supreme God, the True God of Light. Jonas writes, "The transcendent God Himself is hidden from all creatures and is unknowable by natural concepts. Knowledge of Him requires supernatural revelation and illumination."[7] Gnosis is not merely a way to God, then, it is the *only* way.

The Nag Hammadi discovery is formally analogous to gnosis. The Samman brothers smashed a clay urn—akin to the fallen material world—in order to free gnostic texts that offer penetrating insight into the World of Light. Breaking through the worthless clay urn to reach the sacred gnostic texts is analogous to the movement of gnosis.[8] Of course, that is only true if we take the gnostic texts as standing for gnosis itself. But since we must interpretively penetrate "the crust of [their] literal meaning," to borrow Scholem's phrase, then the truer analogy is the movement from the gnostic texts, breaking through their literal meaning to the Eternal Truths they hold via gnosis.

In William Blake's time, London was full of nonconformist, dissenting religious sects that could have been carriers for gnostic concepts. Blake, however, almost certainly absorbed elements of gnostic thought from Jacob Böhme, the founder of Böhmenism. In *Witness against the Beast*, E. P. Thompson establishes a direct connection between Böhmenism and gnosticism: "[A] historian of Gnosticism

[Giovanni Filoramo] affirms that 'we see a veritable efflorescence of Gnostic mythology in Jacob Boehme.' The influence of Boehme upon Blake is undoubted (and was acknowledged) and he could have derived any Gnostic notions through this source."[9] Indeed, G. E. Bentley, Jr.'s *Blake Records* indicates that Frederick Tatham, heir to some of the Blakes' belongings after their deaths, wrote to a book dealer in 1864 that he had in his possession "books well-thumbed and dirtied by [Blake's] graving hands . . . a large collection of works of the mystical writers, Jacob Behmen, Swedenborg, and others."[10]

The important point for our purposes here is not that Blake was influenced by Böhme but that Böhme's influence upon Blake took a gnostic form. In *Fearful Symmetry*, Northrop Frye notes parallels between Böhmenism and gnosticism in Blake's mythology: "Blake follows some of the Gnostics and Boehme in believing that the fall of man involved a fall in part of the divine nature."[11] But even when Frye doesn't explicitly call elements of Blake's thought "gnostic," his descriptions often square with gnosticism. For instance, Frye writes of Blake's religious beliefs: "The only possible cure for the original sin of this Selfhood of the natural man is vision, the revelation that his world is fallen and therefore not ultimate."[12] We could accurately rephrase that statement as: for Blake, gnosis is the only means for overcoming radical dualism. Although his complex mythology cannot be reduced to gnosticism or any single system of belief, William Blake is undoubtedly the best representative of gnostic poetry. Not only was Blake's thought gnostic, but it was increasingly so. In *The Traveller in the Evening*, Morton Paley writes, "What is important is that Blake had a temperamental affinity for Gnosticism, and that this tendency increased in his very late works."[13]

Now let's turn to how specifically Blake's poetry is gnostic.

Blake's most famous image is *The Ancient of Days*. It is the frontispiece for *Europe: A Prophecy*, and today it's just about everywhere you encounter Blake's images—on postcards in museum shops, on webpages about Blake, on dorm room posters, on covers of books (recent editions of *Fearful Symmetry*, for example). Inside the sun, which is surrounded by dark clouds, a god with a long white beard and white hair crouches down, extending an arm into the black below him, wielding a compass. His crouch crumples his body into itself, in contrast to the clean extension of his long left arm. He kneels on his right knee, leaning so far down that his left shoulder is slightly lower than his left knee, which juts up just above his back.

A strong wind blows his hair and beard starkly sideways. The golden compass is a right angle, which he holds at the apex, symmetrically extending light into the deep below.

Blake had visions regularly. As a four-year-old, he saw the face of God out his window. Around the age of ten, he saw angels in every bough of a tree and, later, in a field among haymakers. In dreams, his dead brother Robert regularly communicated with him. In one dream, Saint Joseph revealed a special use of carpenter's glue for mixing paint colors. At Felpham's shore, Blake conversed with historical figures, such as Moses, the prophets, Homer, Dante, and Milton. He even witnessed a fairy funeral.[14] Those were *visions*. Once, however, he saw a ghost. Alexander Gilchrist recounts the story in *The Life of Blake*. In No. 13, Hercules Buildings, in the Lambeth district of London, Blake looked up at the top of his staircase and saw "a horrible grim figure, 'scaly, speckled, very awful,' stalking downstairs towards him."[15] The sight sent him running out of his house. *The Ancient of Days* was inspired by this ghost.

We might call *The Ancient* by another name—Urizen. In Blake's mythology, Urizen is born into the realm of light—or, as Blake would call it, Eternity—but Urizen falls and, as S. Foster Damon distills it, "The result was the creation of this world."[16] Here's Blake's account from chapter VII of *The Book of Urizen*:

> He form'd a line & a plummet
> To divide the Abyss beneath.
> He form'd a dividing rule:
>
> He formed scales to weigh;
> He formed massy weights;
> He formed a brazen quadrant;
>
> He formed golden compasses
> And began to explore the Abyss
> And he planted a garden of Fruits.[17]

Urizen is the inferior Creator God depicted in Genesis and the Hebrew Scriptures—or in gnostic terms, the Demiurge. So—*not* God Supreme. Urizen is, thus, evidence that Blake is working within a mythology of basic gnostic dualism. Urizen is god of the material world, the gnostic fallen world—what Blake calls "Ulro."

As such, Urizen is reason, ratio, symmetry, finitude, doctrine, and corporeality. He is fit for someone like Newton, who, according to

Blake, accounts for reality only by what is empirically measurable, thereby leaving out what is most important. Newton's *Opticks*, for instance, details vision and color brilliantly, but it is blind to Vision. The faculties of Urizen lead humanity to the mistakes of Natural Religion and Deism. Even before he created Urizen, Blake was opposed to what the lesser God would come to stand for. We can read "There Is No Natural Religion," anachronistically, as a treatise against Urizen. Blake writes, "Man's perceptions are not bounded by organs of perception. He perceives more than sense (tho' ever so acute) can discover."[18] In other words, we have the ability to see beyond Urizen's material world but not with our sensory perceptions alone.

It is not only ocular vision Blake speaks of when he begins *Jerusalem* by writing, "I see the Saviour over me / Spreading his beams of love, & dictating the words of this mild song."[19] Indeed, "There Is No Natural Religion" tells us that it is thanks to "the Poetic or Prophetic character" that we can go beyond the material world: "If it were not for the Poetic or Prophetic character the Philosophic & Experimental would soon be at the ratio of all things, & stand still, unable to do other than repeat the same dull round over again."[20] The poetic character is supernatural—a gnostic extrasensory ability to perceive that takes us to Eternity and to God. Thus, Blake claims that "[h]e who sees the Infinite in all things sees God. He who sees the Ratio only sees himself only."[21]

The final line of "There Is No Natural Religion" reads, "God becomes as we are, that we may be as he is."[22] Readers have noted that Blake's line resembles John 3:16: "For God so loved the world, that he gave his only begotten Son, that whosoever believeth in him should not perish, but have everlasting life."[23] But I think the spirit of Blake's line is in closer keeping with the gnostic *Gospel of Thomas*: "Whoever drinks from my mouth will become like me; I myself shall become that person, and the hidden things will be revealed to that person."[24] Blake echoes Thomas more closely than John because John limits humankind's likeness to God to immortality (both shall have "everlasting life"), while Blake and Thomas do not specify the manner of humanity's similarity with the divine (simply, you "will become like me"). But there may be more to it still: Jonas describes gnosis as making one "a partaker in the divine essence," and Blake, too, suggests that possibility.

At the end of *Jerusalem*, the epic's hero, Los, proclaims: "[T]he Worship of God, is honouring his gifts / In other men: & loving the greatest men best, each according / To his Genius: which is the Holy Ghost in Man; there is no other / God."[25] Blakean gnosis culminates in humanity partaking in divinity. Or as Blake once reportedly phrased it: "Jesus Christ was the only God, and so am I and so are you."[26]

To highlight Blake's gnosticism, we will consider two of his four Zoas, Urizen and Los.[27] Urizen is the southern Zoa characterized by reason, and his counterpart is Los—the northern Zoa characterized by imagination. Los is essentially the "Poetic or Prophetic character" Blake mentions in "There Is No Natural Religion." He is Poetic or Creative Imagination, the faculty that renders humankind infinite and capable of perceiving Eternity; he offers solutions to Urizen's deficiencies. Los directly inspires Blake, quite literally in the following passage:

Los descended to me:
And Los behind me stood: a terrible flaming Sun: just close
Behind my back . . .
. . . he kissed me, and wishd me health.
And I became One Man with him arising in my strength . . .
. . . Los had enter'd into my soul:
His terrors now posses'd me whole! I arose in fury & strength.[28]

Then, the Prophet "in the Eternal bosom" speaks through Blake in much the same manner God speaks through Ezekiel in chapter 3 of the Bible, when God visits the prophet:

I fell on my face. / Then the spirit entered into me, and set me upon my feet, and spake with me, and said unto me . . . / when I speak with thee, I will open thy mouth, and thou shalt say unto them, Thus saith the Lord God.[29]

Los is Blake's figure for Prophetic Poetry.

Blake often gives us Urizen and Los even when they aren't named as such. For instance, here is his extraordinary end to "A Vision of the Last Judgment":

"What," it will be Question'd, "When the Sun rises, do you not see a round disk of fire somewhat like a Guinea?" O no, no, I see an Innumerable company of the Heavenly host crying "Holy,

Holy, Holy is the Lord God Almighty." I question not my Corporeal or Vegetative Eye any more than I would Question a Window concerning a Sight: I look thro it & not with it.[30]

With the faculties of Urizen, we see a burning coin. With the faculties of Los, we see a host of innumerable angels. If we look *with* our eyes, we are limited to Ulro—the Corporeal, Vegetative world. By looking *through* our organs of sensory perception, however, we see the Eternal, the Infinite.

Blake's passage rhymes nicely with Pagels's discussion of the Gospel of Mary. She writes, "Mary Magdalene, seeing the Lord in a vision, asked him, 'How does he who sees the vision see it? [Through] the soul, [or] through the spirit?' He answered that the visionary perceives through the mind."[31] This, of course, is partly what Blake means when says he looks through rather than with his eye. Vision is a form of gnosis.

Of course, we mustn't carry dualism too far. Although there are ascetic gnostic schools, equating gnosticism with an outright rejection of the body and the physical world would be too extreme. In his reading of the *Apocryphon of John*, Michael A. Williams shows us that "according to many Gnostic sources, precisely in the human body is to be found the best *visible* trace of the divine in the material world."[32] In the body, we can glimpse a divine spark. Blake would agree. Indeed, in "The Divine Image," Blake writes, "all must love the human form . . . / [where] God is dwelling too."[33] And Oothoon, in *The Visions of the Daughters of Albion*, goes even further, declaring the sacredness of love—including sexual love: "[E]very thing that lives is holy!"[34]

In *Jerusalem*, Erin epitomizes this same principle. She is Los's first creation, and after she comes forth from Los's furnaces, Los and all his kin weep with joy because the spaces of Erin are so beautiful. She is the embodiment of the idea that "all living things, especially the body and its impulses, are holy," as Damon has put it.[35]

It's worth looking at Blake through the lens of gnosticism not only because it helps frame Blake's complex work but also because there is a resurgence of gnosticism among American poets. While most have absorbed gnostic elements more directly from Modernist and contemporary poets, such as Robert Duncan and Nathaniel Mackey, the ultimate source of their gnostic influences is Blake himself.[36] A chief case in point is Peter O'Leary, who is one of the most explicitly and directly gnostic of American poets today. His gnostic movement, dubbed "The New Gnosticism," includes Norman Finkelstein, Patrick Pritchett, Edward Foster, Joseph Donahue, Mark Scroggins, David Need, and Robert Archambeau. The forty-second issue of the literary journal *Talisman* devotes a section to their essays on gnosticism. And a few years ago, the journal *Coldfront* published Henry Gould's write-up of their coterie. There is, however, one poet in particular who—so far as I can tell—has been omitted from current discussions of gnosticism in poetry: Donald Revell.

Donald Revell is perhaps the most Blakean poet writing today. He is a poet of grand vision and of faithful attention whose voice—by turns tender and urgent—often takes the mode of prophecy. And the speaker in his poems looks not *with* but *through* the eye, as Blake urges. So, his poems are constantly discovering an innumerable company of the heavenly host where most would see a round disc of fire. Discussing just that very passage from "A Vision of the Last Judgment," Revell writes in *The Art of Attention*:

> That "disk of fire somewhat like a guinea" condemns craft and all its clever coinage. Blake sees the heavenly host and not something "like" it. The art of poetry, then, involves the sustained and sustaining increase of just this capacity. . . . The capacity of his eye is the direct consequence of his faith: not faith in a dogma or superstition or simple wish, but faith *in* his eye. The poetry of attention is not metaphysical. It trusts the open eye to see. By faith, the eye stays open. And so, the work of poetry is trust that, by faith, is shown to be no work at all.[37]

In his exegesis, Revell shows that, like Blake, he, too, is a "literal realist of the imagination," to use Yeats's phrase.[38] The innumerable company of the heavenly host that Blake sees is not metaphysical in nature, Revell argues; Blake *literally sees it*.

As literal realists of the imagination, Blake and Revell share a key revision of gnosticism: they believe that the senses can participate in the imagination's overcoming of radical dualism. In a system of radical dualism, Jonas explains, "the transcendent God is unknown in the world and cannot be discovered from it; therefore, revelation is needed."[39] But such revelation is metaphysical or mystical in nature. Still, Revell stresses that Blake sees God by having "faith *in* his eye," so sensory experience is involved. Blake sees the innumerable company of the heavenly host not metaphorically "with his mind's eye" but literally *through* his physical eye, which means that God can be known in the world. This point is imperative. We must now come to understand what Blake, and therefore Revell, mean by "through."

For our purposes here, Revell's working epistemology is Blake's. Here's Frye's sketch of it:

> [For Blake] all knowledge comes from mental experience. Mental experience is a union of a perceiving subject and a perceived object; it is something in which the barrier between "inside" and "outside" dissolves. But the power to unite comes from the subject. The work of art is the product of this creative perception; hence it is not an escape from reality but a systematic training in comprehending it.[40]

So, when Blake sees the innumerable company of the heavenly host, he does not abandon his eye. Rather, he looks *through* it, perceiving creatively, which is to say, he sees the heavenly host in an act of mental experience that unites sensory (ocular) perception and imagination. His mind looks through his bodily eye.

Reality, thus, is not a field of objects existing independently of us. Rather, it is mental experience, which is partly what Blake was driving at when he writes, "If the sun and moon should doubt, / They'd immediately go out."[41] Or, as Revell puts it in *Tantivy*, "[I]t is all hallucinations, / And one of them is true."[42] Reality is the unification of the subjective and objective via mental experience that includes imagination; so is Blake's form of gnosis, and so is Revell's, too. For Revell, the work of poetry is the work of placing trust and faith in one's eye. Or in Blakean terms, it involves locating imagination in sensory perception. Once that work is done, no further work is left to do. Or, as Revell writes in "My Trip": "The work of poetry is trust, / And under the aegis of trust / Nothing could be more effortless."[43] Revell's imagination is literal because his seeing is imaginative.

According to Revell's thinking, then, Blake's vision of the innumerable heavenly host is not unlike Pound's in that famous moment in Canto XVII when he writes, "The light now, not of the sun."[44] For Pound, the light is not "of the sun" because it is Neoplatonic, divine light. Henry Chatwick explains the metaphysical nature of divine light in Neoplatonic thought: "Plotinus sees the light of the sun as analogous to the light which is the One, and sharply distinguishes sunlight from the metaphysical Light of the transcendent realm."[45] But in Pound's poem, the light is no mere abstraction. Revell would insist, thus, that the light is not only metaphysical. Pound *sees* it. The light is physically perceptible through his eyes—because he has faith in them. Thus, Pound goes on to describe the quality of the sunlight: "Chrysophrase, / And the water green clear, and blue clear; / On, to the cliffs of amber."[46]

By similarly affirming that God is knowable in this world, Revell's brand of gnosticism perpetually seeks to overcome radical dualism. Unlike traditional gnosticism, which wants to escape from the fallen world into Eternity, Revell's poetry works to see Paradise and Eternity *in* that fallen world: "You are violets. I am broth. / God walks on earth."[47] For Revell, such vision is the task of his poetry.

To overcome radical dualism, Revell often uses metaphors that are really anti-metaphors. Traditionally, metaphor depends on a gap between its two terms. A metaphor—in Greek, literally "to bear across"—conducts a transfer of associations across that gap from the vehicle to the tenor. But the gap remains because we understand that a metaphor is a mere comparison and not an assertion of identicalness. In his anti-metaphors, however, Revell aims to obliterate that gap and show that there is no difference, ultimately, between the two terms, only identification.

In his review of Revell's *My Mojave* that appeared in *Harvard Review*, Robert Schnall contends, "Revell is both fascinated and frustrated by the seeming impenetrability and elusiveness of what he calls 'reality.'"[48] I'd argue, however, that Revell's anti-metaphors show us that reality isn't impenetrable or elusive at all. Rather, they are extraordinarily bold ways for Revell to reveal the true world to himself and to us. They are the fruit of his gnosis. For example, in "O Rare," Revell writes:

> I see an equestrienne
> Riding a plough horse the color of milk
> Along a dirt path towards a sunny upland.
> The rider is Heaven.[49]

Since "The rider is Heaven" takes the form "A is B," we're naturally inclined to treat the line as a metaphor. But to do so would be a mistake that would unnecessarily complicate matters. Revell's simplicity is precisely what makes his poetry so radical. The task he gives us is not hermeneutical. It's visionary.

Looking at the rider and seeing only an equestrienne is akin to looking at the sun and seeing only "a disk of fire somewhat like a guinea." Looking at the rider, however, and also seeing Heaven is to look *through* the eye. This also reveals something about the nature of Paradise—it is not a destination ("a sunny upland"), as we might expect; rather, it is a process, something *en route*. Formulations of the "A is B" variety are only metaphors if the speaker doesn't truly mean the word "is." John Donne's famous formulation, "This flea is you and I," for instance, is a metaphor.[50] We know Donne is merely comparing the "you" and the "I" of the poem to a flea. However, when philosopher Saul Kripke writes, "Hesperus is Phosphorus"[51]—it is no metaphor; it is an equation.[52] Revell's proposal—"the rider is Heaven"—is radical because it asserts that two things that seem so extremely unequal are, in that moment anyway, one and the same. In other words, by saying "The rider is Heaven," Revell in fact means, "The rider is Heaven."[53] What could be more radical than a poetry that requires intelligence and faith but no interpretation?

Revell is at his boldest when we simply take him at his word, as when in "Zion" he writes, "I'm saying that death is a little girl. The apple / There in her hand is God Almighty where the skin / Breaks to her teeth and spills my freedom all over / Sunlight turning deadwood coppery rose."[54] Most of us wouldn't see how death could be a little girl, but that's because we don't tend to see as gnostics do. In verse 113 of *The Gospel of Thomas*, Jesus says:

> [The kingdom] will not come by watching for it. It will not be said, "Look, here it is," or "Look, there it is." Rather, the father's kingdom is spread out upon the earth, and people do not see it.[55]

Revell's gnostic vision lets him see Paradise, Eternity, and Death where most of us see just the everyday world.

Because this kind of vision sets him apart, Revell is antinomian, as was Blake. Morton Paley has observed that Blake would not "have been troubled by apparent contradictions between Gnosticism and antinomianism," but I think we can go even further: Blake is unusually energized by their combination.[56] So is Revell. Antinomianism maintains that true believers are saved by grace and are thus free from moral law.[57] Although dualism remains indomitable for most of us—in the sense that we cannot supersede the sensorial realm—Revell's poetry successfully overcomes the obstacle of dualism, which is where antinomianism comes in. Revell writes in *The Art of Attention*, "Real eyesight is unprecedented and so escapes all names. As it turns out, the optic nerve is an antinomian. Seeing a pretty street in the morning means that everything is new again."[58] So, not to see newly is to fall short of the elect company.

In "A Green Hill Far Away" from *Pennyweight Windows*, Revell writes, "Today is the day / The desert gives up its baseballs, / The day / Its blue-black butterflies and dragonflies / Uncover the real sun no one's ever seen."[59] To see the real sun is salvation, election, gnosis. Poetry is for Revell what walking is for Henry David Thoreau. In his famous essay "Walking," Thoreau writes, "No wealth can buy the requisite leisure, freedom, and independence which are the capital in this profession. It comes only by the grace of God. It requires a direct dispensation from Heaven to become a walker. You must be born into the family of the Walkers. *Ambulator nascitur, non fit.*"[60] If you want to become a walker, it cannot be done through greater effort, enhanced understanding, or cultivated skill. You must get born. In Revell's poem, no one has seen the real sun yet because we must be reborn to see it, in which case, Vision is evidence of grace.

We might better understand Revell's steady surge in prominence if we consider his place in gnostic poetry within the context of the procession out of postmodernism. Postmodernism, after all, is characterized largely by intense and extensive skepticism—skepticism over literature, philosophy, truth, metaphysics, language, personal identity, access to the body, and so forth. That same skepticism extends to poetry, too. Language Poetry, for instance, is importantly and valuably skeptical of expressive verse, the lyrical "I," authorial intention, and the very possibility of apolitical language. Postmodernism, however, is over by now, and poets are still finding ways forward. One way to proceed from a position of skepticism—stretching at least as far back as Descartes—has been via some form of faith or mysticism. [61]

From one angle, a bird's-eye view of contemporary American poetry's various groups shows two particularly prominent ways of branching out from postmodernism's extensive skepticism. One endeavors to recuperate the kinds of voice, expression, and affect that were possible before the postmodern moment. The other, conceptualism (and post-conceptualism), extends postmodernism's skepticism in the form of hyper-rationalism. Revell's work, though, illuminates another viable way—not through atavism or hyper-rationalism but through irrationalism, gnosis as a poetic process. While gnosticism offers another potential path forward from postmodernism, that path will never seem as viable or as significant if we don't include Revell, who is one of its most prominent and important practitioners. And more generally, conversations about contemporary poetry would be further enriched were they to consider gnosticism alongside more popular approaches. It's a category that is both useful and more accommodating than one might initially think. Revell might be the highest profile Blakean gnostic, but there are also many other contemporary poets whose work could be further examined by recognizing their gnostic tendencies.

Gnostic poetry hasn't had its fair shake yet. It awaits further attention, but further attention should also be awaiting it—because the *kairos* is right for gnostic poetry.

Notes

1. Elaine Pagels, *The Gnostic Gospels*, 13.
2. Gershom Scholem, *Major Trends in Jewish Mysticism*, 14.
3. Hans Jonas, *The Gnostic Religion*, 34.
4. Ibid., 34–35.
5. Ibid., 35.
6. Ibid., 42.
7. Ibid., 42–43.
8. For an equally brief example that is literary in nature, see the pasteboard mask passage in chapter 36 of *Moby-Dick*.
9. E. P. Thompson, *Witness against the Beast*, 35. Blake might also have read John Laurence Mosheim's *Ecclesiastical History* or his *Commentaries*— and maybe Joseph Priestley's *Disquisitions* as well (Paley 5).
10. G. E. Bentley, *Blake Records*, 57. Note that "Behmen" is a variant spelling.
11. Northrop Frye, *Fearful Symmetry*, 41.
12. Ibid., 58.
13. Morton D. Paley, *The Traveller in the Evening*, 7.
14. Alexander Gilchrist, *The Life of Blake*.
15. Ibid., 127.
16. S. Foster Damon, *A Blake Dictionary*, 419.
17. William Blake, *The Book of Urizen, The Complete Poetry and Prose of William Blake*, 80–81.

18. Blake, "There Is No Natural Religion," *The Complete Poetry and Prose of William Blake*, 2.

19. Blake, Jerusalem, *The Complete Poetry and Prose of William Blake*, 146.

20. Blake, "There Is No Natural Religion," *The Complete Poetry and Prose of William Blake*, 3.

21. Ibid.

22. Ibid.

23. John 3:16 (King James Version).

24. Marvin Meyer, *The Gospel of Thomas*, 63.

25. Blake, Jerusalem, *The Complete Poetry and Prose of William Blake*, 251.

26. Alexander Gilchrist, *The Life of Blake*, x.

27. For simplification, I'm setting aside a great deal, including the other two Zoas—Tharmas and Orc/Luvah. (The Zoas are aspects of the divine and fundamental parts of humanity/Albion. So while they're presented literally as titanic deities, there are always allegorical layers at work in Blake, too. And, these change and evolve across the full range of Blake's work.)

28. Blake, *Milton, The Complete Poetry and Prose of William Blake*, 116–17.

29. Ezek. 3:23–27 (King James Version).

30. Blake, "A Vision of the Last Judgment," *The Complete Poetry and Prose of William Blake*, 565–66.

31. Pagels, *The Gnostic Gospels*, 11.

32. Michael A. Williams, "Divine Image—Prison of Flesh: Perceptions of the Body in Ancient Gnosticism," *Fragments for a History of the Human Body*, 130.

33. Blake, "The Divine Image," *The Complete Poetry and Prose of William Blake*, 13.

34. Blake, *The Visions of the Daughters of Albion, The Complete Poetry and Prose of William Blake*, 51.

35. Damon, *A Blake Dictionary*, 247.

36. There have been many writers who could be described, to varying degrees, as gnostic—Herman Melville, W. B. Yeats, H. D., William Bronk, Jorge Luis Borges, Allen Ginsberg, Jack Spicer, Robert Duncan, Ronald Johnson, Alice Notley, Harold Bloom, Nathaniel Mackey, Gerrit Lansing, Fanny Howe, Matthew Henriksen, Will Alexander, Brenda Hillman, and Susan Howe, to name a few.

37. Donald Revell, *The Art of Attention*, 12–13.

38. Yeats, *Ideas of Good and Evil*, 182.

39. Jonas, *The Gnostic Religion*, 45.

40. Frye, *Fearful Symmetry*, 85.

41. Blake, "Auguries of Innocence," *The Complete Poetry and Prose of William Blake*, 492.

42. Revell, "Tithon," *Tantivy*, 53.

43. Revell, "My Trip," *My Mojave*, 9.

44. Ezra Pound, "XVII," *The Cantos of Ezra Pound*, 76.

45. Henry Chatwick, *Confessions*, Saint Augustine, 209.

46. Pound, "XVII," The Cantos of Ezra Pound, 76.

47. Revell, "Delirium: A Landscape," *A Thief of Strings*, 7.

48. Robert Schnall, review of *My Mojave, Harvard Review*, 223.

49. Revell, "O Rare," *A Thief of Strings*, 16.

50. John Donne, "The Flea," https://www.poetryfoundation.org/poems/46467/the-flea

51. Frege is pointing out that the Greek names for the morning star and the evening star refer to the same celestial body, not a star at all, in fact, but the planet Venus.

52. Saul A. Kripke, *Naming and Necessity*, 29.

53. Or consider the final lines of *My Mojave*'s title poem: "I'm not needed / Like wings in a storm, / And God is the storm" (14).

54. Revell, "Zion," *Pennyweight Windows: New & Selected Poems*, 196.

55. Meyer, *The Gospel of Thomas*, 65.

56. Paley, *The Traveller in the Evening*, 6.

57. What motivates gnosticism and antinomianism, however, isn't the desire to get off the hook from an ethical standard of behavior; rather, it is a search for newness. E. P. Thompson claims that antinomianism is "a way of breaking from our received wisdom and moralism, and entering upon new possibilities" (20). For Elaine Pagels, the parallel between a religious search for newness and artistry is clear: "Like circles of artists today, gnostics considered original creative invention to be the mark of anyone who becomes spiritually alive. Each one, like students of a painter or writer, expected to express his own perceptions by revising and transforming what he was taught" (19). Gnosticism and antinomianism, thus, have clear aesthetic correlations.

58. Revell, *The Art of Attention*, 75.

59. Revell, "A Green Hill Far Away," *Pennyweight Windows*, 205.

60. Henry David Thoreau, "Walking," *The Making of the American Essay*, 168.

61. Descartes, for instance, concludes that his idea of an infinite and benevolent God could have no other origin than God instilling that idea innately in him, which he perceives clearly and distinctly. This tautological reasoning has been coined "The Cartesian Circle": clear and distinct ideas allow certainty only because Descartes can be certain that God—whom he clearly and distinctly perceives—does not deceive him. That God is the basis for Descartes's "knowledge"—of his own existence, of the outside world, of everything he can claim to know—and qualifies this move in his philosophy as mystical, cf., the *Tractatus*. Wittgenstein explicitly identifies the movement beyond solipsism as mystical in nature: "Not *how* the world is, is the mystical, but *that* it is" (107).

Works Cited

Bentley, G. E. Blake *Records: Documents (1714–1841) Concerning the Life of William Blake (1757–1827) and his Family*. 2nd ed. Yale University Press, 2004.

The Bible. King James Version. *Bible Gateway*, 2013. Accessed July 8, 2013, https://www.biblegateway.com

Blake, William. *The Complete Poetry and Prose of William Blake*. Edited by David V. Erdman. 1965. Anchor Books, 1988.

Chatwick, Henry, trans. and ed. *Confessions*. 1992. By Saint Augustine. Oxford University Press, 2008.

Damon, S. Foster. *A Blake Dictionary: The Ideas and Symbols of William Blake*. University Press of New England, 1988.

Descartes, René. *Meditations on First Philosophy*. 1986. Translated and edited by John Cottingham. Cambridge University Press, 2001.

Donne, John. "The Flea." *Poetry Foundation*, https://www.poetryfoundation.org/poems/46467/the-flea

Frye, Northrop. *Fearful Symmetry*. 1947. Princeton University Press, 1990.

Gilchrist, Alexander. *The Life of Blake: With Selections from His Poems and Other Writings*. 2 vols. London and Cambridge, 1863.

Jonas, Hans. *The Gnostic Religion: The Message of the Alien God and the Beginnings of Christianity*. 3rd ed. Beacon Press, 2001.

King, Karen L. *What Is Gnosticism?* 2003. Harvard University Press, 2005.

Kripke, Saul A. *Naming and Necessity*. Harvard University Press, 1980.

Melville, Herman. *Moby-Dick*. Penguin Books, 1992.

Meyer, Marvin, trans. and ed. *The Gospel of Thomas*. Harper, 1992.

Pagels, Elaine. *The Gnostic Gospels*. 1979. Vintage Books, 1989.

Paley, Morton D. *The Traveller in the Evening: The Last Works of William Blake*. Oxford University Press, 2003.

Pound, Ezra. *The Cantos of Ezra Pound*. New Directions, 1996.

Revell, Donald. *The Art of Attention: A Poet's Eye*. Graywolf, 2007.

Revell, Donald. *My Mojave*. Alice James, 2003.

Revell, Donald. *Pennyweight Windows: New & Selected Poems*. Alice James, 2005.

Revell, Donald. *Tantivy*. Alice James, 2012.

Revell, Donald. *A Thief of Strings*. Alice James, 2007.

Scholem, Gershom. *Major Trends in Jewish Mysticism*. 1946. Schocken Books, 1995.

Schnall, Robert. Review of *My Mojave*, by Donald Revell. *Harvard Review*, no. 26, 2004, pp. 223–25.

Thompson, E. P. *Witness against the Beast*. The New Press, 1993.

Thoreau, Henry David. "Walking." *The Making of the American Essay*. Edited by John D'Agata. Graywolf, 2016, pp. 167–95.

Williams, Michael A. "Divine Image—Prison of Flesh: Perceptions of the Body in Ancient Gnosticism." *Fragments for a History of the Human Body*. Edited by Michel Feher, Ramona Naddaff, and Nadia Tazi. 2nd ed. Zone Books, 1989, pp. 129–47.

Wittgenstein, Ludwig. *Tractatus Logico-Philosophicus*. Translated by C. K. Ogden. Dover, 1999.

Yeats, William Butler. *Ideas of Good and Evil*. 3rd ed. A. H. Bullen and Maunsel, 1914.

BRUCE BOND

Reclamations of the Marvelous

> *When the neighbors complained*
> *the roots of our cypress were buckling*
> *their lot, my landlord cut the tree down.*
> *I didn't know a living thing three stories high*
> *could be so silent, until it was gone.*
> —RICK BAROT, "ON GARDENS"[1]

In his first surrealist manifesto of 1924, the poet André Breton trumpets his singular criterion of beauty as if it were a challenge. Thus, he embodies something of the rebellious vitality implicit in the beautiful itself, something less indicative of formal harmony or bourgeois complacency than the revolutionary summons of the strange. "Let us not mince words," he states, "the marvelous is always beautiful, anything marvelous is beautiful, in fact only the marvelous is beautiful."[2] Pitched to provoke, the statement relies upon a polemical sureness of phrase and purpose that would both liberate and dictate the terms of liberation—a paradox that has come to haunt our memory of the man himself. That said, the rhetoric of secular zealotry contains within it a highly mercurial and revisionary distinction in danger of being obscured by the force of Breton's certitude. Beauty in its alliance with marvel figures as the threshold of the uncertain, a realm without predetermined and thus familiar formal character. Breton needs no logical argument, since, when it comes to beauty, no such argument exists. Rather he summons us to look more closely at the biases implicit in the language of aesthetics, to put extreme pressure on the words "marvelous" and "beautiful" in ways that beg a reconsideration of just what these categories mean as embedded in one another and how the notion of "marvel" brings to "beauty" a sense of dissonant engagement, both psychological and epistemological.

Beauty, defined this way, thrives on the horror and lure of the partially concealed. Thus, the distinction between the sublime and beautiful as we see it in Edmund Burke appears less relevant to

Breton than a broader sense of beauty as imbued with elements of the sublime—the unknown, the irreconcilable, the unnerving, the disorienting, the terrifying—all that intensifies the encounter in honor of some oppositional enormity. It is one thing to be other than utilitarian, logical, and common; it is another to owe one's origin to the defiance of these things. Breton's sense of marvel would give rebellion a central role in aesthetics as the corrective to the repression of the illogical and taboo. Quite apart from the hint of exoticism implicit in the notion of marvel, beauty for Breton is less a form of escape than a means of liberation of the unconscious.

If "marvel" were defined merely as aesthetic awe, then Breton's statement approaches the circular; but indeed, the word plays a larger role in relation to his surreal aspirations, such that, like surrealism itself, its revisionary character changes in relation to a dominant culture. As Breton states, "We are still living under the reign of logic."[3] What he does not state, however, is that the experience of the marvelous relies upon that reign in order to radiate its liberating power. Viewed in context, there is no "marvel" without rationality as its implicit subtext and antagonist; and thus, beauty becomes contingent upon complex negotiations of what we call "the real" and how logic might play and refuse to play a role in our deepest epistemological intuitions, the ones we live by, the ones we suffer, however much we may be dreaming or awake.

Perhaps it goes without saying that Breton's frame of reference is poetry and visual art, both of which, through referential and imaginative tension, negotiate unresolved dependencies between the private and the public, the interior and exterior, the invented and the discovered, the projected and the perceived. Given that the "natural marvel" is likely to be dull in the poem that aspires merely to mirror, the marvelous in poetry must engage greater tension in the realm of how a poem means, how it reads, and how it thereby creates a world. With marvel as central to its power, the notion of beauty in Breton's polemics proves immensely useful in pushing back against both a dominant scientific materialism and a more traditional aesthetics. While poetry's rhetorical beauty gave Plato reservations about the manipulations of readers and in turn a more logical and pragmatic version of truth, for Breton, the virtues of poetry's beauty, as more affectively and psychologically defined, lie in that beauty's resistant enlargement of the category of truth.

Beauty is not, therefore, merely structural; it is semiotic. As such, it participates, as all meaning does, in the contextual relations that make of it a spontaneous process, forever adapting and shifting the terms of adaptation. Less obvious perhaps is the fact that the vicissitudes of aesthetic experience, like those of language, make possible in turn the intimation of a human nature and its repression. For Breton, this is no small matter, for his call for sociological shift contains within it the cry of the animal, of that troubled, human wilderness largely distant from a contemporary liberal discourse of cultural criticism and yet wedded to a tradition of psychoanalysis that was a major liberating voice of its time. At the present cultural moment, Breton figures as potentially new and useful once again, one more resource in the conversation that struggles with concepts such as beauty and nature in their alignment with a less than progressive essentialism. Beauty conceived as the marvelous gives voice to a stubbornly revisionary essence, to nature as vulnerable to appropriation and misreading—nature as the underworld in Breton's cosmos, the repression of which sends our towers higher or sets them ablaze; nature as that stubborn, dark, instinctual soil on which our modern infrastructure rises and falls.

The Limits of Theory

The marvelous as the face of sublimated instinct opens a space for beauty's provocation of desire: how it is unique among forms of arousal, since it intensifies desire even as it in some measure satisfies. Much of this satisfaction comes by way of an appeasement of anxiety—a sense of resolution and empowerment via the simultaneous continuity and distance forged in form itself. Form makes possible a psychic spaciousness and perspective or, as Nietzsche points out, a provisional sense of mastery via the objectivization of the abject, the dreaded, the desired, the broken. This point of Nietzsche's also renders beauty, as we find it in literary texts, open to social critique. Do sensations of aesthetic mastery fuel complacency or denial or displace gestures of sacrificial engagement in favor of the appearance of such? At what point does beauty reach a saturation point of solipsistic decadence that, unlike Breton's revolutionary marvels, reify the normative? When faced with suffering on a massive scale, is it any wonder Adorno made his famous claim as a challenge to "the poetic" as emblematic of beauty at its most refined: "To write poetry after Auschwitz is barbaric."[4]

Breton's defense of beauty's relation to human values is at best implicit when he considers the alternative spiritual impoverishment of a culture dominated by logic, but beauty is not the only antagonist of a rationality and a broader cultural effacement of contradiction and difference. The question remains: What is the specific good of the marvelous to those who suffer something that refuses or, at the very least, resists imaginative transfiguration? Why dabble in apparent trifles of the marvelous in light of the euphemizing mediations of horror that already saturate our media? If beauty justifies itself as the antidote to a compulsive utilitarianism, how might we answer compulsion's anxious reply: What use is that?

The experience of beauty has traditionally flummoxed theory in its search for precision and justification. No Aristotelian sense of beginnings, middles, and ends or Ruskinian sense of the greatness of style can reliably describe or inform the process whereby changing standards of beauty come into a changing world. At best, the poetics engaged in the realm of the aesthetic offers ontological descriptions immune to refutations of logic. We might say something similar about the sense of the marvelous, but what is distinctive there is the way in which wonder relies upon semiotic consciousness evolved at least to the degree of rational skepticism. In the history of literature, medieval romance, with its transportations through the liminal spaces of forests and dreams, marks a place where marvels figure self-consciously in dialogue with the doubt that makes them possible. A similar dialectic appears in Romanticism's corrective to Enlightenment values upon which the liberating energy of the marvelous depends. While beauty in the guise of the marvelous offers a world in conflict with a dominant epistemology, that world depends on an oppressive sense of the real it ostensibly negates. Once again, the obscurations of reverie are never absolute.

Another complicating pressure in theorizing beauty lies in the shifting valences that argue for beauty as mere cultural construction. Indeed, Breton's necessarily flexible and obscure notion of the marvelous anticipates the historicizing impulse that would destabilize the theoretical essentializing:

The marvelous is not the same in every period of history: it partakes in some obscure way of a sort of general revelation only the fragments of which come down to us: they are the romantic *ruins,* the modern *mannequin,* or any other symbol capable of affecting the human sensibility of a period of time.[5]

Marvel as relational, thus contextual, thus historical, need not overthrow the role of some universal in negotiating the terms of that relationship. The deference to "the natural" as revealed and honored in "spontaneous" activity at the heart of Breton's primitivism dramatizes a clash of epistemologies that continues to describe a contemporary unease, where the rising influence of neurology and eco-criticism challenges the anti-essentialism that would relegate beauty exclusively to the status of cultural construction. As scientific experiments with infants suggest that our experience of beauty is, in part, genetic, the post-postmodern reclamation of "nature" as suggestive of biological universals parallels a shift in the emphasis of much social critique. In a culture where an insincere and unsophisticated breed of relativism feeds the discourse of climate change denial, beauty's opposition to logic feels less critical and progressive than its role in catalyzing alliances with the natural world.

Further complicating aesthetic theory is the instability in its terms. In recent times for instance, Kenneth Goldsmith positions beauty as not only haunted by "the messiness of contradiction"—a widely acknowledged notion—but also, more daringly, with the "ridiculous obvious" and the "dumb":

> Eschewing climaxes and crescendos, dumb favors stasis, grids, and predictable systems simply because they require less effort. Similarly, dumb favors re-recontextualization, reframing, redoing, remixing, recycling—rather than having to go through the effort of creating something from scratch. Dumb embraces the messiness of contradiction and revels in the beauty of the ridiculously obvious . . . Smart struts. Dumb stumbles.[6]

Granted, the passage is funny. To put it under thoughtful pressure is to suggest we do not get the joke. Then again, the poignancy of much in Goldsmith's writing suggests that there is more than the campy end-of-seriousness here; and yet, contrary to the argument for greater acceptance, the mode anticipates and deflects any contrariness as belonging to the realm of the formulaic and egocentric. The discourse maintains an ironic control by granting itself immunity from other discourses, so its humor can be read as self-parody bordering on camp. A more discerning language might admit that any discourse, dumb or smart, can become the vehicle of pride and the stuff of formula. The infinite resourcefulness of ego eludes most of all the resourceful ego. The pleasure of the text resembles that of comic release: the sublimated expression of power through identification with the powerless—the paradox of sublimation being, like dreams, a simultaneous manifestation and concealment. In the process, one token of power exchanged is the word "beauty."

The fact that the *phenomenon* of beauty lends itself to ontological description but not to analytic argument destabilizes the discourse, such that the word "beauty" can become too relativized to function. As its meaning pales, so, too, does its power—which figures nicely in a negative dialectic whose target is the aesthete. Goldsmith's energy of daring, however familiarly Dadaist, relies on the counterintuitive as widely disseminated for its oppositional charisma. If granted only the tiny or compliant audience, Goldsmith's claims wither. The conventional wisdom about messiness and contradiction as elements in beauty—an idea whose acceptance reaches far beyond surrealism alone—does nothing to support the new claim here about the beauty of the "ridiculously obvious"—akin to "the uncanny" but minus the element of wonder as the threshold of inner knowledge. We might find the obvious made once again not obvious by virtue of aesthetic habits and formulae that have us looking beyond it, but such an interpretation of Goldsmith's subtext threatens to domesticate it. True, his example of grids as icons of the dull and dumb and therefore beautiful suggests something of the mercurial nature of wonder that is so quick to occupy the space it abandoned. True, a thing can be both beautiful and not beautiful at the same moment, such that a newly engendered experience of beauty swells to include the contradiction. But Goldsmith's text is funnier and more provocative without such claims. His notion of the beauty of the obvious derives an art-like energy from a contrariness of reconceptualization, such that one is left to wonder if this energy is accurately speaking of creativity as opposed to beauty. Has Goldsmith, unthinkingly or not, conflated the two in the spirit of creative defiance?

We find ourselves in an echo chamber of ironies, the subtext of which is the infinite plasticity of objects of intuition. Goldsmith's notion of beauty as counterintuitive needs no logical grounding or support, because beauty as object of ontology has none. In such a world, the counterintuitive and the rhetoric it engenders displaces both reason and intuition (or what we perceived as such) as authoritative. Intuition as the faculty that perceives inner states appears historicized to the brink of conceptual extinction. Thus, Goldsmith performs without any possible rational challenge a skepticism about beauty's relation to some essential nature and the biological limits that circumscribe the powers of cultural construction. If we agree that no person is any more intuitive than any other, beauty then becomes whatever we say it is, and ontological precision an illusion, its art form trumped by a flattening of values, by a skepticism that distrusts the notions of an objective psyche and a resilient givenness of inner states. On the one hand, this sounds rather great—democratic, liberating, refreshing, fun, "rerecontextualizing." We take ourselves way too seriously as it is. But the authority of the counterintuitive not only rejects a societal norm, it leaves aside any marveling deference to beauty as entangled in a natural order, a wilderness whose inner life is ours and forever strange.

Aesthetic Play and Pressures of the Real

No doubt Goldsmith's humor is more conducive to creative play than formulaic didacticism, and once a text announces the value of contradiction, it loosens its grip on the importance of theory. Breton's speculations, too, conspire to undo themselves, since he did not always give such clear voice to the importance of beauty in the surrealist poem; but his concern is less theory than an infusion of vitality in poems to come. When, in his description of the surrealist method, he recommends proceeding without "aesthetic or moral concern," the irony remains that such a process gives rise to a new aesthetic based on juxtaposition and, in future manifestoes, a new sense of poetry's politically dialectical role.[7] That said, irony need not suggest contradiction, since the possibility remains that aesthetic and moral goals are better served without "aesthetic or moral concern." The elusive distinction between the efficacy of the product and the psychology of the process lies at the heart of Romantic primitivism as both an ethical and aesthetic corrective to the relatively self-conscious, artificial, and "unnatural." A primitivist faith in the spontaneous similarly informs the associative method in its psychoanalytic function. The fact that the fruits of Breton's automatic method are not described as "beautiful" stands as an early example of a trend in twentieth-century poetics wherein the word "beauty" will appear less and less frequently, perhaps because of its less progressive connotations.

Charles Olson, for example, invested as he is with questions of poetic form, will justify his process by way of its epistemological function, its inclusiveness, its "stance toward reality." The word "beauty" on the other hand can invoke memories of a lyric tradition that, in Olson's poetics, represents a self-consciousness, phoniness, and egotism. While Olson's attack inherits a rather limited view of what the lyric might be and how its beauty might arise and function, his spirit of resistance to artifice helps to breathe energy, albeit Romantic in origin, into the theory and practice of poetry since the fifties. His poetics, while eschewing the diction of "beauty," does not so much refute its viability or importance as sidestep the problems associated with aesthetic rhetoric. In the years that followed, one of those problems emerged increasingly as political.

Since Olson, the horrors of world conflict have put increasing pressure on poetry to bear witness: a goal that challenges beauty's place in responsible engagement. A complex evolution of culture, including at its center the Vietnam War, prepared the American soil for its receptivity to the work of South American surrealists, such as Pablo Neruda, who manage to blend political message with a post-rationalist wonder. What we see in Neruda, however, is psychic dissonance over the conflation of impulses. In his famous poem "I Explain a Few Things," Neruda laments the passing of the "light of June" that "drowned flowers in your mouth," but there it is—the word "light" as elegy and testament to the beauty abandoned. Thus, the tension between beauty and necessity in the poem's final plea:

And you will ask: why doesn't his poetry
speak of dreams and leaves
and the great volcanoes of his native land?

Come and see the blood in the streets.
Come and see
The blood in the streets.
Come and see the blood
In the streets![8]

Of course, we see no blood, only the summons of it and the nomenclature of beauty that leverages that summons. Here, then, we might broaden our sense of what both beauty and marvel mean. To marvel at something is, after all, to look at it, to bear witness; and yet, the marvelous likewise relies upon unfamiliarity and disorientation. Wonder, in its liberating power over reason, also registers our powerlessness faced with what we cannot fathom or represent. Robert

Bly's "Counting Small-Boned Bodies" and W. S. Merwin's "To the Asians Dying" stand as two of many Vietnam-era examples where elements of the absurd create the intimate distance of matters so deeply felt they must also contain elements of imaginative play and distraction. This play paradoxically authenticates the poem's engagement and, in the process, evokes greater participation to enter the space of the unresolved. The result is less a conflation of beauty and horror than a complexity whose contradictions are seminal to beauty. To marvel then is to become negatively capable in a new sense—not only to bear the horror because of the beauty but also to bear the beauty, the horrifying pleasure of that complexity.

The rather directive poetry of transparency and reportage that would eschew beauty, however broadly conceived, begs the question: What is the gift here? Might the eschewing of beauty impoverish poetry and create an equally insidious distortion, a ghost of moral pride incapable of candor? After all, value, including ethical value, is a form of power and its discourse a currency (though more insidious than seeking validation through moral empowerment is the self-cruelty that finds this unacceptable). It is common now to see the animating tension between witness and beauty in an oddly gothic breed of realism whose beauties thrive on conflict. The flower that is the bloodied handkerchief in Keats's pocket contains within it a simultaneous force of repression and expression that, like angry comedy, gives to the unresolved the release of form and voice. That said, such ironies can be more stable than perhaps intended, since their appearance now is so frequent. The poem that operates as an irony machine has become so familiar one can often hear the gears as subtext and motive force in lieu of vision. The question remains: What are the resonances here that open up a space of seeing?

Given the historical evolution of beauty, it is commonplace now to see the tonal simplicity of the "pretty" or the gratuitous nature of the "ornamental" as unbeautiful, even distasteful because, aside from whatever imaginative familiarity they may possess, they are only ever "about" themselves. Given how beauty, in forms that mean, cannot be extricated from that meaning—as Pound noted, its speed and abundance—an act of kindness might be viewed as "beautiful," as if to suggest an aesthetics of selflessness. As with the natural marvel, the ready-made nature of such beauty is precisely what makes it problematic for imaginative form. A poem's engagement of the beautiful act relies heavily on some greater complication of new meaning spilling over the poem's particulars, lest it fail its own summons as gift. Beauty seems to participate in some elusive gift-exchange of identities, where the beautiful as mirror keeps dissolving our face inside it, thus enacting the death of the sentimental and the liminal threshold of something far too vast for the form it is in. The paradox remains: to destroy that otherness is to destroy ourselves. To eschew beauty is to participate in a larger cultural tendency whose assaults on the natural are forms of self-hatred. What we see in contemporary poetry is less a working out of the tensions that beauty inspires than a longing to give voice to them as endemic to both our flawed condition and our resilient humanity. We see a heightened awareness that either extreme of literality or exoticism constitutes a form of exploitation—that is, a failure of imagination's capacity to animate the other in the self, the self in the other, the ghost in the beautiful that exceeds its formal delineations (as meaning necessarily must) and thus, in speaking, listens.

Barot: Obscurations of the Garden

Two living poets who interrogate with emotional force and distinctive vision the call of beauty as a source of possible revelation, redemption, or exclusion are Rick Barot and Donald Revell. Their most recent volumes of poetry explore beauty's relation to human suffering with a complexity that refuses easy polemics or a failure to consider priorities in conflict. They are both writers of a mercurial questioning who engage the resources of the surreal to do more thoughtful work than Breton exemplified. Both Barot and Revell give voice to the vital, resistant blessings of absurdity in the paradoxical service of a more meditative intellect whose strangeness labors to be wise.

In his book *Chord*, Barot explores the hazards and marvels of beauty in relation to those of language, with its potential to connect and divide, clarify and obscure. Words repeatedly appear as failed mimesis and, by virtue of this, politically fraught. Barot's allusions to the writing process appear less self-focused than expansive, concerned as he is with the enlargement of our empathy, desire, and sense of wonder for that which must lie, in part, beyond representation. The tarps of the opening poem entitled "Tarp" figure as forms of obscuration and protection that gather resonance as the need for representation and charity become more salient. Few would disregard the sense of marvel in portions of the poem, and more largely the book, that owe something to a surrealist sense of the uncanny: "Another flew off the back of a truck, // black as a piano if a piano could rise into the air.[9]

Mercifully, the poem offers us a small marvel, a relief from the literal; and, just as mercifully, it returns us to the limits of the imagination amid the realities of a difficult world. It makes its implicit claim for the marvelous, for a quality akin to music in its airborne flight, but then moves to the tarps under bridges, a suggestion of the homeless, the fiercely literal treated in the quiet, efficient, indirect style made beautiful by its lack of aesthetic embellishment and strain: "I have seen the ones under bridges, // the forms they make of sleep."[10] By itself, the passage is not saturated in wonder, and yet the rhetorical flatness and indirection are key to accommodating the wonder of the whole—beauty as the mercurial performance of a process, eschewing an insistence upon beauty.

With gathering force then, the poem opens its concerns to that of writing the book itself. Thus, the language becomes more discursive, clear in ways that confess to the necessity in some measure of the unclear. The more language knows of itself and the world, the larger the experience of the unknown:

> There is no tarp for dread

> whose only recourse is language
> so approximate it hardly means what it means:

> He is not here. She is sick. She cannot remember
> her name. He is old. He is ashamed.[11]

The language of elegy becomes the language of recovery. To say, "[H]e is not here" is to invoke the presence of a "he" whose identity would indeed be elusive whether here or not. The mention of shame begs the question of its relevance to the writing act. Is there not a residue of shame involved in the "cover up," the obscuration of both those in need and the presumption that language—particularly language that aspires to be beautiful—is a substitute for what they need? Might language connect us by simultaneously placing a deep suspicion in us about the overestimation of that connection?

The paradox of language as severed and thereby charged with the longing that binds runs through the entire book. The music of elegy and lamentation provides a figure for this quality of language, invoking those who, like music, are ever in the process of becoming lost. The chord of the title poem points to its own identity as musical lamentation and so registers a coming together of parts that must remain just that, parts, in order for its chords to cohere. The chord is indeed a "cord," though made of desire, of what Barot calls "grief's appetite."[12] So, too, that appetite is made of memory. The lyricism here embodies and validates beauty of a gift given in gratitude and in defiance of a more skeptical realism that sees only alienation in language's failures:

> why not see it simply as lost   blood
> pressure   the breath ceasing
> one unreleased grasp   why not see it
> as body   parting with its function
>
> her face is   a fall leaf parchment
> I am writing   her face
> I am writing   a parchment love
> the parchment   I am writing upon.[13]

Deftly, the poem refuses to negate the implicit anxiety and urgency of the initial question. It does not directly answer the plaguing skepticism, the need to give voice to suffering and the irrevocable nature of loss. That voice remains. And what follows is less a correction than a juxtaposition, part of the emotional and conceptual complexity of contraindication that is the poem's form of precision. Not only do we have an act of recovery via writing, we also have new light coming into being. To say one is "writing her face" is to call into question to what degree we have exhumed the past and to what degree the new displaces it. The word "her" in "her face" aches with what it cannot say. Once again, language "hardly means what it means." The result has something of the marvelous in its defiance of rationality, though the tone is more delicate and affirming than defiant, more amorous in its priorities, more open to the face of the beloved as the threshold of the unknown.

Throughout Barot's book, yet another face of the beloved is the beauty of the natural world formalized in some way, into gardens, for example, or rendered in a soldier's poems before battle. As counterpoint to human suffering, such beauty would call Barot's own lyricism into question. In the poem "On Gardens," for instance, nature as cultivated now becomes emblematic of privilege:

> I know it's not fair
> to see qualities of injustice in the aesthetics
> of a garden, but somewhere between
> what the eye sees and what the mind thinks
> is the world, landscapes mangled
> into sentences, one color read into rage.[14]

Such gestures, although self-reflexive, are the opposite of self-regarding; they figure as expressions of a troubled conscience whose stakes are ethical and political, as well as aesthetic. It is the very beauties of traditional consolation, such as the blossom, that register now the horrors of exclusion that give permission to the colonizing sensibility:

> If you look at the word *garden*
> deep enough, you see it blossoming
> in an enclosure meant to keep out history
> and disorder.[15]

Meanwhile, what we encounter in such lines is a formally culti-vated poetic structure (octets), the beauties of which are never merely ironic. The final image of raccoon tracks "like a barbed-wire sash on a white gown" suggests the garden has not obscured from view the malice of exclusion any more than the poem has.[16] The image also renders difficult any clear sense of "nature" as something apart from human nature and its forces of creation and destruction. Just as haunting as the more obvious ethical summons of the poem is the undeniable power of the natural world and how it might in-spire our desire to care for it.

We see this more affirmative face of natural beauty and its rela-tion to poetic beauty in the poem "Exegesis in Wartime." Much like the middle section of "Chord," we have two competing areas of concern delineated somewhat by alternating stanzaic columns. On the one hand: war, murder by bandits, the explosion that took with it 30 citizens and a book bazaar; on the other hand: beauty, that of the natural world and that of the elegance of poetic form. The power of the poem's closure lies in part in the stubborn won-der that comes through in the soldier's journal as he takes pleasure in nature. In similar fashion, the poet takes pleasure in the soldier's writing in light—and in spite—of the embedded notes of trepida-tion and disgust:

When I read the soldier's online journal, I am
impressed by the pleasure of language: birds' names
like jewels, landscapes exalted somehow
into clarity, even when they have become a theater
of trash, sulfur, and dread.[17]

With the poem's final lines, the luminosity of the countryside "var-
nished" by dawn argues for natural beauty and the marvel of those
who participate in language as fundamental to a spirit of preserva-
tion. Aesthetic reverie figures as inextricable from the eros and the
attachment that invigorate ethics, the sense of the given as gift, of
inherent value, the light as "light itself, simple as it was."[18] With the
line that follows this affirmation of innocence, the time before the
"soldier's errand" that "would make the scene remarkable," Barot
once again weds the experience of beauty to the horror of experi-
ence, both of which lie embedded within the language of place.[19]
Beauty therefore cannot be extricated from all that it is not.

Revell: Wonders of Engagement

In Donald Revell's book *Drought-Adapted Vine*, we find the inimi-
cal style of a contemporary master whose spellbinding lyricism and
mercurial argumentation work in a similarly dialectical fashion.
Like Barot, Revell relies upon a large measure of surreal wonder—
swift juxtapositions, tensive metaphors, hyperbolic absurdities that
gather significance in context, frequent metonymies with vaguely
determined referents. Such stylistic tendencies open up the world
to play with an implicit and liberating spirit of rebellion against the
more directive and dull modes of utilitarian literalism. That said,
the meditative vocation of Revell's work positions it in opposition
to the equally dull arbitrariness that haunts the aleatory strain of
the surrealist tradition. Much like the work of Wallace Stevens,
Revell's poems gather meaningful power when we become in-
creasingly acclimated to the new vocabulary emergent within the
old—that is, how words such as "Eden" acquire new resonance in
the context of sustained meditation. Such poems aspire to enlarge
the medium itself.

As with all speculative poems that would bring the distinctive
powers of poetry to bear, the breed of philosophy that Revell's
meditations most invoke is ontology—that is, the art of attention

that, at its most precise, registers a sense of what must go unseen and/or unsaid. A tireless logical consistency would obviously be antithetical to poetry's ontological calling, but the vastness of the visionary requires both associative logic and a tolerance of disorder. It takes an elusive and feeling intellect that makes of both a new diction and syntax, a new conversation. We see in Revell's poems a mind working at such speed that the affect and conceptual resonance of one metonymy swiftly conjures its opposite—a phenomenon that potentially enlarges any one gesture in feeling and idea, even as it threatens to make obscure a forward momentum. Take, for instance, these lines from his poem "Letters to an English Friend":

> We are killing each other,
> Not skating. These are
> The last days and no
> Kidding. The undersong
> Perfected me, adored you.
>
> Hart and hind, heart in hand.
> William James places a white hand
> Upon white Henry. The picture
> Sets fire to the hair
> Of two oceans.[20]

Identity becomes tenuous throughout Revell's work, as indeed it appears to those who examine the phenomenon with relative clarity. The recurring wonder here relies on how resilient and memorable the swiftly and amply associative lines become, how they swell in the mind to reveal more upon successive readings. The above mixed metaphor (by way of metonymy) of the picture setting fire to the hair of oceans relies upon efficiency to work. The problem with most mixed metaphors, aside from whatever lapses in wit have occurred, is the clumsy cognitive sluggishness that breaks the affective spell. But rhetorical speed, when handled with other manifestations of precision, can not only accommodate the mix but make of it one of those haunting, memorable clusters of associative intelligence.

The poem's "undersong" becomes the pretext for brotherly love as it moves from the realm of William James, philosopher, into the realm of Henry, whose imaginative structures rely on the critical moment of the unrepresented, the "figure in the carpet" for instance. "White" is one of those words that gathers significance when we consider its recurrence throughout the book as evoking effacement, disease, apartness in the forms of race and innocence, not to mention the persistent albeit reductive black-and-white photos of the past. While the debt to Ashbery may be obvious, we see here a more consistently lyric embodiment of the surrealist-turned-speculative-musician. In Revell, the imperfect, the threatening, and the disorderly need not break the spell of wonder but rather figure as necessary to both his elusive realism and his transformative aesthetic.

Thus, even more than Barot's book, Revell's is saturated with the marvelous, unabashed in beauties that gather energy, not from any euphemistic exclusionary force but rather from the inclusive tensions that would re-conceptualize and revalidate the role of innocence as critical to the experience of the wise. If the voice of these poems is that of an ecstatic, a man high on the bold, imaginative play that would make of Hell an Eden, it is nonetheless one who is grounded in the real, in the flawed human condition, which is at the mercy of time yet invigorated by something outside it. Loss and suffering appear in constant dialogue with a stubborn vitality as figured in images of natural beauty. The drought-adapted vine provides one lens through which to read the opening poem, "Chorister," with its tropes of childhood and Eden that come to dominate the book:

> Cello or clarinet, it was smoke, smoke,
> Just as Paradise fading over time at the road's
> End is a black and white photograph
> Of Paradise. Elementary schoolboy
> Leaning into the hedgerow somehow still,
> Such am I. A car passes. And then no
> Traffic at all, for hours, for years it seems.
> Make a little music, boy.[21]

Paradise lost is not lost, not entirely. Time passes; and yet, the hedgerow is still. Everywhere in this book, the irrevocable nature of time conjures the newly adapted assertion of the opposite. The man remains the child and yet is also his own elder, offering up encouragement, the spirit of which is music ("Make a little music")—as is the boy's reply. The charm of the voice lies in part in the levity of tone that belies a grandeur of scope.

Suffering in Revell's work, especially as it relates to the problem of time, also figures as necessary to an abiding sense of the "marvelous" as something "marred." As he states in the poem "A Shepherd's Calendar":

> For now,
> Joy. For an hour at least,
> The effortless white of the wheels.
> Boy, to mar is to marvel.
> To be the wound of the sun
> On Time's face is beautiful.[22]

The gift Revell brings to a contemporary unease about the role of beauty in relation to the troubled conscience is a revival of the Romantic trope of the child as paradigm of an intelligence that recurs transformed in some measure to redeem us, to console us, to create a necessary and powerful space for play in light of—and in spite of—the horrors beyond.

It is in this spirit that the ensuing alphabet poem, "Alphabet City: An Autobiography," embraces the childlike even as it sketches Hell. Such Hell suggests not only the personal suffering in any one autobiography but also the imaginative construct of a moral nature that outlives each story. When we get to the letter "D," for instance, we find: "DANTE // Has a box of crayons he'd like to share."[23] What is shared is not *The Divine Comedy* alone but the capacity to make one. Revell's entire book offers a highly intimate and personal breed of Christianity—more obviously a relation to Jesus than to the Church—an imaginative engagement wherein Christ manifests in forms of beauty, childhood, and contemporary crucifixion whose unlikely blessings are their imperfections.

In the sonnet-sequence "The Watteau Poem," Revell's meditation on the troubled nature of the ideal—"beauty / Bent to the breaking point"—allows into the poem the speaker's own shadow so as to implicate his wretchedness as the pretext for a more inclusive voice:[24]

> Christ promised me American catastrophe
> All my own. My erst friends, beloved,
> Would hurry away down the white, white snow,
> And I would pound into the window panes
>
> White names, their names. Below the eye, self-made
> Imaginations of a colored spree
> Plays hangman. Wretched man. Wretched tree.[25]

The uneasy friction between "American catastrophe" and "all my own" opens up possibilities of parody or confession; yet, the lines also point to the dark ground of the individual psyche that introjects and projects its personally inflected cultural constructions.

One does not need the specificity of something like a 9/11 tragedy to unearth the essentials here. In fact, such specificity might divert us from Revell's transformative and meditative (versus narrative and journalistic) priorities. The elusive dialectic that would avoid the euphemistic or the sensational would likewise open our eyes to hard truths while engaging in a child's game of hangman. The child deserves some measure of protection, which is one point of the story Revell tells in *Invisible Green* when he describes his eventual response to the redundant inundation of news after the World Trade Center disaster. Here, too, we see a righting of priorities in a politically charged context:

> It is October 15, 2001. We have stopped taking the newspaper, and this morning my son complained that he was missing the news. I thought of the bombs falling somewhere in his little name, and I opened the window shade. I pointed to the red sunrise reflected on the near Spring Mountains and said "There's the news."[26]

It is a testament of love that the immediate world below the eye is seen through the lens of cultural disaster; but the question remains whether these associations at some point threaten to obscure our place in the world and thereby turn us away from the gift of being. At what point does the spectacle of disaster become a lively entertainment, a "colored spree," as "The Watteau Poem" calls it, such that the wretched object of our gaze is our own impoverished interiority in denial of its all too human failures of attention?[27]

Hangman, as a child's game, casts the shadow of the child as narcissist, voyeur, and, albeit playfully, as sadist; just as the "wretched tree" casts the shadow of a crucifixion whose more distant "other self" is the stubborn spirit of grace. The wretched human condition, as something that binds us, opens a space for human charity and forgiveness and, moreover, the beauty of hymns as the reincarnated reverie of the child. In Revell's work, time is not so much conquered as put into relation with the stubborn persistence of a marveling wisdom and the role of Eden as the articulation not merely of who we are but of who we might become and therefore of what we value.

It is a testament to the broadly humane, inclusive, and genuinely humble imaginations of both Barot and Revell that the movement from beauty's self-evident gifts to its self-secluding hazards is never simple. What they offer cannot be accurately described as aestheticism or its utilitarian, moralistic opposite. More radical than their passion is their precision, and precision requires the vulnerability of the open eye. Not that the presumed exclusivity of the chambered garden tells us lies. But rather, it *is* a lie. Exclusion is repugnant. Beauty seen precisely as relational, semiotic, marvelous in its dialogue with human difficulty, cannot exclude the world without in turn excluding us. As it is in dreams, aesthetic wonder invites us to consider more closely the very thing it would conceal. While dreams intimate a cypher, such cyphers do more than merely conceal or reveal. They summon. They seduce. They make us marvel— not because they are the core of some autonomous identity but because they problematize the notions of identity and autonomy. They open our eyes in wonder, even as they shake us, or confuse us, or frighten us awake.

Notes

1. Rick Barot, "On Gardens," *Chord*, 5–6.
2. André Breton, *Manifestoes of Surrealism*, 14.
3. Ibid., 9.
4. Theodor Adorno, "An Essay on Cultural Criticism and Society," *Prisms*, 34.
5. Breton, *Manifestoes of Surrealism*, 16.
6. Kenneth Goldsmith, "Kenneth Goldsmith on Dumb Culture," *The Utne Reader*, par. 5.
7. Breton, *Manifestoes of Surrealism*, 26.
8. Pablo Neruda, *Selected Poems*, 150–51.
9. Barot, "Tarp," *Chord*, 3.
10. Ibid.
11. Ibid., 3–4.
12. Barot, "Chord," *Chord*, 41.
13. Ibid., 43.
14. Barot, "On Gardens," *Chord*, 6.
15. Ibid.
16. Ibid.
17. Barot, "Exegesis in Wartime," *Chord*, 11.
18. Ibid., 54.
19. Ibid.
20. Donald Revell, "Letters to an English Friend, *Drought-Adapted Vine*, 11.

21. Revell, "Chorister," *Drought-Adapted Vine,* 3.
22. Revell, "A Shepherd's Calendar," *Drought-Adapted Vine,* 4.
23. Revell, "Alphabet City: An Autobiography," *Drought-Adapted Vine,* 5.
24. Revell, "The Watteau Poem," *Drought-Adapted Vine,* 57.
25. Ibid., 57.
26. Revell, *Invisible Green,* 65.
27. Revell, "The Watteau Poem," *Drought-Adapted Vine,* 57.

Works Cited

Adorno, Theodor. "An Essay on Cultural Criticism and Society." *Prisms.* Translated by Samuel and Shiery Weber. MIT Press, 1967.

Barot, Rick. *Chord.* Sarabande, 2015.

Breton, André. *Manifestoes of Surrealism.* Translated by Richard Seaver and Helen Lane. University of Michigan Press, 1972.

Goldsmith, Kenneth. "Kenneth Goldsmith on Dumb Culture." *The Utne Reader,* 2015, http://www.utne.com/arts/kenneth-goldsmith-on-dumb-culture-zm0z13ndzlin.aspx?PageId=2

Neruda, Pablo. *Selected Poems.* Edited by Nathaniel Tarn. Dell, 1972.

Revell, Donald. *Drought-Adapted Vine.* Alice James, 2015.

Revell, Donald. *Invisible Green: Selected Prose.* Omnidawn, 2005.

KATHRYN COWLES

Recuperating the Brilliant Picture
Language as Transubstantiation in Donald Revell's Later Poems

In "The Poet," Ralph Waldo Emerson writes, "Every word was once a poem."[1] Poets, he argues, name the stuff of the world, and the names are initially fresh and full of the essence of their subject matter; indeed, as he writes, "The etymologist finds the deadest word to have been once a brilliant picture."[2] But over time, words lose their luster and clarity. Now, "Language is fossil poetry. As the limestone of the continent consists of infinite masses of the shells of animalcules, so language is made up of images or tropes, which now, in their secondary use, have long ceased to remind us of their poetic origin."[3] Language is full of the dead junk left behind by old generations of long-dead namers. "But the poet," Emerson continues, talking about the best writers writing now (or in the now of his essay), "names the thing because he sees it, or comes one step nearer to it than any other."[4] True poets can make words back into the brilliant pictures of their origins. True poets can revivify the fossils, can raise the dead.

Every so often in my reading life, I have encountered a writer who is a true poet according to this definition, who causes a profound shift in my understanding of what language can do, a poet who makes words mean again. Donald Revell's poems have done this for me—have reinscribed language with long-dead capacities in a way I had thought was impossible.

Revell's poems are alchemical. They take little strange ingredients, sometimes the most everyday things you can imagine, and mix them together; then, a kind of chemical reaction occurs, and suddenly, miraculously, the language lifts up off the page. Dead words resuscitate. They transubstantiate. They somehow say things, deeply human things, that aren't actually possible to say, at least not directly. They help words regain their mystery, their gravity, their grace. They rescue language from the grim lonesomeness of poststructuralism.

Lately, I've been rereading, side-by-side, three of Revell's most recent poetry collections—*The Bitter Withy* (2009), *Tantivy* (2012), and *Drought-Adapted Vine* (2015)—paying special attention to these moments of transubstantiation the way one might look at the insides of a timepiece: prodding little gears and levers and hammer springs and pinions trying to intuit how the whole thing moves, why it moves me, what causes which part to tick. I don't want to explain craft here so much as to witness and name moments of this process of word revivification. In tracking some of these moments, I hope to make it so I can feel my way through the poems in the future with an eye on more of their parts at once, so I can sense their little tickings more clearly, so I can teach myself how to take in and hold what is miraculous about them.

Telescoping Scale

> *"God is in the kitchen drawer, / And His love is infinite"*
> —Donald Revell, "Alphabet City: An Autobiography"[5]

Sometimes reading a Revell poem involves a dizzying shift in scale, like looking through a microscope, then binoculars, then a telescope, all in the course of a line or two. In these particular lines, the shift in scale overlaps the quotidian with the infinite. God in the kitchen drawer can be intimate and everyday and endlessly huge at once. This vacillation between huge and tiny, between universe and kitchen drawer, somehow, for me, reinvests the concept of God with mystery, with miraculousness. I get closer to the infinite via the kitchen drawer.

See also:

From "Victorians (5)" in *Tantivy*: "The fossil record quietly accounts for me . . ."[6]

From "Victorians (10)" in *Tantivy*: "Whichever way I go was once an ocean."[7]

From "Tithon" in *Tantivy*: "God counts only up to one / His hands are small / And in God's hands even / Mountains are sparrow-sized."[8]

Collapsing Time

*"Even as their shadows / Move, still leaves remain still. The pas-
sage / Of time is indescribable."*
— "THE LIBRARY"[9]

That's the trouble, for many poets, with too many things in the
world: they're indescribable. And yet, I often find Revell describing
the effects of time in a way that reminds me *of* time, in a way that
feels like time feels. He does this, for instance, with that description
of the leaves. Something about shadows moving while their leaves
stay still unhinges the time of the poem, makes it wobble, physical-
izes its passing-ness for me, as if I'm seeing a few seconds of the
leaves through stop-gap animation or a time-lapse film depicting a
leaf budding and then opening out before it fades, all within sec-
onds. I know what it means, even though it's unparaphrasable. I
know what its time looks like. Likewise with the poem "Days of
Illness":

> I can hear the rain 900 miles from here.
> Nearer, two eyes open, vacant and pure,
> Timelessness . . . there's no such thing. It would kill me.
> I think of two small children, brother and sister
> They shelter small together beneath one tree.
> Behind them, motionless in a rain-swept field,
> Women in stiff, outdated clothing stand
> Waist deep in the blowing grass. I would choose
> To be the grass, to be moving, hoping
> Somehow to draw the children's attention
> And to draw them into the field. The women are dead
> Long since. The children are old. The rain
> 900 miles from here is speaking through the grass,
> From field to field in me so I might live.[10]

In this poem, Revell describes an indescribable thing when he
edges in on what I'll call his concept of eternity—and one thing it's
not is timeless. Instead, its time is collapsible and expandable. The
small children are simultaneously small together and old. The
women are waist deep in grasses and long since dead. The here
overlaps the hereafter. Time is simultaneously now now and always
now, and I really feel it when I read this poem.

I suspect that the rain 900 miles away is important to this felt time the way the shadows and still leaves were important to the passage from "The Library"—that distance is operating as a kind of metaphor for the simultaneous smallness and bigness of time, for its temporal vacillation between near and far. Everything can exist together in the now of the poem. And somehow, this conception of eternity circumvents the sorrow of decline or death, if only for a moment.

See also:

> From "Little Bees" in *The Bitter Withy*: "Low suns glow in the river. / I am losing my days to them. / I miss the days, but not too much. / Wherever they go, they make a meadow."[11]
>
> From "Drought" in *The Bitter Withy*: "Eyesight is nobody. / Perspective dies before it lives, / And it lives a long time after death // Like birdsong. // When I die, I will begin to hear / The higher frequency, / A whine, as though the moment were a lathe. / It will be a true lathe, / All my life spinning off from it."[12]
>
> From "Lay of Waters" in *The Bitter Withy*: "The actual past weeps from future wounds."[13]
>
> From "A Painting of Cezanne's" in *The Bitter Withy*: "Whatever lives at all, lives a long time."[14]
>
> From "Tithon" in *Tantivy*: "And a child my child myself as a child waiting."[15]
>
> From "Graves Variations" in *Drought-Adapted Vine*: "Genesis / Makes nonsense of our Christmases."[16]
>
> From "Foxglove" in *Drought-Adapted Vine*: "And poetry. Jesus please slow down. / The bad men are far behind us now. / Lunching among postcards of the Last Judgment, / We can breathe. We have time. We have plenty of it."[17]

Metaphors via Big Time

> *"An epochal sun sees / Mountain ranges, and the mountains melt away."*
> —"GRAVES VARIATIONS"[18]

When William Blake compares two things using figurative language, they could be any two things. As he writes in *The Marriage of*

Heaven and Hell, "Everything that lives is holy."[19] It stands to reason, then, that if everything that lives is holy, if everything is touching the holy, everything is as everything else: all holy. Metaphors are easy in this world.

I want to present Revell's notion of eternity as parallel to Blake's notion of "Everything that lives is holy." Revell's Everything can be compared to everything else via a kind of radical temporal contiguity: everything is like everything else because it's all touching time. Or, seen a different way, Everything is like everything else because even things that are on the opposite ends of eternity are still in eternity, and eternity is always happening now. As Revell writes in one of the splendid footnotes to "The Watteau Poem," "The parts of a world are alone with God, crowded together."[20] I would go so far as to say the times of the world are also alone with God, crowded together.

And so, as Revell writes, "An epochal sun sees / Mountain ranges, and the mountains melt away." Mountains can turn to not-mountains if you just wait long enough. And the wait can collapse time into a single present tense. All of time can take place now in the space of the poem. A speaker can be a young boy and an old man. Multiple Christmases can happen at once.

Furthermore, time is never done. In "A Shepherd's Calendar," Revell writes,

Out of marred and moving whiteness
Wisdom consists entirely
Of afterwards, of far ahead
Where time is finished with itself
Just as the mountains over there
Are finished with the sun. For now,
Joy. For an hour at least.[21]

The mountains, of course, are not finished with the sun at all—just finished *for now.* (The line break helps us read over the punctuation and see "are finished with the sun for now.") Likewise, joy is temporary, but we have it for an hour, and that means we have it now. And we have plenty of it.

Even language is never finished with itself. Later in "A Shepherd's Calendar," Revell revisits the word "marred" when he writes, "Boy, to mar is to marvel."[22] If we wait long enough, the marred whiteness from earlier shifts to marvel. There is always the possibility of a complete turnaround, even at the level of the word. Sometimes all we need is the patience to wait for a few more letters. Or, for a cycle to begin again, as with "West Agate": "Winter really is the end, but only one at a time. / And then the summer rushes in, lauding / The life's work, the legacy only now / Bursting into flower and flame."[23] Yes, winter is the end. And then comes summer.

See also:

> From "Homage to John Frederick Peto" in *Tantivy:* "Creation's a funny word. / I think of noises rounding a corner / Becoming names, and then a child for each / Of the names climbs down the sun. Creation's the soul of haphazard. / I was old. I was young. I was old again. / Anymore Johnny, all I feel is fine."[24]
>
> From "For John Riley" in *Drought-Adapted Vine:* "Go apple, apfel, apples fall in parallel, / Each alone. Likeness is no likeness nor / Contrast a divide."[25]

Part-and-Whole Metaphors

> *"Vision runs up a hill called Vision. It never / Comes down."*
> —"FOXGLOVE"[26]

Paradox is at the heart of some of Revell's most visionary metaphors. In them, a thing acquires a metaphorical relationship with itself. So, in the lines above, Vision can be both part and whole. The slippage between part and whole makes a word difficult to conceive. And this difficulty sharpens my attention, activates the terms of the metaphor, creates a charge. A concept that seemed stable or contained ("Vision") is revealed to be uncontainable ("Vision" becomes a hill "Vision" can run up). A thing throws itself outside itself, breaks out of its container, and this breaking has the capacity to re-mystify this thing that has otherwise been run down by the everyday nature of language. A word finds a way to be magical again.

Sometimes, in the paradoxical turn of a part-and-whole metaphor, a seemingly literal thing ("Angels") becomes figurative, as in "The Creation of the Stag": "Let all / Angels become the angels of themselves."[27] The tenor of the metaphor becomes its own vehicle, and it drives itself out of the confines of the metaphor, remystifying the relationship between signifier and signified.

See also:

> From "Tithon" in *Tantivy*: "Creation is the miniature of creation."[28]
>
> From "Alphabet City: An Autobiography" in *Drought-Adapted Vine*: "HEART / Is a hollow island / With hands of its own. / Those hands crush the heart."[29]
>
> From "Crickets" in *The Bitter Withy*: "If she ever steps out of that entryway / Into the full sunlight, my heart / Will leave my heart. / What happens then?"[30]

Vehicles on the Move

Although I just used them myself in the previous section, I want to say that I've always found the terms *vehicle* and *tenor* to be relatively unhelpful when discussing figurative language. For I. A. Richards, the tenor, the thing the metaphor's supposed to be talking about, the original thing to which some other thing is being compared in order to teach us something about that original thing, is fairly distinct from the vehicle, the thing from which one is stealing terms of comparison. Me, I like when the literal blurs with the figurative. I like, as with epic simile in Homer, to forget the tenor in light of the fascinating thing to which it is being compared. I like a vehicle that drives away, as happens with "My Name Is Donald" in *The Bitter Withy*:

> Like a fish on a hedge, the horsefly
> Lands on my wife's lipstick.
> That is sobriety.
> That is the end of my hayride with oblivion.
> I wonder: how long will it be until no one
> Knows what a hayride is,
> Or was? I've never been,
> But the happiness I've seen in movies—
> All the kids piled up in hay & a fiddler driving—
> Is very real. It was real for a while.
> Only a child can watch a movie sober.
> He is younger than the mule pulling the wagon.
> He is unshamed by the fiddler's expertise.
> His birth trumps all, which is to say he's flying.[31]

Here, the comparison of a fish so deeply out of place on a hedge to a horsefly on lipstick—the weird, bold attractiveness of the nouns, the attachment of them all via a gestural "that" to sobriety, to "the end of my hayride with oblivion"—draws all the attention in the first lines of this poem. But it's that hayride that won't sit still in its vehicular positioning. The poem starts to think about hayrides, and the vehicle gets going, gets to driving away. The poem is Rimbaud's drunken boat, oars thrown overboard. The poem takes a hayride.

And so, the completely figurative "hayride with oblivion" becomes a specific kind of hayride—a movied, moving-picture hayride. The perfect-looking kind. And that might make for a mildly interesting metaphor. But then the vehicle takes a detour. It's like a trick rollercoaster ride, with quick turns and reversals and secret doors that throw themselves open to reveal new ways to go. It distracts itself from its own sobriety with a vehicular kind of oblivion. The poem repaints the tone of the hayride with temporariness: "It was real for a while." And then, "Only a child can watch a movie sober." So, we're back to our original term of comparison, our sobriety, our tenor, as it were, but it's a changed thing. Its bags are packed with new and different connotations. Drunkenness seems suddenly to be the only rational response to a world stricken with perfect pictures no one ever lives in, the world that differs so much from the world of ideal hayrides.

And then the child climbs in the vehicle. He becomes specific; he becomes real, takes on qualities of his own that feel resonantly figurative, even though they're readable as literal. "He is younger than the mule" and "He is unshamed by the fiddler's expertise." Something is being said here that's other than what is literally being said. And so, the last line, "His birth trumps all, which is to say he's flying," which feels suddenly like a second coming, and which shoots us out of the poem going in a completely different direction than the one we came in, also follows what came before, according to the drunken logic. The vehicle's takeover of the tenor gets us to the poem's second coming.

See also:

From "Debris" in *Drought-Adapted Vine:* "Antiquity shivers in the unbuilt tree. / She laments (antiquity is a widow, braided /

Into the rained–upon color of desert trees / After a wind-storm) her perfected dead."[32]

From "Tithon" in *Tantivy*: "The dome of heaven is a nest / It trembles and the nestlings / Fall into this world their mouths / Agape their mother already gone / To God yet something / Is it death comes to gather them / Mends them and they arise / Singing their one note the green sound / Shaped by the updraft"[33]

Syntax-Resisting Sentences

> *"Violets are the anniversary of something / Youthful covers the next hill hurrying."*
> —"TANTIVY"[34]

Sometimes in Revell's poems, especially the later poems, individual words shake loose from their syntax, as happens with the above lines. Often, this means that two sentences join together at the hip, sharing a word or phrase that is necessary to each. The loosened syntax holds together multiple grammars and possibilities.

For instance, the line breaks in "Tantivy" make it easy to read the words "Violets are the anniversary of something" as a single sentence. But the sentence doesn't end there. Instead, it rushes into another seemingly self-contained sentence: "Something youthful covers the next hill hurrying." The pivot at "something" enacts the hurrying. There are two gravitational pulls in the two lines—two sentences, each pulling "something" into the arms of their syntax. The two internal sentences cause a continual rereading, a vacillation, and there is life in vacillation.

In her "Two Stein Talks," from *The Language of Inquiry*, Lyn Hejinian talks about how Stein's work, which doesn't stylistically resemble what we think of as realism at all, is actually a modern kind of realism, perhaps a more realistic version of realism, because it resembles the way life works—it acts like life.[35] In this sense, Revell's disrupted and dual syntax, his sentences that resist their lines, look like life to me. They feel alive.

See also:

From "The Watteau Poem" in *Drought-Adapted Vine*: "Life in heaven not alto, but the freight / Train's higher register a shriek of couplings / In the February night are bedside / Table bedside telephone 1982 / Resembles her, resembles the two of us. / We are an old married couple in Corinth, // Tennessee. How is any child's / Eyesight a heaven?"[36]

Also from "The Watteau Poem": "The heaven-sent harries our evidence / Each sign each second of extremity / All rescued by the Lord gives freely / Unhappy we cannot say He."[37]

Devices for Thinking

> *"Either everything is music or nothing is. / Either we live in the past or there are more birds / Than can be counted. / Everything is music."*
> —"HUNTING"[38]

Revell frequently uses poems as devices for thinking. In the above example, the poem poses a question to which it doesn't know the answer—and then it finds its way to an answer. While some poets begin their poems knowing in advance what their (therefore artificial) revelations will be, Revell never knows his conclusions or resting points in advance. The poem is always an act of faith, a walking out into the darkness only to discover a path appearing under one's foot. The poem makes its propositions or asks its questions; then, the task of the poem is to address these propositions and questions, to find out what it thinks.

See also:

From "Pine Creek" in *The Bitter Withy*: "Only the one chair. / Is it because my dead are happy standing, / Perfectly at ease, each in his own flower? / Of course it is."[39]

From "Long-Legged Bird" in *The Bitter Withy*: "No one knows. A moth knows."[40]

Image as Metaphor

> *"Otherwise, / I am toys / Lost on the polar ice."*
> —"CRICKETS"[41]

Sometimes Revell will put an image in place of a terrible fact. Or a true fact, or a powerful fact. In such a case, merely saying the fact would lend it little of its gravity. Saying a fact is a newspaper lede. It is information without any feeling. The right image, conversely, can come at something indirectly, can quote how it feels. An image can be a kind of telepathy. It can transmit a felt fact via the conduit of words on the page directly without ever saying the fact. It can say one thing and point to something else entirely.

And thus, the above lines from "Crickets" in *The Bitter Withy*. The toys carry with them so many other things. They carry children, obviously, but children in a place where no children would ever be. They are toys without any possibility of children. They are useless. They are more than abandoned. They are completely outside the possibility of use. And utterly alone. The extreme cold of polar ice is made colder by the grim thought of children there. In a poem with so many Christmases, this is one where the toys didn't make it to the children—became frozen out of time almost, having entered a new brutal reality outside the possibility of Christmas. In a poem that invests boyness and Christmas with the accumulated meaning of repetitions in new contexts, this image, which ends the poem, echoes and holds together all of those previous contexts. And the fact that the toys are being compared to an "I" matters. There's a kind of implied, hollowed-out, lost childhood in it. Something more complicated than either "I am toys lost" or "I am polar ice." There's a pictureable absence with lost toys.

In truth, I can't explain it, what's happening in these seemingly simple lines. It is unparaphrasable, and yet feelable, tangible. I can't explain what and how the lines mean, but I know what they mean, immediately, intuitively, as soon as I read them.

See also:

> From "Lay of Waters" in *The Bitter Withy*: "Love never fails. / I met a woman in Kentucky. / There's no going back. / If I am in a woodland, / She is the woodland, / The warm, soft hand extended on the leaves."[42]

> From "Odysseus Hears of the Death of Kalypso" in *The Bitter Withy*: "She was mast and sail. She was / A stillness pregnant with motion, / Adorable to me as, all my life, / I have hidden a cruel, secret ocean / In sinews and in sleep and cowardice.

/ She forgave me. Once, she wept for me. / Our child died
then, and she is with him."[43]

Eye-Trusting Trajectories

*"The rainbow seems to breathe / And so it breathes. // When it
speaks it makes / The birds in our black trees // Glad and brave."*
—"BETWEEN STORMS"[44]

In order for there to be the possibility of the miraculous, poems
must be able to believe a miracle when they see one. Sometimes
poems must talk their way into believing what they see. I love how
in poems like "Between Storms," Revell lets us in on the process,
relinquishing the poet's traditional infallibility and authority in or-
der to give himself over to the greater authority of the miraculous.
Thus, "The rainbow seems to breathe" leads to "And so it breathes."
The poem teaches us to trust what we see, to believe our own eyes'
miracles.

See also:

From "Can't Stand It" in *The Bitter Withy*: "A cloud is a cloud
that looks like one."[45]

Kaleidoscopic Methodologies

Many of the poems in Revell's later books, most especially the lon-
ger poems and series poems, have what I'm calling kaleidoscopic
methodologies. This is one of the most difficult concepts in Revell's
poems for me to describe and yet one of the most pervasive, char-
acteristic, original, and compelling. The pieces from one line or
section, the images and bits of language, will undergo a spatial and
temporal shift and appear again in another section, newly arranged
like the pieces in a kaleidoscope, reconfigured with a twist of its top
and echoed with mirrors and light. The relationships between these
words, these pieces, changes with each reconfiguration, and the cu-
mulative effect is such that by the end, the words have picked up
shorthand associations and carried them through to the end, cover-

ing ground with great efficiency. They are resonant with new meanings, are more than the sum of their parts. A good example of this appears in "Chorister" from *Drought-Adapted Vine:*

> Cello or clarinet, it was smoke, smoke,
> Just as Paradise fading over time at the road's
> End is a black and white photograph
> Of Paradise. Elementary schoolboy
> Leaning into the hedgerow somehow still,
> Such am I. A car passes. And then no
> Traffic at all, for hours, for years it seems.
> Make a little music, boy. Light a cigarette
> Found in the roadway, a sign from God.
> I remember the bitter taste of small berries
> Before the summer began, and then
> A bitter taste again in early autumn. Sweetness,
> A little portion, like a wisp of smoke
> Mistaken for music. A lonely car
> Is all the traffic ever comes. Walk on.
> I am entering a photograph fades with me
> And no one else. Ahead, a derelict
> Sound in the shape of cellos disappears
> Into pale, gray foliage. Childhood's
> Amazon River hounded out of church,
> Out of the painfully small portion
> Of ripe berries any soul can find,
> Empties into Paradise one white boy.[46]

In "Chorister," I'm focusing on the recurring words and concepts of music/cello, smoke/cigarettes, boy/childhood, something fading, berries with a little sweetness, and Paradise (though there are other little pieces in the poem's shifting kaleidoscopic repertoire— the car, the traffic, or lack thereof, elements of time, lifespans, etc.). So, the initial metaphor in the poem, "Cello or clarinet, it was smoke, smoke," reappears a little later with "Make a little music, boy. Light a cigarette / Found in the roadway, a sign from God." God is linked to the previous "Paradise fading over time" like "a black and white photograph" of itself. Then small berries are described as having "Sweetness, / A little portion, like a wisp of smoke / Mistaken for music," and so back to the music and the smoke. The faded photograph of Paradise reappears with, "I am entering a photograph fades with me," and then "a derelict / Sound in the shape of cellos disappears" or fades, smoke-like. Then, finally, the poem ends with "Childhood's / Amazon River hounded out of church, / Out of the painfully small portion / Of ripe berries any soul can find, / Empties into Paradise one white boy." By the end of the poem, each recurring word holds together a constellation of pieces, reflects what came before. And so, the final incarnation of each word feels pregnant with meaning, feels like it's holding together disparate elements. We're closer to the unnameable origins of words, past the limiting and lonely restrictions of communication described in twentieth-century linguistic theory.

This effect is even more pronounced, and significantly more complicated, in the longer poems, such as "The Watteau Poem" in *Drought-Adapted Vine* and the "Tithon" section of *Tantivy*. In "The Watteau Poem," footnotes further complicate the recurring words and images, sometimes coloring previously repeated words retroactively, sometimes shifting all the pieces of the kaleidoscope around to accommodate the new one. And, in fact, the magic of recurring images and phrases plays out across whole books and between books, with little beautiful threads of Revell's lifelong concerns and interests and landscapes visible in the stitching, holding together the body of his work and adding the resonance of whole books' worth of associations to later recurrences of a word or an image. His entire oeuvre is kaleidoscopic and readable as a singular entity, continuous.

Finally

I could go on. There are as many ways to traverse a Donald Revell poem as there are Donald Revell poems. I have chosen here examples that resonate especially with me and that enact a miraculous transubstantiation of words, that make words meaningful again in the way Emerson describes.

I encounter words constantly in the quotidian world that are merely utilitarian devices for the most basic communications (like Emerson's "fossil poetry")—words that are good enough to help me order food or ask directions, but that are remarkably imprecise or general. Using words this way can be lonesome. Communication becomes approximate, always halfway, or halfhearted. I feel the gap between me and others, between me and the world, when I use a word as "elegy to what it signifies," as Robert Hass writes (and refutes) in "Meditation at Lagunitas."[47]

Revell's words are not elegies to anything. They don't point at absences; they are themselves presences, alive and mysterious, infinite and immediate. They throw me outside of myself and into the actual world. They hit the ground running. They are difficult to pin down, are unparaphraseable. I take them on faith. They pack their bags with cumulative meaning, take on new resonances, new layers. They feel to me like the world feels; they act like it acts. And so they restore for me its brilliant picture, its miraculousness, its grace.

Notes

1. Ralph Waldo Emerson, "The Poet," *Selected Essays*, 269.
2. Ibid., 271.
3. Ibid.
4. Ibid.
5. Donald Revell, "Alphabet City: An Autobiography," *Drought-Adapted Vine*, 5. Note that this and all remaining epigraphs are from poems by Revell. Titles appear in the body of the text, along with additional bibliographic information in the corresponding endnote.
6. Revell, "Victorians (5)," *Tantivy*, 7.
7. Revell, "Victorians (10)," *Tantivy*, 12.
8. Revell, "Tithon," *Tantivy*, 43.
9. Revell, "The Library," *Drought-Adapted Vine*, 33.
10. Revell, "Days of Illness," *The Bitter Withy*, 45.
11. Revell, "Little Bees," *The Bitter Withy*, 50. The concept of days making a meadow here again intersects time with space to give the feel of days slipping. I think of Robert Duncan's famous meadow in "Often I Am Permitted to Return to a Meadow" as a "field folded" (7). I've heard Revell say before that a meadow is a place without an edge, which fits with these lines.
12. Revell, "Drought," *The Bitter Withy*, 52.
13. Revell, "Lay of Waters," *The Bitter Withy*, 29.
14. Revell, "A Painting of Cezanne's," *The Bitter Withy*, 36.
15. Revell, "Tithon," *Tantivy*, 43.
16. Revell, "Graves Variations," *Drought-Adapted Vine*, 42.
17. Revell, "Foxglove," *Drought-Adapted Vine*, 75. These are the very last lines of *Drought-Adapted Vine*, a book mightily concerned with its own passing. "We have plenty of it" is the only underlined text in all of Revell's oeuvre and seems to me to point clearly to a loosened and specifically Revellian conceptualization of eternity.
18. Revell, "Graves Variations," *Drought-Adapted Vine*, 42.
19. William Blake, *The Marriage of Heaven and Hell: The Complete Illuminated Books*, 133.
20. Revell, "The Watteau Poem," *Drought-Adapted Vine*, 53.
21. Revell, "A Shepherd's Calendar," *Drought-Adapted Vine*, 4.
22. Ibid.

23. Revell, "West Agate," *The Bitter Withy*, 24.

24. Revell, "Homage to John Frederick Peto," *Tantivy*, 16.

25. Revell, "For John Riley," *Drought-Adapted Vine*, 67. Here, as with mar/marvel, "apfel" is a kind of shorthand word that accordions out into "apples fall" and then "apples fall in parallel." The word is a squeezing together of these things. In "Some Notes on Organic Form," Denise Levertov writes, "there must be a place in the poem for rifts too—(never to be stuffed with imported ore). Great gaps between perception and perception which must be leapt across if they are to be crossed at all." And then, "The X-factor, the magic, is when we come to those rifts and make those leaps. A religious devotion to the truth, to the splendor of the authentic, involves the writer in a process rewarding in itself; but when that devotion brings us to undreamed abysses and we find ourselves sailing slowly over them and landing on the other side—that's ecstasy" (425). It seems counterintuitive, but Revell's compression actually creates the gaps that lead to my ecstatic leaping. This space for leaping is, I think, characteristic of his work.

26. Revell, "Foxglove," *Drought-Adapted Vine*, 75.

27. Revell, "The Creation of the Stag," *Drought-Adapted Vine*, 22.

28. Revell, "Tithon," *Tantivy*, 44. This line has the effect of infinitizing creation—insisting that it's much bigger than one originally thought.

29. Revell, "Alphabet City: An Autobiography," *Drought-Adapted Vine*, 6. Heart is conceptual before it is physical. It vacillates between the conceptual and the physical. It's on the move, so it breaks free of the clichés that often cling to the word "heart."

30. Revell, "Crickets," *The Bitter Withy*, 15. The paradox here—the part shifting out of its whole—is necessary to the saying of this concept; it has the dizzying effect of a heart skipping a beat.

31. Revell, "My Name Is Donald," *The Bitter Withy*, 10.

32. Revell, "Debris," *Drought-Adapted Vine*, 32. The parenthetical here whiplashes me out of the syntax of the sentence momentarily; and yet, the imagery is continuous, even as the sentence splits apart.

33. Revell, "Tithon," *Tantivy*, 48. Here, the nest outshines its heaven, distracts from it, gets in the car and drives.

34. Revell, "Tantivy," *Drought-Adapted Vine*, 41.

35. Lyn Hejinian, "Two Stein Talks," *The Language of Inquiry*, 86–90.

36. Revell, "The Watteau Poem," *Drought-Adapted Vine*, 49. The initial sentence here turns and turns on its syntax, allowing for a wrinkle in the time and space of the poem—allowing life in heaven to shift to a bedside table telephone in 1982, to an old married couple in Tennessee, then back to heaven. Perhaps this is what a child's eyesight can encompass?

37. Revell, "The Watteau Poem," *Drought-Adapted Vine*, 53.

38. Revell, "Hunting," *Drought-Adapted Vine*, 70.

39. Revell, "Pine Creek," *The Bitter Withy*, 46.

40. Revell, "Long-Legged Bird," *The Bitter Withy*, 55. The poem contradicts its conclusion immediately after making it. It tries again. Contradiction is a door, the "sudden portal" of the next line, toward some place of new revelation.

41. Revell, "Crickets," *The Bitter Withy*, 17.

42. Revell, "Lay of Waters," *The Bitter Withy*, 29.

43. Revell, "Odysseus Hears of the Death of Kalypso," *The Bitter Withy*, 53.

44. Revell, "Between Storms," *The Bitter Withy*, 19.

45. Revell, "Can't Stand It," *The Bitter Withy*, 6.

46. Revell, "Chorister," *Drought-Adapted Vine*, 3.

47. Robert Hass, "Meditations at Lagunitas," *Praise*, 4.

Works Cited

Blake, William. *The Marriage of Heaven and Hell. William Blake: The Complete Illuminated Books.* Thames & Hudson, 2000, pp. 107–33.

Duncan, Robert. "Often I Am Permitted to Return to a Meadow." *The Opening of the Field.* New Directions, 1960, p. 7.

Emerson, Ralph Waldo. "The Poet." *Selected Essays.* Penguin Classics, 1985, pp. 259–84.

Hass, Robert. "Meditation and Lagunitas." *Praise.* Ecco, 1979, pp. 4–5.

Hejinian, Lyn. "Two Stein Talks." *The Language of Inquiry.* University of California Press, 2000, pp. 83–130.

Levertov, Denise. "Some Notes on Organic Form." *Poetry,* 106, no. 6, 1965, pp. 420–25.

Revell, Donald. *The Bitter Withy.* Alice James, 2009.

Revell, Donald. *Drought-Adapted Vine.* Alice James, 2015.

Revell, Donald. *Tantivy.* Alice James, 2012.

JACQUELINE LYONS

Participant in the Larger Force
Perception and Presence in the Poems of Donald Revell

Presence and Present

Charles Olson, near the end of his essay "Projective Verse," writes, "It comes to this: the use of a man . . . lies in how he conceives his relation to nature . . . to which he owes his somewhat small existence. If he sprawl, he shall find little to sing but himself . . . [but] if he is participant in the larger force, he will be able to listen, and his hearing through himself will give him secret objects to share."[1] The act of listening described by Olson and its way of attending to the world allow a poet to create open or projective verse, the "artist's act in the larger field of objects, [which] leads to dimension larger than the man."[2]

Thoreau, in "Walking," wished a radical conception, to see each of us as "inhabitant, or part and parcel of Nature."[3] In nature, our true and only home, we come to our senses, tune our perception, and engage in thought without constraint. Thoreau laments the separation of body and mind, noting times when he has walked his body for hours through the woods, spirit lagging behind, and celebrates the joyful realignment of body and mind when he returns "with a sudden gush" to his senses.[4] To be aligned with the self shores up resolve against regret, and the unified body and mind create a position of integrity from which we can turn to the world, not with a sprawling or grasping, but with an open embrace.

The experience of reading Donald's Revell's poems, line by line, image by image, thought by thought, is to witness a listener and participant of the larger force; to be continually restored to the senses, body and mind together, in the same place, at the same time. The poems, as reflected upon by Revell in *The Art of Attention*, exist as a presence, in the present. The poems do not force a sequence; there is no hierarchy or consequence. They move, as Olson describes, "instanter," "one perception [leading] directly to the next."[5]

The gate in "Arcady Again" neither causes nor controls the grass it reveals to the listener upon opening. The attention, completely present, makes each moment reveal a new perception, an unveiling of what exists for the participant, if he sustains attention, if ear and breath stay tuned.

The etymology of the word *perceive* leads us to the Latin roots "seize, understand," and "entirely" alongside "take." Inhabiting the present—and one's own nature—is to inhabit the body, and to take in moments through the senses. "Stand," linguistically, extends roots to variations of place: town, role, position—creating fanciful and practical connections between receiving the sensory world, and the site of that reception, with deference to understanding (standing under) the nature of the experience.

Olson's "the HEAD, by way of the EAR, to the SYLLABLE and the HEART, by way of the BREATH, to the LINE" reflects a physiological phenomenon: that data received via the physical senses is processed by the brain's limbic system, which produces physiological effects (change in heart rate, quickening of breath) associated with emotion.[6] Words of emotion do not incite emotion; rather, description of sensory experience reaches the reader's brain, i.e., *emotion is communicated through the physical body.* The physical world vibrates variously with rhythms, and Revell conveys them bodily, writer to reader, in spare lines, deft repetition of word and image, and swift passage from one perception to the next—the kind of composition that recreates attention's effortless leaps. Tuning into sound leads the poet to sense, which he then imparts through word, rhythm, and vision. Readers experience a progression of energy, of times and places brought simultaneously into a single frame. If the poems appear less familiar than the everyday life of the mind, it is because we are not in the habit of attending to our own train of thought, of knowing our mind's busyness, of seeing our leaping thoughts assembled across the field of the page.

Eadweard Muybridge, challenged to employ his photographic skills to seize a vision unavailable to the human eye, tuned his camera to twenty-four frames per second to capture the motion of a running horse. Through a technological exercise, comparable to poetry's meditative one, Muybridge exaggerated the physical sense of sight to lead to insight—when the horse runs, all four legs do in fact leave the ground at once. Muybridge's assembly of the photographs recreates, slow enough for the naked human eye to receive, the easeful—natural and naturally complex—interaction of a horse's legs in motion. Revell's poems (like Muybridge's images) recreate, frame by frame, the flow of one perception leading to the next—a way of being in the world always possible, yet often closed by inattention.

Far and Equally

"Arcady Again," the prelude poem in *My Mojave*, begins in motion, with a prepositional phrase:

> Beside the house a path

and identifies the sensory self in terms of its surroundings, participant in a larger force:

> Green leaves as low
> As my eyes and a low
> Gate into the rainy yard
> Opens and even the little
> Grass is very wide[7]

The repetition of "low" and the poem's spatial sequencing create sonic and visual rhythms. Enjambment adds a bass line. One perception leads to the next in a manner that mirrors movement along a path, beside a house, through a gate. The grass, both "little" and "wide" (and a third, implied, "low"), inhabits dimension and color. Echoes multiply as every other line begins with "g," and the green of the leaves in the first line echoes intuitively the presumed color of the grass in the fifth line. There is no sprawl here, but a close sustained attention that can leap with ease to

> God help the man who breathes
> With nothing leading him
> Here or someplace like it
> Inside him which he opens
> Wide enough to walk through
> And walks through[8]

The self-referential "lead," the simultaneity of "here or someplace like it," and the quietly shocking "inside him" all guide us to where attention lives. Or where, with deference to Olson, the speaker is participant in the force. The speaker opens himself wide enough to walk through, and walks through—and then is

> Surprised to find deer and turtles
> Living so near his house[9]

To follow the poem's attention is to follow the poet turned inside out, passing through himself, led beyond himself and back to the place where the poem begins—surprised at actual deer, noticing them, noticing anything alive and "so near." The word "find" glows within an aura of noticing and active seeing. The figurative sense of "find" waits somewhere aside from the poem—the speaker is surprised to find *himself*—near deer and turtles, or here, or someplace like it, or anywhere in particular. Thoreau's "with a sudden gush" manifests here as "surprise," body and mind together like lovers leaping to the next perception.

"For Thomas Traherne" begins with "The ground," which "is tender with cold rain." The declared tenderness will emerge again in the poem's middle stanza, uniting the series of perceptions by the quality of tenderness, as will the repetition in the poem's final words, "underground as rain."[10]

The tenderness, and the poem's second line "Far and equally," referring to coastlines ("our" coastlines), which "grow younger / With tides," perceive an equanimity among natural forces, and position the speaker as part and parcel of immensity. The poem gathers (parts of) the physical earth, vast and various, into the poem, allowing our naked and time-bound eyes to see changing shorelines, to see "Beautiful winter" apart from spring, and to stand in the presence of "earth everywhere," which exists "above all festivals or praise." Earth remains constant, a constant presence, and winter, by "Not becoming spring today and not tomorrow / Has time to stay."[11] We who identify with winter find a sense of season most leisurely and securely itself when not compared to spring, or to any phenomenon other than itself.

The next stanza's "Easter will be very late this year," sharpens the distinction between weather, which is sensed, and a holiday, which is constructed. Easter can be early or late according to the calendar. Earth remains above all Easters, the only one who can always be on time. The poem wants to reach past its elbows into this sense of season and time and feel around: "Thirty years ago / I saw my church / All flowery / And snow / Melting in the hair of the procession / As tender as today."[12] Readers familiar with Revell's larger body of work know there are brick and wood churches; in this poem, the ambiguous descriptions could refer to a building, religiously codified, or to a site outside, in the spirit of Emily Dickinson's "an Orchard, for a Dome."[13] The church in "For Thomas Traherne" is "flowery," and "snow melt[s] in the hair of the procession," a procession that could consist of girls in Easter dresses, snow in their hair, or trees and squirrels, snow melting on bark and fur.

The poem's three stanzas, seven lines each, raise a solid structure within a broad visionary sweep across land and water, season and time, today and thirty years ago. In the final stanza, the poem returns to earth. The "coastlines grow younger" of the first stanza morphs into "all things here / Becoming younger."[14] Paradox resides in "growing younger," as does an implication that perception of the new and present moment requires cultivation—we grow into new attention. If attention is new, intimate and tender, then what is being attended to is also new, young(er), finally present.

Arrival and Return

Innovation characterized Muybridge's explorations, and curiosity directed him toward the intersection of the human sense of sight and the phenomenal world in motion. To better see motion ("the kinetics of the thing"), he broke it down and reassembled it, creating insight from new technology.[15]

Olson emphasized kinetics, "a poem as energy transferred" from poet-seer to reader, and poetry's "essential use," urging that poetry must contain "laws and possibilities of the breath, of the breathing of the man who writes as well as of his listenings." Both Muybridge's and Olson's innovations depend on a "certain stance toward reality" and a means of conveying that stance to an audience.[16]

We have motion and energy and the poet coming into relation with them. The following, from the second section of Revell's "Pandemonium," instructs:

I remember my son in tears
In the apple tree, ashamed
Because he could not climb it,
Not realizing he had already climbed it

And was being photographed in the blossoms
Eight feet above violets and dandelions.[17]

The boy's error is all of ours, difficult as it is to see where we stand in relation to an abstraction, like tree-climbing or success—without a sharp image of it, we cannot recognize whether or not we have arrived. Or, not in the habit of seeing, we cannot identify our location. Lost in ourselves, we need a larger hand, or a better eye, to register our location. We need someone to photograph our location within, and relationship to, our surroundings, a better eye to see that we are "Eight feet above violets and dandelions." In sustained attention, we could capture each moment, and our movement, and know our place, maybe for the first time.

Such seeing is difficult. It requires continual practice and effort, and, as Revell suggests in *The Art of Attention,* proliferation—attention "begets a present attention."[18] Attention is travel without having to go far, and the reward is the familiar place made new, which puts us in mind of Eliot's "We shall not cease from exploration / And the end of all our exploring / Will be to arrive where we started / And know the place for the first time."[19]

Such circumnavigation can be found in varying degrees in Revell's poetry, as in "Zion," where the first line's "Suddenly copper roses glow on the deadwood" becomes, in the fourteenth and final line, "Sunlight turning deadwood coppery rose."[20] The unexpected inversion alludes perhaps to closing sight's paradoxical relationship to traveling the circumference (which was, let us recall, Emily Dickinson's business).

Where does continuous attention lead us? Back to ourselves ("God help the man"), back to the beginning, to the pleasure of aligned body and mind, to a well-tuned perception, to energy, to perspective ("Eight feet above"), to everything "Becoming younger," to the place we started from and knowing it for the first time, to understanding, to compassion for the nature of our near universe, to, as Olson observes, a "stance toward reality outside a poem as well as a new stance toward the reality of a poem itself,"[21] and to sustained and meditative attention, for the deep peace of knowing ourselves.

Notes

1. Charles Olson, "Projective Verse," *Poetry Foundation,* https://www.poetryfoundation.org/articles/69406/projective-verse
2. Ibid.
3. Henry David Thoreau, "Walking," 35.
4. Ibid.
5. Olson, "Projective Verse," *Poetry Foundation,* https://www.poetryfoundation.org/articles/69406/projective-verse
6. Ibid.
7. Donald Revell, "Arcady Again," *My Mojave,* 1.
8. Ibid.
9. Ibid.
10. Revell, "For Thomas Traherne," *My Mojave,* 32.
11. Ibid.
12. Ibid.
13. Emily Dickinson, "Some keep the Sabbath going to Church—," *The Poems of Emily Dickinson,* 106.
14. Revell, "For Thomas Traherne," *My Mojave,* 32.
15. Olson, "Projective Verse," *Poetry Foundation,* https://www.poetryfoundation.org/articles/69406/projective-verse
16. Ibid.
17. Revell, "Pandemonium," *My Mojave,* 5.
18. Revell, *The Art of Attention,* 6.
19. T. S. Eliot, "Four Quartets," *The Collected Poems,* 208.
20. Revell, "Zion," *Pennyweight Windows: New & Selected Poems,* 196.
21. Olson, "Projective Verse," *Poetry Foundation,* https://www.poetryfoundation.org/articles/69406/projective-verse

Works Cited

Dickinson, Emily. "Some keep the Sabbath going to Church—." *The Poems of Emily Dickinson.* Reading ed. Edited by R. W. Franklin. Harvard University Press, 1999, p. 106.

Eliot, T. S. "Four Quartets." *The Collected Poems, 1909–1962.* Harcourt, 1991

Olson, Charles. "Projective Verse." *Poetry Foundation,* https://www.poetryfoundation.org/articles/69406/projective-verse

Revell, Donald. *The Art of Attention: A Poet's Eye.* Graywolf, 2007.

Revell, Donald. *My Mojave.* Alice James, 2003.

Revell, Donald. *Pennyweight Windows: New & Selected Poems.* Alice James, 2005.

Thoreau, Henry David. *Walking.* Cricket House Books, 2010.

MICHELLE MITCHELL FOUST

The God Paintings
The Geometry of Donald Revell's "Tithon"

The nineteenth century brought us the Romantic Imagination. Poets of period understood the necessity of the mind's return to childhood and to those first encounters of darkness and light in the natural world that nourished the gothic. The nineteenth century, via Felix Klein's *Ernlangen Programme* (1872), also ushered in the first systematic use of transformations within geometry: reflection, rotation, translation, dilation, and tessellation. On Descartes' coordinate plane, images move according to the tenets of each transformation. Similarly, images shift on the heavenly planes of Donald Revell's "Tithon," an epistolary poem that embraces creation stories, ghost stories, and fairy tales peopled with children and lit by color theory that we saw first in the experiments of Isaac Newton. A girl wanders the planes of the poem, and on those planes are solar axles. She is blind as only someone who has stared at the sun unflinchingly can be.

With a Romanticist's vision, Donald Revell threads "Tithon" with comparisons among Creation *(C* majuscule), creation, and transformation. With a child, his child, and his child self as protagonists of "Tithon," Revell also uses the tropes of geometry—reflection, tessellation, and dilation—in a transformational approach to painting pictures of God.

"Shadows of leaves" follows "Shadows of leaves" at the onset of "Tithon."[1] There begin the transformations of the poem, the shadows being reflections, a host of them repeated. These are shadows and not their leaves. They fall on and onto each other. To repeat them is to tessellate, and if we consider the equation of "Shadows of leaves" and "Shadows of leaves," a composition of transformations has taken place (i.e., reflection and tessellation). Revell repeats these phrasal reflections throughout the poem. The inaugural shadows, however, are punctuated with a prince's announcement: *"Je suis le prince / D'un pays aboli,"* or "I am the prince / Of a country *aboli.* "[2] The speaker is the protagonist of the fairy tale residing in "Tithon," and his country is an abrogated one, from the French understanding of *aboli*. But according to the Hindu definition of *aboli*, he is the prince of a country with the name of a flower, a girl's name. Both interpretations of *aboli* can find a home in "Tithon." A country continually abolished is a country in its natural state should a child be its creator. A prince can end or cancel a world indefinitely through transformations such as reflection and tessellation (think of blocks, of Lincoln logs). Escheresque, in this country *aboli*, each image, each world, is always becoming another.

> How wonderful,
> How entirely human it is to dream the death
> Of all creatures, leaving the planet to itself
> In starlight.[3]

The prince dreams the children up in smoke. He dreams his tabula rasa: the black ice enshelling Ganymede, the Jupiter of Jupiter, Jupiter's moon. This is creation in the hands of the prince and of the poet protagonist who was himself once the prince. Even the poet's son walks out of his eyes "Never to be seen by me."[4] But unpeopled silence is the sound of creation, and "We mend in death."[5]

> The mothers are glad with God
> As we are glad to be alone
> Broken mirrors thrown into flowing water
> Become souls[6]

Reflection on reflection here. "Shadows of leaves / Shadows of leaves." Reflection and tessellation, together with rotation and translation, are also called isometries, because the images are reoriented on the plane—the images are flipped or are repeated or are turned or slid—thus, the leaf shadows maintain their integrity. They are no smaller or larger. Their shape has not changed. Green makes love to them in another kind of transformation in the poem, that of color, often accompanied by sex in "Tithon." Nineteenth-century color theorist Thomas Young

> assumed the existence of three independent response functions in the human eye: one predominantly sensitive to the long-wave light and yielding the response red; a second predominantly sensitive to the middle-wave light and yielding the response green, a third predominantly sensitive to short-wave light and yielding the response violet.[7]

Over the years, many variations have been proposed, each a linear transformation from one triplet of color-matching functions to another triplet of color-matching functions.[8]

In "Tithon," color is not a physical response so much as a divine gift. Every color is matched to white, where, "At the center of creation," shadows are "Dying unafraid into real colors / in [God's] sunlight," like a rainbow in the real world.[9] According to Newton's corpuscular theory of light, sun enters rain and reflects off the back of the drops, retracting as it leaves. The bow centered on the shadow of the watcher's head at the anti-solar point reveals a collection of colors carrying more than light. In "Tithon," color is born out of water whose surface imagery/reflection is the city (for the prince) and Heaven (for the protagonist). God is the protagonist's "lost reciprocal," and he asks of God, "Will you read will you bring a color only one / Here to the mirror / White is water from which the colors rise."[10]

No one needs be called to the mirror. God holds it up to the child protagonists. God is the fountain whose reflection is Heaven. When the children plunge their hands in, the mountains and clouds fly. They do not see themselves. They are blinded by the axle of sunlight much the way Newton was in his monastery room. He stared at the sun for as long as he could. He stuck pins in his eyes. He was alone with the light. The sound was the sound of the leaves' shadows.

Reflection is the primary transformation of "Tithon"—"Green I can see when I see nothing"—and yet dilation is the only transformation whose image changes shape in this text, which gives the transformation a different primacy in Revell's poem.[11] In "Tithon," God's image is dilation or contraction. What God creates is also a dilation or contraction. After all, as the poem observes, "Creation is a miniature of creation."[12] God is small when small means immense. It's a game of proportions. God's image in "Tithon" is measured in sparrows. His hands are measured in sparrows. How else paint God except by ratio?

God counts only up to one
His hands are small
And in God's hands even
Mountains are sparrow-sized[13]

God need only count to one because the images between zero and one are infinite: as x approaches one, y approaches infinity. Those "axles of sunlight" recall those axes of the unit circle whose radius is the span between the origin-locus-center and one. Zero to one recalls the periodic functions of the nineteenth century, particularly the sine function and its line mounting upward on the plane from zero to one, sine that helps us measure a shadow over time. So much happens in so small a space, as in the palm of a hand.

> God is holding a mirror
> No bigger than my eye
> Beloved lost reciprocal
> Restore to me
> My infant eye[14]

"Tithon" is not a creation story that portrays the creation of the earth or the world. It is verse on creation. The speaker wants creation from the moment of creation. He wants to create from the moment of his own creation and to see with his original eyes, to address with his infant "I." The poem is also verse on the relationship among creators. When the speaker talks with God, he says, "we spoke paint," a medium of color.[15] When Donald talks to Nathan in the letter within the poem, he applauds Nathan's poems of ghosts, saying, "[Y]ou have made a purist origin." Transformation begins at (o, o), at "Once upon a time," where the x and y axes cross on Descartes' plane:[16] "Once / Upon a time, the sun in the morning / Was painted like a mouth.[17]

Like the onset of a fairy tale, this image. The sun is immortal to a child. It speaks, companion-like, in the morning and afternoon. It goes away, but it never disappears. In "Tithon," "The shadows of leaves are addressed to immortality" through transformation.[18] In the poem, Revell references three immortals whose stories are reminders of this very idea: Tithonus, Ganymede, and Jesus. "Ganymede again and again but never quite the same," because we need only one.[19]

On earth as it is in Heaven, we need only the original point "A," the one "A." When point "A" is transformed, "A'" (A prime) is its ghost, whether the point is reflected or translated. "A" might even be three-dimensional, such as the nest in the dome of Heaven, reflected in the bowl of the fountain full of souls, mothers mended, ascending: "Nothing but one road in all this world there is nothing

/ But God myself alone as a child and counting / Up to one the garden number."[20]

Creation is the return to childhood. Creation is solitary, is communion. In the world of geometric transformation, creation needs only the span from zero to one. One leaf in Heaven, one note, one color, one road. Because this is a world of transformation, we can tessellate. We only need one to begin: "And a prince beside himself with joy at the axle of sunlight / Knows that it is all hallucinations / And one of them is true."[21]

Notes

1. Donald Revell, "Tithon," *Tantivy*, 43.
2. Ibid.
3. Ibid., 51.
4. Ibid., 52.
5. Ibid., 48.
6. Ibid., 48.
7. Quoted in Stephen D. Songden and Emeka E. Ike, "On the Models of Colour Vision," *Journal of Natural Sciences Research*, 166–67.
8. Quoted in Jozef Cohen, *Visual Color and Color Mixture: The Fundamental Color Space*, 85.
9. Revell, "Tithon," *Tantivy*, 45.
10. Ibid., 46.
11. Ibid.
12. Ibid., 44.
13. Ibid., 43.
14. Ibid., 45.
15. Ibid., 44.
16. Ibid., 49.
17. Ibid., 51.
18. Ibid., 52.
19. Ibid., 44.
20. Ibid., 52.
21. Ibid., 53.

Works Cited

Cohen, Jozef. *Visual Color and Color Mixture: The Fundamental Color Space*. University of Illinois Press, 2001.
Revell, Donald. "Tithon." *Tantivy*. Alice James, 2012.
Songden, Stephen D., and Emeka E. Ike. "On the Models of Colour Vision." *Journal of Natural Sciences Research*, 4, no. 19, 2014, pp. 160–71.

REBECCA LINDENBERG

Et in Arcadia Ego

Don't tell anybody / This is only for the good to know
—DONALD REVELL, "LEARNEDLY"[1]

In 2009, just three days before I was scheduled to sit for my doctoral exams, my partner, Craig Arnold, who had also been a student of Don's, went missing on a small island called Kuchinoerabushima in the south of Japan. He'd gone for a solo hike and had never returned. Don naturally let me postpone my exams for the duration of the search for Craig and for a period after, during which I came to terms—officially, legally, and ritually—with Craig's death. About an hour after I finally did submit the last of my exams, my phone rang, and Don said, "Now, buy a plane ticket and come home." I did, and I spent the next few weeks floating in the pool with Don and his wife, Claudia, letting myself be fed guacamole and smoked fish and white wine, sleeping late, napping often, talking a lot, and now and then picking up Don's beautiful and visionary book *Arcady*, written in the wake of his sister's death, and reading a poem or two. A few months later, I finally had the strength to read the book all the way through. I had looked at all of the words before, but that was when I read *Arcady* for the first of many times.

As I sit down to write this essay, I have just come from teaching *Arcady* to the graduate poetry workshop I am teaching at the University of Cincinnati. I say "teaching," but these poets are quite impressive, so what I really mean is that I'm simply the one who gets to choose the books we discuss. And that happens to be work I take very seriously. I have a kind of spiritual algorithm for doing that work, too—balancing books I love, still warm in my hands, with books I haven't read yet but have wanted to feel new energy from; texts I understand to be canonical, texts all poets should know, with texts I mostly wish were already canonical, that I delight in for their risk and their ambition, their experiment and their novelty, all balanced with a desire to draw into company poets of our tradition and our future who come to us from many places and races and human experiences to make for a fuller vision of the range of aesthetics, subjects, methods, and *raisons d'être* that make up the sublimely varied fabric of (predominantly) Anglophone poetries. It feels somewhat like sacred work, ensuring that certain voices are heard. It is not idly that I suggest that Donald Revell's should be one of them.

Stephanie Burt has rightly pointed out that Don's poetry has transformed dramatically from book to book, but that *Arcady* marks an especially notable change. This is, of course, explained in the moving prefatory note. In this book in which she is mostly absent—though her absence is felt throughout—the poet's sister is named only once, and her name, Roberta, almost like an apostrophe or an invocation, is the book's opening word. Roberta's sudden death ruptures the language of poetry in almost the way a stroke might do, requiring a profound reimagining, or perhaps I should say re-visioning. Don writes, "It takes two (never fewer, rarely more) to language. I was suddenly one. My native language lapsed."[2] In the summer of 2009, just a few months after Craig disappeared, I picked up my copy of *Arcady* one evening, for the company and comfort of a trusted mentor and friend and read those words. And something that had been troubling me greatly but which I hadn't made any words for yet—the feeling that what I had once cherished as a private kind of language and conversation had become suddenly and terribly secret and silent—became astonishingly clear to me for what it was in that passage, and I experienced one of the things I think we often hope to experience when we read: I suddenly didn't feel alone.

Of all Don's books, *Arcady* most gives me hope. It gives me hope for my own poetry, that I, too, may change and change and come to feel that "To dream like this / Was worth the trouble / Getting here."[3] But perhaps more importantly, and the reason I share it with students instead of merely cherishing it, is that it also gives me hope for poetry. "Best poetry has never been written," Revell writes.[4] Of course, this suggests that many unlanguaged things might be poetry—"Flowerily than ever / Unspoken and wide open // Leave death to ripen / Flowerily."—but it also supplies the hope, and indeed the provocation, to poets who often write in the shadow of belatedness—hearing the death knell of their art rung again and again in this or that journal, digging in a field fenced-in by all the posts- (modernist, feminist, avant-garde, etc.)—to imagine that "best poetry" might be yet to come.[5] The poetry of Donald Revell, vatic, ecstatic, and affirming, is a strong tincture against cynicism.

When I teach *Arcady*, which I dearly love to do, I often begin by asking students how they would react if any of the poems in the collection were brought into a workshop. The answer, almost invariably, is a kind of skepticism, which is the pale of most workshop experiences. It is not the students' fault that these poems seem to elude the kind of critical engagement that they are most familiar with. While I believe in poetic collaborations, the conventional workshop model seems almost coercive to me, designed to cultivate a limited series of expectations in young poets, so that when a poem satisfies those expectations it gives delight, and when it does not satisfy them, whether by the poet's perceived ineptitude or the poet's deliberate resistance to them, the poem creates confusion. The poems that seem to excite the widest approval in most classrooms are those poet Lyn Hejinian has described as "'closed' texts," meaning the poet has wrought the poem in such a way that all of its formal, thematic, and linguistic elements corroborate a single fairly visible interpretation.[6] In her essay "The Rejection of Closure," she calls this the "coercive epiphanic" mode.[7] An open text is one that, to put it plainly, just doesn't do that. Donald Revell writes open texts. They may be provocative, they may be ecstatic, and they are certainly visionary. They are *not*, however, coercive, nor are they epiphanic. How, a student asked recently, isn't the following statement epiphanic?

> I think there must be a place
> In the soul for perfection
> I think it moves around
>
> And no mistake[8]

The reason these final lines aren't epiphanic is because the poem doesn't move by that kind of logic, the kind of cause and effect logic by which narrative, for instance, progresses. Something about epiphany requires the reader's confirmation—*yes, yes, I would never have thought of that. Yes, you're right, how important this is. And yes, this is precisely and perhaps the only thing really that logically follows from what comes before.* Not so here. As Don himself observes, "A story asks to be followed; Arcady remains to be seen."[9] It remains. It's not just that you haven't seen it yet—for all you know, you've been there all along—but that it *remains*. It'll keep. It'll be there when you need it. To be seen. To be perceived. And this poem reads as a fragmentary, dreamlike record of perception. The mind moving between planes of awareness. It moves around. It shines because it moves. Uninvolved with perfection. And no mistake. "And no mistake." There would be no room for the workshop to correct this poem, because how can you correct experience? How can you correct evidence? The poem, aware as it is of all its awareness, feels visionary. But not in that "closed text" way, not epiphanically. The difference between epiphany and vision is the difference between getting a lukewarm plate of what you ordered for your dinner on a cruise ship and being in another country offered a fruit you've never tasted. One gives delight by somewhat tepidly satisfying an expectation, the other by altering and enlarging the whole idea of what one might imagine as expectation.

Vision is not exactly something commonly taught in the creative writing workshop. (Nor really re-vision, despite the somewhat unexamined ubiquity of the term.) Mostly, the workshop purports to teach poetic craft. To be honest, I have never taken comfort in this idea. It has always seemed to me a little bit of a con. The way Phillip Larkin grumpily explained it, poets find themselves "in the unprecedented position of peddling both their work and the standards by which it is judged."[10] But, I think my objection started as an undergraduate, when I began to recognize, somewhat resentfully, that the more or less standardized lexicon of critique was heavily gendered. Praise was always offered in the most unreconstructed masculine terms for writing that was "strong," "powerful," "terse," "brave," "bold," or—still it persists—"muscular." Critique was equally feminized for chastising writing that was "soft," "sentimental," "shrill," "melodramatic," or "flowery." I was even offered, once, the dubious praise of "being something of an intellectual tomboy."

I resisted these formulations of "craft." I felt diminished by them. I also had an intuition that while they might be the tricks of the trade, they were not, in fact, the trade itself. I tried to trust my cluttered gut. I found myself in a workshop at the University of Utah in Salt Lake City, sitting expectantly at a long table with others who, I think now, only seemed less nervous than I was. Don's entrance, because Don is very tall, as are the mountains that were visible through the windows behind him, felt somehow monumental even before he thumped a copy of Pound's *Cantos* on the table and said,

"I will not be grading you this semester on the quality of your poems. I will be grading you on the quality of your souls."

Donald Revell's poems teach me that there are many, many (I call them in my head) sites of virtuosity in poetry that long precede the page. This really has nothing to do with craft and everything to do with vision. I wish to distinguish virtuosity from the notion of mastery. In fact, I sometimes think the idea of mastery is anathema to that of virtuosity, at least in regard to poetry. Virtuosity is intuitive, ambitious, daring, feral. Don writes, "Wild work / needs wilderness."[11] I needed the wilderness of Utah. I needed the wilderness of a Donald Revell workshop. I still need the wilderness of his poems—and I want to share that wilderness with my students, too. But being wild can be scary. Mastery makes "coercive epiphanic" poems that feel safe and controlled and that give the impression that one knows what one is doing. Virtuosity gets the better of us. Or, virtuosity becomes possible when the poet lets the poem get the better of her or him.

When we speak of things like "risk" and "experiment," even of "ambition" in poetry, I think—perhaps I hope—that we speak of writing beyond the reach of our own organized understanding. This is not to say that we suddenly become possessed, oracular poets, just that we are willing to trust that we're smarter than we are and that in our poems we may discover how that is the case. To enter into that willingness, that trust, requires great faith.

> Heart I agree
> Is a heavy f
> Lower now *lour*
> *De* THAT[12]

Throughout *Arcady*, "atom" and "void" recur. Language, too, is atomized, so that the unit of meaning in these poems is often not the line, not even the word, but the letter. "Is a heavy f," a resonant alto; "Lower" now *"lour,"* a scowl, perhaps of doubt; "De," a note close below f. And these lines are followed by a kind of musical notation:

S	H	
I	I	
M	D	L
P	D	I

It is difficult to know how to bow across the strings here—the words are chords, not individual notes. They are atomized but played simultaneously. The whole poem is played simultaneously. Simultaneous with "Is a heavy f / Lower now *lour* / *De* THAT" is "fLower now lourDE" and "fLower now *flour.*" And yet, there is "hardly room for an echo."[14] How can that be? Because as atomized as things might seem—letters in words, words in ideas, people in families, stars in constellations—faith is what gets the poet across the void.

The poem finishes on a higher, more celestial frequency than that lower f and even lower D (though we do move from minor to major in that case), and "[m]y son and wife whistling / Shake the stars in Orion."[15] Whatever we may assume about the intention of all these remarkable elements of the poem, the poem is entitled "Heart I Agree." It is an affirmation, a realization, of something a priori to the poem. Something heart, not mind or eye or ear, something that has asked something of the poet, to which the poem is the poet's response. I like the idea of the poem as a reaction to one's self, particularly if we agree upon the notion of "self." That, too, is a struck chord. That, too, is something atomized we need a bit of faith to cross the void of.

Don also offers in his prefatory note that this project is coeval with his intense involvement in "the pictures of Poussin, and the writings of Thoreau."[16] Poussin's most famous painting, which hangs in the Louvre in Paris, *Et in Arcadia Ego* (1637–38), depicts a group of classical pastoral figures gathered around a stone sarcophagus which they gesture toward animatedly. The phrase "I am also in Arcadia" refers to death—its ubiquity so thorough as to be in Arcadia, Elysium, making "Tombs in Heaven too."[17] Some art historians have speculated that one of the figure's gestures toward the tomb trace the shadow of the dead on the stone and are meant to depict the origin of art-making as elegiac, memorial. Whether that interpretation of the painting is correct or not, the sublimation of love, once lost, into art, is one of the most ancient of faiths—just as the knowledge that death transforms us all is among the most ancient of truths. And yet, as Don writes:

It is impossible
Not to suffer agonies
Of attachment to the world
Is really so wonderful[18]

I love these lines. They remind me of something Don said to me once while I was in the throes of my deep grief. I was floating in the below-ground lap pool in the back yard at Don and Claudia's, trying to fall out of my grief into the sky, and Don said, "Rebecca, just because the world is beautiful doesn't mean it will satisfy us." Even though my relationship with Don has always been affectionate and respectful, we have certainly not been without our share of disagreement. I did not come to my understanding and appreciation of Don's way of thinking, of being, of poeming, by sitting reverently. It's not my way, I suppose, and happily for me, Don understood that. He said one day, "I understand that sometimes you need to listen by talking. You echo-locate." On another occasion, when I said that I felt angry, he replied, "Just remember, there is a difference between anger, which is energy, and abuse, which is captivity." And one time while we were on a stroll in the Mojave Desert near his home, gazing somewhat wistfully into some brush rattling with birds, he announced, "I aspire to be a minor poet."

I aspire to someday aspire to such a thing. For now, I aspire to vision, and to the encouragement of vision. "No, no," Don once said, shaking his head. "Not writers at work. Writers at peace." Poetry cannot be laborious or contentious when it is visionary— neither to read nor to write nor to discuss. I want to learn to teach, as well as to practice, the risk, the ambition I find in Donald Revell's poems. I want, as a teacher, not to "demystify the writing process," as it is often described in composition pedagogy, but rather to entirely re-mystify it. There are some things one cannot exactly teach but can aspire to cultivate in oneself and in one's students, just as Don observes in "Thales," "No one taught me a magnet / Because it moves iron / Has a soul,"[19] and in "Hymn Completed in Tears," "This is an explosion / An exact white lollipop / I refuse to stop."[20]

Notes

1. Donald Revell, "Learnedly," *Arcady*, 19.
2. Revell, "Prefatory," *Arcady*, ix.

3. Revell, "Nature a Corner for Me," *Arcady*, 15.

4. Revell, "In Buenos Aires as Large as Small Apples Hail," *Arcady*, 31.

5. Revell, "Strange Little Doors," *Arcady*, 7.

6. Lyn Hejinian, "The Rejection of Closure," *The Poetry Foundation*, https://www.poetryfoundation.org/articles/69401/the-rejection-of-closure

7. Ibid.

8. Revell, "The Stars Their Perfection," *Arcady*, 33.

9. Revell, "Prefatory," *Arcady*, ix.

10. Phillip Larkin, "The Pleasure Principle," *Required Writing: Miscellaneous Pieces 1955–1982*, 82.

11. Revell, "Conforming to the Fashions of Eternity," *Arcady*, 14.

12. Revell, "Heart I Agree," *Arcady*, 24.

13. Ibid.

14. Ibid.

15. Ibid.

16. Revell, "Prefatory," *Arcady*, ix. N.b.: I treat the prefatory note as a poem in this book, and I learn a great deal from doing so, especially as a poet.

17. Revell, "A Bird Sick on the Pavement," *Arcady*, 16.

18. Revell, "July 4th Blue Diamond," *Arcady*, 25.

19. Revell, "Thales," *Arcady*, 46.

20. Revell, "Hymn Completed in Tears," *Arcady*, 4.

Works Cited

Hejinian, Lyn. "The Rejection of Closure." *The Poetry Foundation,* https://www.poetryfoundation.org/articles/69401/the-rejection-of-closure

Larkin, Philip. "The Pleasure Principle." *Required Writing: Miscellaneous Pieces 1955–1982*. Faber and Faber, 1983, pp. 80–82.

Revell, Donald. *Arcady.* Wesleyan University Press, 2002.

PART 2

Reviews, Interviews, and Online Texts

MARJORIE PERLOFF

Alcools
Poems by Guillaume Apollinaire,
Translated by Donald Revell

At last: a first-rate, lively, and imaginative translation of Apollinaire's
Alcools to set side by side with Ron Padgett's *Complete Poems of
Blaise Cendrars*. I say at last because both these great French avant-
garde poets have been poorly served by their U.S. translators and
publishers. Until recently, the only large-scale English translation of
Cendrars available was the New Directions selection, edited and
translated by Walter Albert, just as the only Apollinaire available was
the New Directions Selected Writings by Roger Shattuck. Both
were at least 30 years out of date. Shattuck is a great Apollinaire
scholar, but the Selected Writings includes only about a third of
Alcools and the formal language and syntax of the translations ac-
cord with the New Critical norms for poetry prevalent in the late
40s when the book was first published. The same holds true for
Anne Hyde Greet's 1965 translation of *Alcools* (California). Like
Shattuck's, hers is a literal translation designed to help the reader
who knows at least a little French. Greet has good notes on the
individual poems, but her *Alcools* (long out of print) was not exactly
calculated to win Apollinaire a new readership, any more than was
Albert's translation of Cendrars. There is a further paradox. From
Samuel Beckett, who was commissioned to translate "Zone," to
Paul Blackburn and W. S. Merwin, a good number of poets have
tried their hand at translating Apollinaire, even as other poets like
Frank O'Hara and Allen Ginsberg have claimed him as their master.
Yet, just as Padgett was the first poet to take on Cendrars in any-
thing like systematic fashion, Revell is the first poet to give us a
full-scale Apollinaire—an Apollinaire, moreover, who is very much
our contemporary.

   "I chose," Revell explains in his preface, "to translate many pas-
sages in *Alcools* as 'incorrect' mixes of high and low diction, of Lati-
nate and slang, of abstracted concretes and concretized abstractions,

because it is just such mixes that have made Apollinaire so enabling to our contemporary poets." And again, "I have tried, in translating Apollinaire to the end of his century, to present him a new suit of grammars, a suit cut after his own audacious style." Such updating is necessary, Revell posits, today when "an exaggerated sense of 'now' suppresses the more genuine, more useful sense of 'for now' inscribed within the etymology of 'modern.'"[1]

Let's see what this means in practice. Here is a passage roughly halfway through the volume's opening poem "Zone." It is the moment when the exuberance of the poet's stroll through the noisy Paris streets begins to give way to something darker:

Maintenant tu marches dans Paris tout seul parmi la foule
Des troupeaux d'autobus mugissant près de toi roulent
L'angoisse de l'amour te serre le gosier
Comme si tu ne devais jamais plus être aimé
Si tu vivais dans l'ancien temps tu entrerais dans un monastère
Vous avez honte quand vous vous surprenez à dire une prière
Tu te moques de toi et comme le feu de l'Enfer ton rire pétille
Les etincelles de ton rire dorent le fond de ta vie
C'est un tableau pendu dans un sombre musée
Et quelque fois tu vas le regarder de près

Aujourd'hui tu marches dans Paris les femmes sont ensanglantées
C'était et je voudrais ne pas m'en souvenir c'était au déclin de la
    beauté[2]

Anne Hyde Greet renders this as follows:

Now you stride alone through the Paris crowds
Busses in bellowing herds roll by
Anguish clutches your throat
As if you would never again be loved
In the old days you would have turned monk
With shame you catch yourself praying
And jeer your laughter crackles like hellfire
Its sparks gild the depths of your life
Which like a painting in a dark museum
You approach sometimes to peer at closely

Today in Paris the women are bloodstained
It was as I would rather forget it was during beauty's decline[3]

Compare Revell:

You are walking in Paris alone inside a crowd
Herds of buses bellow and come too close
Love-anguish clutches your throat
You must never again be loved
In the Dark Ages you would have entered a monastery
You are ashamed to overhear yourself praying
You laugh at yourself and the laughter crackles like hellfire
The sparks gild the ground and background of your life
Your life is a painting in a dark museum
And sometimes you examine it closely

You are walking in Paris the women are bloodsoaked
It was and I have no wish to remember it was the end of beauty[4]

Greet's translation is the more accurate of the two: "Des trou-
peaux d'autobus mugissant" literally means "bellowing herds of
buses;" "dans l'ancien temps" means "the old days," not quite Rev-
ell's "the Dark Ages;" and, in line 82, the reference is, as Greet trans-
lates it, to "beauty's decline," not to its "end." But the great feat
Revell has brought off is to render Apollinaire's racy, nervous, col-
loquial French in comparable paratactic clauses, specifically in sim-
ple subject-verb-object units that render the sense of presence and
simultaneity central to Apollinaire's montage. "You are walking in
Paris alone inside a crowd": given the cataloguing of images in the
stanza, the reference to "Now" ("Maintenant") is gratuitous, "are
walking" is much more effective than "you stride," and "alone inside
the crowd" emphasizes the poet's growing alienation much more
fully than "you stride alone through the Paris crowds."
    In the next line—and here is a favorite Revell device—the
modifying participle becomes an active verb: "Herds of buses bel-
low and come too close," the latter construction signifying the un-
derlying meaning of "près de toi roulent." Throughout the stanza,
the "as if" and "which" constructions, constructions that rationalize
the fluidity of Apollinaire's unpunctuated verse, are replaced by a
collaging of equally weighted fragments. In lines 79–80, for exam-
ple, Revell dispenses with Greet's cumbersome simile ("your life /
Which like a painting") and lets the observation stand alone: "Your
life is a painting in a dark museum / And sometimes you examine
it closely." The covert reference here is to the painful scandal in
which Apollinaire was accused of having stolen the Mona Lisa from

the Louvre and had to spend a few days in jail before being cleared. It was the sort of incident that made the poet, himself an exile, "examine" (Revell's rendition of "regarder") himself in a rare moment of introspection—a moment that leads to the vision of Paris as a city of "femmes ensanglantées," followed by the famous line in which the second-person self-address (whether "tu" or "vous") abruptly switches to "je," echoing Rimbaud's "Je est un autre." The dissolution of self is prefaced by "C'était," the verb left hanging with no predicate. It was . . . what? Greet rationalizes this famous line by turning the "et" into an "as"—"as I would rather forget it was during beauty's decline." Revell restores the ambiguity and again proceeds paratactically: "and I have no wish to remember it was the end of beauty," which is more matter-of-fact, less posturing than "during beauty's decline."

Revell thus gives us an Apollinaire who is, in David Antin's words about Charles Olson, "a man on his feet, talking."[5] "You are ashamed to overhear yourself praying," for example, has the note of actual conversation—a note absent from Greet's "With shame you catch yourself praying." And so, this remarkable poet of the avant guerre, an urban poet whose proto-Dada, proto-Surrealist, comic-fantastic inflections look straight ahead to O'Hara's "I do this, I do that" poems, to Ginsberg's manic catalogues, and to John Ashbery's journeys to mysterious places that turn out to be right in the poet's own backyard. Once unencumbered by the baggage of neo-Victorian diction characteristic of most earlier Apollinaire translation—for example, "you stride alone," "With shame you catch," "jeer," "peer at closely" in the Greet translation above—the poems in *Alcools* become astonishingly contemporary. Even the early quatrain poems now get a new life. Take the last stanza of "The Gypsy" ("La Tzigane"):

On sait tres bien que l'on se damne
Mais l'espoir d'aimer en chemin
Nous fait penser main dans la main
A ce qu'a prédit la tzigane[6]

Revell retains the rhyming tetrameter quatrain but takes liberties with the meaning:

A person knows damn well he's damned
But hope of loving along the way

Compels us to consider hand in hand
The words the gypsy meant to say[7]

"Meant to say" puts an unexpected spin on "prédit;" but, come to think of it, Revell's reading is perfectly in keeping with the mordant irony of this love song, with its recognition that the gypsy's predictions are worth no more than we make of them.

Thus modernized (or perhaps postmodernized), Apollinaire deserves to have a wide audience in late twentieth-century America. If Roger Shattuck's Apollinaire was primarily the avant-garde poet of *The Banquet Years,* the disseminator of Cubism and the father of Surrealism, the wistful lyrical love poet of "La Chanson du mal-aimé," the new Apollinaire emerges as one of us. A French poet who was in fact not French at all but half-Polish, half-Italian (he was christened Wilhelm-Apollinaris de Kostrowitski by his Polish mother, who refused to divulge the identity of his father—probably an Italian army officer named Francesco Flugi d'Aspermont), he prefigures the poets of our own hybrid nationalities and origins. Like Cendrars (né Freddy Hauser), Apollinaire compensated for his outsider status by becoming the most patriotic of Frenchmen and rushing to enlist in the Great War, a decision that led to his premature death at thirty-eight from the head wounds he had received in battle. Again like Cendrars, his poetic diction is an amalgam of solecisms, archaisms, foreign phrases, street slang, and eclectic religious and mythological vocabulary. The precariousness of his sense of identity is the subject of many of his finest poems, especially "Cortège," where the poet in a dream-vision sees "[t]ous ceux qui survenaient et n'étaient pas moi-même" ("the many who passed and were not me"), and who "carried fragments" of a self that could never come together.[8]

Apollinaire's Paris is a long way from Baudelaire's; it is the Paris of refugees, whose odor fills the hall of the "gare Saint-Lazare," who carry "red eiderdowns" even as the poet himself carries his heart. It is also the Paris of "Christs of another shape another faith / Subordinate Christs of uncertain hopes" in the form of "South Sea and Guinean fetishes."[9] And, most of all, it is a Paris that the poet adores but is always leaving—to go to Marseilles, to Coblenz, to Amsterdam, to the trenches . . . almost anywhere else. It is thus that Baudelaire's imaginary voyage has become real, only to be even more disillusioning than its precursor.

Revell's translation is not without its faults. The rendition of the last line of "Zone," for example, the famous "Soleil cou coupé" as "Sun cut throated"[10] strikes me as awkward compared to Greet's "Sun slit throat,"[11] or Shattuck's "The sun a severed head."[12] The great last stanza of "Cortège" is marred by the translation of "Rien n'est mort que ce qui n'existe pas encore" as "Nothing has died that never existed," which undercuts the poet's conclusion that nothing dies except that which has never existed.[13] In the same poem, "Baisse ta deuxième paupière" is curiously rendered as "Abase your other eye," where "Lower" would, I think, have done nicely.[14] And in "Les Fiançailles": "la lune qui cuit comme un oeuf sur le plat" ("the moon that sizzles like a fried egg") is deprived of its sizzle and, contrary to Revell's usual predilection for active verbs, becomes "The moon is a fried egg."[15]

But these are minor flaws in what is an ambitious and important poetic project. My own hope is that Revell will now take on the *Calligrammes* as well and give us a Collected Poems. We need one, and Revell, whose visual sense is as acute as his verbal, is just the person to do it.

Notes

1. Donald Revell, preface to *Alcools*, xi.
2. Revell, "Zone," *Alcools* [Apollinaire], 6.
3. Anne Hyde Greet, "Zone," *Alcools* [Apollinaire], 43.
4. Revell, "Zone," *Alcools* [Apollinaire], 7.
5. David Antin, "Modernism and Postmodernism: Approaching the Present in American Poetry," *Radical Coherency: Selected Essays on Art and Literature, 1966 to 2005,* 195.
6. Revell, "The Gypsy," *Alcools* [Apollinaire], 96.
7. Ibid., 97.
8. Revell, "Procession," *Alcools* [Apollinaire], 64, 65.
9. Revell, "Zone," *Alcools* [Apollinaire], 11.
10. Ibid.
11. Greet, "Zone," *Alcools* [Apollinaire], 45.
12. Roger Shattuck, "Zone," *Alcools* [Apollinaire], 127.
13. Revell, "Procession," *Alcools* [Apollinaire], 66, 67.
14. Ibid., 62, 63.
15. Revell, "The Betrothal," *Alcools* [Apollinaire], 140, 141.

Works Cited

Antin, David. "Modernism and Postmodernism: Approaching the Present in American Poetry." 1972. *Radical Coherency: Selected Essays on Art and Literature, 1966 to 2005.* Edited by David Antin. University of Chicago Press, 2011, pp. 161–96.

Greet, Anne Hyde, trans. *Alcools.* By Guillaume Apollinaire. University of California Press, 1965.

Revell, Donald. Preface in *Alcools,* by Guillaume Apollinaire. Translated by Donald Revell. Wesleyan University Press, 1995, pp. ix.–xii.

Revell, Donald, trans. *Alcools.* By Guillaume Apollinaire. Wesleyan University Press, 1995.

Shattuck, Roger, trans. *Selected Writings of Guillaume Apollinaire.* By Guillaume Apollinaire. New Directions, 1971.

Donald Revell

An Interview by Tod Marshall

TOD MARSHALL: You've spoken of a "lack of generosity" as a failing point for some poets and poems. Who among the moderns do you see as least generous and why would you dub them so?

DONALD REVELL: The modernist enterprise is fundamentally ungenerous because it is conceived in opposition to time. And since time is where we live, is what everything we do is made of, setting up shop contra time is explicitly ungenerous. I find myself moved by how several of the moderns became postmoderns, sort of understood that their original idea of time as degenerative mode, time as destroyer, as chaos, as unmaker of civilization, needed to change. Ronald Bush's book on Eliot talks about this a lot, how the Eliot of *The Waste Land* is a very different creature from the Eliot of *Four Quartets* because *Four Quartets* moves toward an affirmation of time. April is not the cruelest month; there is no such thing as a cruel month. Whose ruins are they and who says they're fragments? To say the word fragment itself is to imagine a preexisting whole, and what was that and why are we privileging that which does not exist over that which does?

Stevens I find, because of his insistence that art provide durable forms of happiness and pleasure, ungenerous. I think he's so fundamentally disappointed with the world that he overprivileges art and, in doing so, is ungenerous to what actually happens. And I believe he realizes this in his later poems. What makes Stevens's later poems his best is the fact that they confront the failure, the parsimony, of his attitude towards change and the world.

On the other hand, Williams understood that time is a mess, the world is a mess, and therefore time and the world are simultaneous. To affirm anything real, whatever it is, whether it's a painting or a piece of broken glass in the gutter, is to affirm time. Williams is generous to the medium that includes all media. It's in useless opposition to time that Stevens and Eliot take themselves out of the creative, i.e., the generative, genital realm. Eliot is an uncreative writer. Stevens, until late, is an uncreative writer because he abjected the very medium in which creativity occurs. It's like saying, "I love to study fish, but only when they're out of water."

TM: And *The Cantos?*

DR: If you read *The Cantos*, you can see a progressive change. Pound is in hell when he opposes time. The first movement of *The Cantos* is hell because of Pound's attitude toward time. And as the poems go along, they reach Paradiso, they reach paradise, which is a paradise of the affirmation of time—in *The Pisan Cantos* he looks out of the cage and says, "O Moon my pinup, / chronometer."[1] That's when he gets it, that time is all right, and then he can go on to write those beautiful *Drafts and Fragments.* "I cannot make it cohere . . . / i.e., it coheres all right."[2] It was a modernist fantasy that order could somehow be imposed upon reality, when in fact reality always imposes an order of its own, and if we fail to see as much, that's our problem. Pound is happy in the later cantos because he loves time. Time works for him; he understands it as a benign, loving process, and that's where Eliot was beginning to arrive in *Four Quartets,* understanding that eternity exists only because at certain points it intersects the temporal.

TM: Certainly someone who changed her work over the course of her entire career, who revised incessantly, is Marianne Moore; Moore was very resistant to the notion of finishing the poem, of putting a final layer of finish on it. How do you read her? How does she fit in?

DR: I like her mind better than her poems. I think she was trapped because she was such a counter of syllables. She never trusted her lines to duration. She had a musician's heart but a sculptor's craft.

TM: The matrix was made before the music came into being.

DR: Yes. She never was trusting in that way. I think there is something self-mutilated about Marianne Moore. I like the idea of her better than I like any of her poems simply because all the poems panic and fall back onto number, onto counting, onto some sort of sculpted—however eccentric, however unique—form of aesthetic.

TM: Do you see her use of quotations as a generous invitation to enter the poem or as an exclusionary act?

DR: I like the fact that she is willing to find and understand that art is more finding than it is making. I think a lot of what differentiates postmodernism from modernism is this understanding that mostly we find things because if you say that you find your poem then you've already said that time is where it happened. Anyone who finds anything finds it in time. So Marianne Moore, like Joseph Cornell, has this *trouvère* mentality that is wonderful. But then they put it into boxes. They somehow panic at the critical moment and seek to contain: Moore containing it through her numbers, counting syllables; Cornell literally containing it in boxes; whereas you get someone like a Rauschenberg or a Jasper Johns and he's not interested in containment. Just put it out there, put it on the floor, tack it to the canvas.

TM: Containment is the great contrast I see between Stevens and Williams. In early Stevens, we have a sort of clipped-wing Epicureanism sinking, landing time and time again in a gorgeous yet static "Palaz of Hoon."

DR: Well, there's something very mandarin about Stevens. Until those later poems, when he finally realizes that everything he'd written was a dismal, morose failure, and he throws open the shack in *The Auroras of Autumn* and steps out and sees the northern lights and they just extinguish, they exterminate him, and he realizes that the music of time, the music of change, is so much more beautiful and durable than any of the brittle little squeakings he's produced.

TM: Williams's notion of the imagination—as he articulates it in *Spring and All*—is so very different from Stevens's; so many of his poems are of the moment or multiple takes of the moment, of, to borrow Breton's phrase, the "magic-circumstantial."[3] Could you elaborate on this?

DR: Circumstantial is the word. What excites me about Williams and why I always go back to him as our best poet of this century is his fundamental discovery. In *Kora in Hell*, as well as *Spring and All*, he realizes the uselessness of the Orpheus myth. The idea that the poet is looking back or not looking back, that the poet therefore is in charge of the circumstances, of the circumstantial nature of the poem, is just wrong. The poet's not in charge. That's not the poet's role. What happens in *Kora in Hell*, what happens in *Spring and All*, is that Williams sees that Eurydice had better be in front of Orpheus, that if she is in front of him, everything is going to be okay. The reason everything went wrong in the myth is that Orpheus had Eurydice behind him, whereas the poet should always keep her or his subject out in front. Poetry is a way of getting to the world, not a way of getting out of it or beyond it. It's a way of just getting there. Poetry is a vehicle by which we hope, nearly, to arrive at reality. In *Kora in Hell* and *Spring and All* and all the best of Williams, that's what's going on. The understanding that the world is ahead of the poem and that what we have to think of as poetry is an order of words, an event of words that will very nearly get us there.

That's why Olson is always writing about cars and their various troubles. Or, as in *Spring and All*, "No one to drive the car."[4]

TM: Or Creeley.

DR: Yes, exactly. Creeley, too. Poetry is the vehicle; the world is the purpose. The world is not an afterthought of the poem.

TM: In *Spring and All*, Williams uses the expression "the eternal moment."[5] His notion of the eternal moment seems very different from, say, Czeslaw Milosz's, even though the expression is the same.

DR: The moment is eternal; that's just a fact. It's not a question of, "Ah, what we want to do is find that moment which has the potential for eternity." Eternity is a moment. And then it's the next moment, and then the next moment, which is also eternal. So, it's this whole endless sequence of eternities, not an eternity that hovers around like some besotted psychiatric angel on the outside of reality.

TM: With Williams, though, there seems to always be that forward vision, whereas Milosz seems to want to look back and find an eternal moment that he can pluck from the past in order to make meaning.

DR: He's fundamentally a Classicist. This is not the case with Williams. Williams does not locate the golden age anywhere except out in front.

TM: A concordance of Williams's *Collected Poems* would surely uncover that two of his favorite words are "edge" and "edges." I certainly see a connection between that and what you've just been saying—that awareness of what is going to come next. Such a movement toward the future certainly manifests itself in his line breaks. Do you see any point where he suddenly became more aware of this and began using the line more conscientiously toward this end?

DR: I think it's in *Spring and All*. It's so sad that most people know Williams through the *Selected Poems,* the one that Randall Jarrell assembled. Why would anyone trust Randall Jarrell's selection of William Carlos Williams? It's almost as bad as what happened to Poe in the nineteenth century; *Spring and All* is a poem and there's no sense pretending that it's a book of poems from which you can excerpt. In there, in the throb and pulse, in the throb between the prose and verse, we see Williams discovering his "edges."

TM: In Williams's poetry, although there is this "beautiful carelessness," as you've called it, there also seems to be a contradictory compulsion to fulfill more rigorous demands, or at least more expected demands, of what a poem is, as if he feels a need to trim, get the carelessness under control.

DR: Well, I agree with Marjorie Perloff in her understanding that the later Williams was a falling off, but why I continue to honor Williams is that he knew it, too. What I love about the second half of Williams's career is its honoring of time. He understood that one's abilities, one's nerve, one's courage were nonrenewable resources, and it's almost as if he wrote the later poems in that understanding, saying, "Look, I'm getting older, I'm frightened. I'm panicked, and I'm doing all sorts of things that I'm not really proud of, but I don't really have any choice because that's what happens in this phase of a human being's life."

I'm not one of those who says, "'O Asphodel' . . . how spiffy." I prefer *Kora in Hell* to "Asphodel." I prefer *Spring and All* to *Pictures from Brueghel*. I agree with Marjorie when she says that *Paterson* was the poem everybody was ready to read, that it's not really the great Williams. The great Williams is the stuff that's in the New Directions volume *Imaginations: Kora in Hell, Spring and All, The Great American Novel, The Descent of Winter*. But Williams was a good doctor, and he understood that the body starts to deteriorate before it dies. Why shouldn't the poetry? The poetry that understands the process of its own deterioration, its own death, can be beautiful if it doesn't pretend that something else is happening. So many poets pretend that the withering away of their gift is actually a form of wisdom. I don't think Williams was fooled. He understood that his loss of courage, his loss of nerve, was part and parcel of the aging and dying process. His poems age and die. They lose their "edge," to use your word, and they talk about it forthrightly and candidly. I never feel deceived in Williams.

TM: This century certainly has been one in which we've seen the influence of many imports on American poetry: from Pound's efforts at bringing Chinese poetry into the modern scene through *Cathay* to the impact of several French poets, including, for instance, Laforgue, Eliot's great stimulus, to various Eastern European poetries. What influences from abroad do you think have been most productive? Which ones do you think have been the most destructive?

DR: However inaccurate it was, what Pound was doing with the ideogram was very helpful for reasons that I don't even think

Pound predicted—let's treat words as physical things rather than as symbols or totems. Poems are things made of stuff. The stuff is words. The fundamental demystification was enormously helpful, but the idea that the ideogrammatic method was possible in English was not. We see the same input having both deleterious and salubrious results. On the one hand, we strayed off into thinking we could write ideogrammatic English; English is not an ideogrammatic language. But we could *begin* to think of our words as things, as objects in the field. And that's what led to Olson, to Creeley. Very helpful.

The French—you know we like to think of French as one thing, but French is many things. I adore Rimbaud. I do not enjoy Baudelaire. And normally, they turn up in the same anthologies. They have nothing in common. Again, Baudelaire is looking at the world, in that central poem of *Flowers of Evil,* "Correspondences," as if somehow these symbols, these clusters of words made reference to some eternal world outside, whereas Rimbaud knew that poetry does not go all the way, language won't go all the way. Language won't solve anything. It ends as an "O," which is why Olson picked up that best of Rimbaud's poems "O Saisons O Chateaux," because of its "O, O, O." The language just falls apart.

And of all the French poets, Apollinaire shines most brightly, most instructively. In *Alcools,* language celebrates the fact of our being, the malleability of all things, words included, the endless multiplication of perspectives that occurs in any act of saying. In *Alcools,* materiality and temporality become the perfect expressions of human love and of the possibilities of joy.

I found the ideogrammatic method enormously useful because it insisted upon the materiality of language. That helped. Poets like Apollinaire and Rimbaud, who insisted upon the fact that language is just one of many things in an enormous field of things and that to rely upon it as some sort of key is ludicrous, they were also helpful. So, whatever came in and chastened us, humbled us, worked. Whatever came in and offered us shortcuts, offered us alternatives to responsibility of presence, proved to be a curse.

Same thing with Eastern European poets. They're not a single category either. I think of Attila Jozsef, who's about ideology breaking itself into pieces against the facts, the coming apart and exposing of the nakedness of language in ways that I don't think occurs, necessarily, in all Eastern European poets. I think Milosz still trusts language to convey something. Jozsef fell to pieces because he knew it didn't. You think of the difference between Akhmatova and Tsvetayeva. Akhmatova still had a certain confidence in what poetry could do; Tsvetayeva lost it. I honor Tsvetayeva over Akhmatova for that reason. She understood that the necessities of humanity could not be satisfied by poetry alone, whereas Akhmatova really thought she could describe the Stalinist terror. Tsvetayeva screamed, which makes more sense to me.

And you can do the same thing with almost any European poetry. There were people there who exaggerated the possibilities of what poetry could contribute and those who painfully, but voraciously, admitted that poetry has fierce limits. That's why I really can't love Rilke. Rilke had too high an opinion of poetry. He thought it could do too much, that its role was too wonderful. But someone like Trakl understood that poetry would never suffice, that it wasn't enough, that human suffering was larger than language and that language was no balm for catastrophe. And so I honor him above Rilke.

TM: Another "import" in a very different vein is Auden, who wrote the famous line "for poetry makes nothing happen."[6] What do you understand as the limit of what poetry can do in the public sphere? What do you think its role is?

DR: I think that by the time Auden was writing that poem he'd already shrunk from the "low, dishonest decade" of the thirties.[7] Understandably so; it was a horrible time to be anybody and to understand the criminality of language. English as a language was an accomplice of fascism; it was an accomplice in the whole horror of Hitlerite Europe. To feel disgraced and to want to just take language out of it all was an honorable if flawed intention.

Poetry is where the language gets made. It's where the language gets examined, where, if we're lucky, the rigors of truthfulness and responsibility are applied to words. Consciousness is made of language; therefore, when we subject language to rigors, we subject consciousness to rigors. It is the fundamental building block of what people think and what people see because they see everything through a filter of words, they see everything through a screen of words. The world comes to us through words and is expressed by us in words. Therefore, poetry is tinkering with a primary material of human activity: language. I think that terrified Auden. I think it ought to terrify everybody. Nobody much reads poetry, but that's not the point. Nobody much knows about genetic engineering. We're all affected by it; the history of the species is going to be changed forever by genetic engineering. It doesn't matter that people aren't lining up in bookstores to buy the latest book by a genetic engineer just as it doesn't matter that people aren't lining up in bookstores to buy the latest book of poetry. Poems are where the language gets made. It gets cleansed or it gets soiled. It gets healed or it becomes sicker—through poetry. When something goes right or wrong in language it goes right or wrong first in poetry.

Poetry is not about making things happen. That's what language does. Poetry is about making language happen. *People* make language do things in all human spheres.

TM: So, the conflict is at the level of the word, of syntax, of grammar, rather than within any specific political upheaval.

DR: Yes, poetry is prior to all that. Poetry is language languaging. Which is why it's so silly that they call some poetry "language poetry." All poetry is language poetry. The subject matter is incidental. What's really happening is that language is becoming its next self in poetry, and if that next self is depraved or mendacious, things are pretty bad. But if that next self is forthright and clear, perhaps things get better. I honor Williams and Creeley simply because, in their poems, language becomes a cleaner next self, a clearer thing, a more honest thing, not a more swaddled or concealed or duplicitous thing. Poetry is political the same way that poetry is biological, the same way that poetry is agricultural, economic, philosophical. Everything that human beings do is made of words, and the words come from the workshop of poetry.

TM: How then would you articulate your attitude toward the trend of appropriation of certain political upheavals, the wreckage of history, by American poets in order to assume a political stance? Do you think it irresponsible, immoral, or perhaps just irrelevant?

DR: It's most often adolescent but sometimes immoral. No one should ever feel sad that the secret police aren't breaking into his apartment, thus depriving him of poignant material. The fact is that we all participate in these catastrophes anyway; but we shouldn't be distracted by the glamor of catastrophe, the easy, outward, identifiable enemy, because the enemy in Eastern Europe, the enemy in Tiananmen Square, the enemy in Palo Alto, is always the same. It's people lying to themselves. Poetry is about trying to put a stop to people lying to themselves. Before a tank can run over a boy in Tiananmen Square, before someone can be tortured to death in the Gestapo basements, somebody has to lie to himself. Poetry works at the subatomic level. Things go wrong when you tell lies; language, when it goes wrong, is a lie we tell to ourselves, and I think that an infatuation with history avoids the central issue of history in a weird way. Writing about "bad stuff" that happens in—fill in the blank: Central America, Eastern Europe, Mississippi—that's not the issue. Something more fundamental went wrong before that stuff went wrong, and you don't have to go out of your own room to see the holocaust happening. The holocaust happens when someone consents to lie to himself, and he lies to himself in the form of words. Therefore, we should sit very still and be very rigorous with every syllable we pronounce. That's a way of participating in the resistance to totalizing inhumanities, whether they're happening in China or in the pet store down the street. It doesn't really matter.

TM: So, whatever misdirection his enthusiasms may have caused, Pound's Confucian notion of calling things by their right names is fundamental.

DR: Right. If you can tell the truth to yourself about your daily life, you are in the resistance. It's adolescent, this desire of American poets to vampirize other people's suffering. Sure, it's easy, but it has nothing to do with what's really happening, and the people who are there would be the first to say it. And, it's happening everywhere. There are certain hallucinations called Stalinism, and there are certain hallucinations called free market economy. The issue is to demystify the hallucinations, whatever they happen to be. Whether they are fast-food franchises or five-year plans, it doesn't really matter. Somebody's using a lie to conceal a truth. Language is there to debunk lies in real poetry.

TM: Speaking of real poetry and its impact, you've written of being "floored" by *The Double Dream of Spring*. Can you think of other moments of being floored by poetry when you first encountered it?

DR: Besides Ashbery? I would say when I read Olson's "The Distances," that poem. "So the distances are Galatea / and one does fall in love and desires / mastery."[8] That astonished me. Jorie Graham's second book, *Erosion*. I was on my way to an opera in Virginia, and I stopped at a bookstore, and there was *Erosion,* and I bought it, and I sat down and read it and wept on the sidewalk. Ashbery again with *Houseboat Days*. When that book came out, I was at the bookstore before it opened, knowing that they would have *Houseboat Days* that day. These books have simply taken the top of my head off. Jabès, when I first read *The Book of Questions,* I had no idea that such things were possible—that writing could be writing. It didn't have to become something; it could stay writing—for a long, long time. And Breton. When I read *L'Amour Pou, Mad Love.* The idea that the only thing worth doing was keeping oneself in a position to fall in love, that the only thing worth doing with your life was throwing it away with both hands. Marvelous.

TM: In the same essay on Ashbery, you describe his "spontaneous interiors." In Williams, one might be inclined to describe his "spontaneous *exteriors.*" I wonder if they have become two poles of a dualism, two different guides for you?

DR: People are always talking about how much Ashbery comes out of Wallace Stevens, and of course, Ashbery benefited enormously from Stevens's project. Yet, I see Williams in Ashbery as much as I see Stevens. I think it's part of Ashbery's genius to understand that the inside is outside, too. Part of what happens in the making of poems and the reading of poems is the understanding of one's inner life as being outside and all around you. So, I don't see them as being poles at all; I see them as being orchestrations in the same moment of music. I think Ashbery daunts people in some ways because he is so accessible. They can't quite cope with a poetry that is so on the page. In a sense, he is the most approachable of American poets because nothing is being concealed, and that's why I'm always astonished when people say Ashbery is a difficult poet, because he's not. He's quite the opposite. He's the most available, the most welcoming of poets I know. Everything is what it is. It's not a symbol for anything else. It's this entire exteriorization of the inward life, this humility that says there is nothing in me that didn't come from the world. It's not as if the world were some pale substitute for my splendid inner life. If I have an inner life, where do you think it came from? It came from the world.

TM: If you can make such a choice, which of his books have meant the most to you?

DR: Well, they change all the time, which keeps me nice and humble. I think when I started reading Ashbery it was *The Double Dream of Spring* and *Self Portrait in a Convex Mirror* that most mattered. As I get older, I love most of all *Three Poems*. I don't want to call them prose poems, but we'll call them prose poems. What happens in there is so enormous I can hardly begin to speak of it. All I know is that Ashbery is the first poet who taught me that the poem begins when you stop reading. You read Ashbery and it's beautiful and it's lovely, and then you look up from the page and realize the world is different. What happened as I was reading is that my eyes were changed. My head has been changed and now I'm a different person in the world. So, I guess now *Three Poems* is my favorite, along with *Hotel Lautréamont,* where he seems to give authority away with both hands. I don't know of a poet who can be considered more generous than Ashbery. His learning is enormous. His wisdom is enormous. His memory is capacious, and he never asks to be admired for it. He just gives it away.

TM: Which connects to what his poems have to offer through their resistance to tight closure.

DR: I think Ashbery has said in a variety of circumstances that poetry is continuous. Any given poem is just a cross-section of what was going on before the poem started, and it continues long after the poem ends. It's almost like poetry is a coming attraction for poetry.

TM: You've written of the need to recapture largeness, to revive the grand gesture. How does Whitman figure into your notion of largeness? Is the Whitmanic presence and its vastness of gesture part of your definition?

DR: There's no way around Whitman. He's both a blessing and a curse. One that I suppose every poet, especially an American poet, has come up against. On the one hand, he understood that things like "a self," "a voice," "a poem" are always in the process of being put together. He understood that these things were always under construction, and therefore, any gesture had to be large because it was part of an enormously long project. We weren't beginning with little lyrical exposures of an already completed self. We had work to do; we had to make a self. The genius of *Leaves of Grass* is that the self is something you make. A soul is not something you have and then understand. A soul is something that you put together as a result of living in time.

The trouble was Whitman believed you could finish the job, that eventually you did put together a soul. That led to a political creepiness, a sort of manifest destiny idea that, once you had put this soul together, you could use it as a form of authority. Ashbery goes beyond the limits of Whitman because of this. He understands that yes, the self, whoever you are, is something you're always putting together from pieces that float along toward you, and that you never finish the job. I think Whitman thought you could finish the job, that eventually you got someplace where this was "I." Ashbery realizes that it's an endless improvisation until you die. The job is never completed. The task is never completed. The gesture is never finished. Whitman held onto the idea that, well, I'm starting from zero and I'm the new man in the new country, in the new place, and I'm going to put together this thing—I'll call it "Walt." His insistence upon revising and changing *Leaves of Grass* instead of just writing another book betrays that. Ashbery knows that nothing can be perfected, and that's perfect. Everything we have is perfectly fine, and then we're going to have to do something else that's perfectly fine, too.

TM: The notion of the "unfinishedness" of the soul is important to your essay "The Moving Sidewalk," a very powerful autobiographical piece. In that essay, you argue against any notions of essentialism in regard to class. Do you think your arguments are applicable to a debunking of those same beliefs in regard to, say, gender or ethnicity?

DR: As I get older, I become more and more of an antinomian. I distrust any name. I think it's the project of poetry, the project of writing, the project of reading, the project of doing almost anything: to unname things. I get very sad when people latch on to names because I know there's one way of being sure that someone is wrong, and that's if they're trying to make the world smaller. I'm not really good with ethics, but I know diminishment is always wrong. Somebody does something the result of which is a world smaller than the world he or she received, that's a bad person, that's a bad activity. And so I oppose anything that seeks to define because I think poetry is about undefining. And not just poetry. I think that being human is about that. The more you live, the more you understand the uselessness of definitions and the inutility of seeking to make definitions. All human beings transcend class, all human beings transcend gender, all human beings transcend race, nationality.

TM: The willing indeterminacy of your poetics, the provisionality you were just speaking of and have written of—"nextness," revisionist approaches to genre, the paradoxical openness of the most generous closure—I understand these as profound gestures of humility. Is humility the building block of the creative process? A necessary step toward transparency to the world? What role do you think you play in the creation of the poem?

DR: Well, I think that I'm a better poet the more I unbuild myself. Transparency is something that fascinates me; it's my career goal. It's wonderful that Wittgenstein's last book, *Remarks on Color,* was a hymn to transparency. The idea that if I can be something through which light passes undamaged, I'll have done a good job. If somehow truth can go into my work and come out of it unharmed—because that's the original meaning of innocence. Innocence does not mean "not experienced." Innocence means "I do no harm." If I can somehow put words together that do no harm, allow the free passage of the facts, of the real, it's a Raoul Wallenberg kind of thing. If I can get people out of danger, if I can get words out of the camps, if I can rescue a few phrases from becoming murderous or murdered, how wonderful! And to the extent that I can become transparent, to the extent that I'm not there at all—I'm doubly honored by my Guggenheim fellowship because what I asked the Guggenheim people to fund was a project in which I would look for ways to write poetry as if I were nobody at all. And to my delight, they funded it. To my delight also, it helped. What I found living in regions of Europe where no one spoke any English at all, where I did not come in contact with English on a daily basis, was that I became no one at all, that I had no marketable, commodifiable self. All I could do was invent something every day. Whatever language I spoke on any given day was something I made from my useless English and my inadequate French. It was marvelous.

Everything is about free passage. Wittgenstein talks a lot about prisms. What does a prism do? It does not create. It does not contain light. It is not a creative thing. But light, passing through a prism, is revealed as itself. The light comes in and then emerges as its entire spectrum. Nothing is in the prism, nothing has been created by the prism, but because the light passed through it, it became knowable as itself, as being a spectrum of red, orange, yellow, green, blue, indigo, violet. I would love to know that someday I could write a poem that was prismatic in that way—we're back to Marianne Moore and "In the Days of Prismatic Color." The idea that language would somehow come into me, since I didn't create language, I didn't make any language, I didn't invent a single word in the dictionary, and that language passing through me, not remaining in me would, as a result of passing through me, be more visibly itself.

This goes along with what I've been trying to teach my students: that meaning does not reside in poetry, meaning *passes through* poetry. The point of making a poem is to make something out of words through which meaning can pass without impediment and without significant loss of energy. It's like when you design an electrical circuit. You want as much of the energy that leaves the battery to arrive at the light bulb. The best circuit is the one that allows the least loss of energy. Same with poetry, I think. Whatever truth the language had coming in, you want the greatest amount of that to arrive at the other side of the poem. And to that extent, the poem is best that draws the least attention to itself as a form. It's a middleman, a poem. A prism.

TM: Do you see your four books as progression, revision, retreat? Or perhaps you can supply a more accurate word?

DR: Well, it's in hindsight, so any such gesture is going to be self-congratulatory. I'm not about to say that they've just gotten worse—they've deteriorated over the years. *From the Abandoned Cities* was in a lot of ways a very, very formal book. Formal for the reasons that you would expect: I was young; I was insecure; I was coming from a physically very bad circumstance—the environment I grew up in was a chaos with which I was unable to cope. I found in the ritual of ordering words a way of coping, a way of not drowning. The Bronx is a beautiful, terrible place that is so much larger than an individual that you have to talk yourself out of it. So, that first book was sort of "whenever I feel afraid, I hold my head erect and whistle a happy tune." Whistling, formalism, as a way of talking myself out of the dark. I'm not ashamed of the book at all; I'm very pleased with its reception and what I was able to do. But I think it shows youth, the idea that I needed to wear a magic coat, I needed to have a decoder ring—all the things that are in contemporary boy mythology. You know, we have to have some sort of talisman to get us out of a scary place, and I got out of the scary place through the talisman of poetic form.

The Gaza of Winter was very much a transitional book where I was trying to exorcise my feeling that personal tragedy was unique, that somehow it gave me super privilege or that it was enough to make poetry from for the rest of my life. What *The Gaza of Winter* finally sees is that all the terrible things that happen to me happen to everybody and that I had better find something else to talk about because it's not really news. That's why the book ends with a poem about the raft of the Medusa, a group of people exposed to an extent to which I've never been exposed and reduced to circumstances of violence and horror to which I've never been reduced. Subject matter is not what poetry is made of.

Realizing that, I was able to write *New Dark Ages,* a more explicitly political book. Still very much understanding that there is no such thing as a distinction between private and public life, but rather that there are certain nightmares that result when we treat public life as though it were private and private life as if though it were public. When we try to blur the words, we become irresponsible. Taking history personally and thinking of your girlfriend leaving you as some sort of political catastrophe, that's what makes a "dark ages." The first dark ages were made by a failure of nerve. These days are our "new dark ages" because our nerve has failed again. In the middle eighties, historically, whether we deserved it or not, we were presented with an opportunity to do things anew, to make a new polity, to make a "new world order," as they say. We panicked and decided, "Well, the old world order was pretty good. If it weren't for these guys like Stalin and Karl Marx and Adolph Hitler, everything would have been fine, so let's just go back to the old world order and pretend none of this ever happened." Which means, of course, that it's all going to happen again. And it is. Failure of nerve.

Erasures is a book of despair about that. The presiding genius of that book, the consoling friend, was Karl Kraus, whose line "Let him who has something to say step forward and be silent" inspired it all.[9] The idea that something so horrible has happened in this failure of nerve that the results are going to be incalculably awful.

TM: And yet, through the book, you step forward and speak, so there are grains of hope.

DR: I don't know if I'd call it hope. There are certain circumstances where it is possible to say something not untrue. There is no moment in *Erasures* when there is any expectation that that event will have consequences. The book ends with the line "The unborn have been revoked. They will not be kind."[10] Yes, from time to time we can stand up and say something that is not untrue, but I don't know that anything is going to come of it. To me, if there is one great work of literature in the twentieth century, it's *Endgame*. If anything survives from the twentieth century, I hope it's *Endgame*. I know that in *Erasures* I try very hard to say things not untrue, and I don't know that I should. I don't know that I wasn't congratulating myself for being able to say something that was not entirely false. Hubris? Ego? Narcissism? In my work now, I'm trying to explore ways of saying nothing at all. We'll see what happens.

Notes

1. Ezra Pound, *The Pisan Cantos, The Cantos*, 559.

2. Pound, *Drafts and Fragments of Cantos CX-CXVII, The Cantos*, 816–17.

3. André Breton, *Mad Love*, 19.

4. William Carlos Williams, *Spring and All, The Collected Poems of William Carlos Williams*, Vol. 1: 1909–1939, 219.

5. Ibid., 178.

6. W. H. Auden, "In Memory of W. B. Yeats," *Poets.org*, https://www.poets.org/poetsorg/poem/memory-w-b-yeats

7. Auden, "September 1, 1939," *Poets.org*, https://www.poets.org/poetsorg/poem/september-1-1939

8. Charles Olson, "The Distances," *The Distances*, 94.

9. Quoted in Walter Benjamin, "Karl Kraus," *Reflections: Essays, Aphorisms, Autobiographical Writings*, 243.

10. Donald Revell, "Last," *Erasures*, 47.

Works Cited

Auden, W. H. "In Memory of W. B. Yeats." *Poets.org*. Academy of American Poets, https://www.poets.org/poetsorg/poem/memory-w-b-yeats

Auden, W. H. "September 1, 1939." *Poets.org*. Academy of American Poets, https://www.poets.org/poetsorg/poem/september-1-1939

Benjamin, Walter. "Karl Kraus." *Reflections: Essays, Aphorisms, Autobiographical Writings*. Translated by Edmund F. N. Jephcott and edited by Peter Demetz. Schoken, 1986.

Breton, André. *Mad Love*. Translated by Mary Ann Caws. University of Nebraska Press, 1987.

Olson, Charles. "The Distances." *The Distances*. Grove, 1960.

Pound, Ezra. *The Cantos of Ezra Pound*. New Directions, 1996.

Revell, Donald. *Erasures*. Wesleyan University Press, 1992.

Williams, William Carlos. *Spring and All. The Collected Poems of William Carlos Williams, Volume I: 1909–1939*. Edited by A. Walton Litz and Christopher MacGowan. New Directions, 1986, pp. 175–236.

TOD MARSHALL

From "Review

Forrest Gander's Science and Steepleflower *and Donald Revell's* There Are Three"

Some readers may find Donald Revell's poetry challenging. Revell's poems reveal how language, incarnate as both word and phrase, can resonate both as referential signifier and musical notes. This method can disrupt expectations, but eventually one realizes that "what belongs together / ignores the barriers."[1]

Thus, when Revell's poetry breaks barriers of syntax, usage, formal expectation, and the usual dichotomies of referentiality versus free play of language, his project becomes less a statement of avant-garde allegiances and more a conviction that disrupted expectations help open the interstices through which grace shines. In "Scherzo," Revell quotes Thoreau: "The snow is made by / enthusiasm."[2] Such sentiments speak to how Revell envisions and shapes "a music of variation"—strong and singular and charged.[3] Once a reader becomes accustomed to the manner in which Revell's poetry asks that we think about how language works as a way to think about how other ordering systems work—and Revell is profoundly concerned with questioning, interrogating, and dismantling the ossified systems, whether social, syntactical, grammatical, or aesthetic—the enthusiasm of the poetry takes hold, and the challenge diminishes.

Although, as in his previous three books, *New Dark Ages, Erasures,* and *Beautiful Shirt,* the elegiac continues to be one of Revell's most powerful modes, *There Are Three* is propelled by diverse energies. Motivated by both the loss of a father and renewal through the birth of a son, the poems attempt to understand a world from which "God is gone," and we are left with "only a window and a wilderness / remaining."[4] Windows, though, allow vision, and clear vision is the beginning of revelation. The title poem of the collection reads "An hour along / the groundless tangents / of a meadow is not wasted / until it ends."[5] The lines imply that there is no loss until we impose the barrier of a conceived closure upon the experience, an ordering principle. Other poems articulate similar sentiments. For instance, "Overthrow," where "On such a night, the stars could not consent to constellations."[6]

In some ways, Revell is a religious poet, but having declared that, I feel the need to qualify. He is a religious poet the way that Kandinsky was a religious painter or that Thoreau was a religious writer. His aim is always toward revelations of the provisional interstices through which grace emerges. The quotations from Blake, Hutchinson, and Thoreau; the emphasis on time as durational; a musical score onto which history hasn't scratched its notes; and the revisions of grammar and syntax all embody Revell's dedication to searching for wilderness, a place of possibility for the Arcadian vision in which contradictions can blossom and coexist like "flowers / fist[ing] their beautiful / contentions without choice."[7]

As in his previous three books, Revell organizes this collection as a cluster of brief musical pieces around the scores of the longer poems: "Overthrow," "For the Lord Protector," "Scherzo," and "Outbreak." In many of his poems, Revell repeats words and phrases like notes and themes in a piece of music. At the same time, these words and phrases frequently change meaning and function within the context of different sections, as in musical progressions, offering the effects of counterpoint and dissonance so often utilized by a musical idol of Revell's, Charles Ives. The progression of the poems is not argumentative; they are not discursive. Instead, the phrases accrete and transform. Consider the short poem "Elegy":

> myself the other
> winter even more
> myself the other
> still as obscure
> a milk white one
> a coal black one
> winter even more[8]

Like a rondel, the music of this poem brings us around, but the poem does more than just offer a brief melody. After exploring the many ways that the syntax can enjamb the lines, one might notice the poet's decision to present the lines as exactly the same length (by justifying the text); this lends a formal emphasis to "myself the other": same length equals same weight, same emphasis. Given that the poem is an elegy, such a weighting gives a poignant pathos;

when one recognizes the self in an "other," and there is "loss" involved, then "winter"—that figure for loss and despair—is "even more" felt, apparent, harsh.

Silence is also an important aspect of Revell's aesthetic. If the words sometimes clang and chime like musical notes, then it is also important to note Revell's attention to the ways in which silence textures a poem, functions as both absence of sound and presence, into which anything may be introduced. He uses the short line masterfully—sometimes juxtaposed with prose inserts, sometimes yoked to a halting syntax, sometimes for descriptive purposes, and sometimes as a way to break and drape a quotation from Thoreau or Hutchinson over two or three lines to further concentrate the reader's attention. Revell's work has achieved a minimal music that is reminiscent both of Williams's attentiveness to shape and sound and of Dickinson's grammar of the spirit. Unlike contemporaries such as Jorie Graham or Robert Hass, who have sought a longer line in order to accommodate the snowballing density of commentary and perception, Revell's work achieves an almost ideogrammatic minimalism, as in Japanese ink drawings or the sketches of Joan Miro.

But given Revell's utilization of musical shaping in the book, the music of Ives is probably a strong point of comparison. Ives's signature dissonance finds embodiment when ample silence allows for juxtaposition of discordant sounds and discordant emotions. Revell is similarly attentive. For example, "Scherzo" is simultaneously a poignant announcement of suffering—"Something I trusted / apart from solitude / died with my father / o worse than lonely"[9]—endurance—"My soul is alive alright, but nothing / to do with me"[10]—and, perhaps amid such loss, even hope—"Claudia brought in flowers."[11] The presentation of these three themes is achieved by counterpointing repeated diction and themes in different contexts and usages. Difficult to explain without lengthy excerpting, the effect over the course of the long poems is exhilarating.

Silence and sound, death and birth, the seasonal continuance that the poems articulate: Revell's *There are Three* is a haunting and graceful book. It is haunting in the same manner that Forrest Gander's *Science and Steepleflower* is: both collections remind the reader of lost connections. Similarly, although propelled by different poetic sensibilities, they both ambitiously attempt to reconnect, rediscover, relearn, even invent syntaxes and silences that allow the possibility of realizing grace.

Notes

1. Donald Revell, "Outbreak," *There Are Three,* 47. Note that this and all subsequent excerpts are from *There Are Three.*
2. Revell, "Scherzo," 32.
3. Ibid., 30.
4. Revell, "Outbreak," 48.
5. Revell, "There Are Three," 15.
6. Revell, "Overthrow," 3.
7. Revell, "Scherzo," 38.
8. Revell. "Elegy," 12.
9. Revell, "Scherzo," 34.
10. Ibid., 37–38.
11. Ibid., 38.

Work Cited

Revell, Donald. *There Are Three.* Wesleyan University Press, 1998.

NICK TWEMLOW

An Interview with Poet Donald Revell

Donald Revell grew up in The Bronx, New York. He received his PhD from SUNY-Buffalo, and he splits his time between Nevada and Utah, where he is professor of English and Creative Writing at the University of Utah. Wesleyan University Press published Revell's seventh book of poems, *Arcady*, in February of 2002. Written as a response to the death of his sister and only sibling, Roberta, in 1995, *Arcady* draws its vision from the well of Arcadia—the utopic Greek realm described as paradise by Virgil, painted by Poussin, scored by Charles Ives, and contemplated by Thoreau.

Revell describes it in the prefatory section of the book as a place that "remains to be seen," not followed, as narrative requires.[1] He further meditates on the death of his sister and the profound effects it had on his thinking and his approach to writing.

Poets & Writers Magazine asked Revell how he expects readers of *Arcady* to respond to the book's preface.

DONALD REVELL: I intend the preface to serve as an explicit and public dedication in the old sense: i.e., as a task. I wrote the poems meaning to go to Heaven and to make my best report from there. Of course, I have no wish to distance the readers. Rather, I hope to convince them to take me literally, with all the rigors and consequences thereof.

POETS & WRITERS: Would you elaborate on what this old sense of public dedication is, this task?

DR: By "old sense" of dedication, I mean something to be done with myself, as myself. The only way to write an *Arcady* is to go there, or to see oneself fail in trying. This is somehow connected with the one thing of importance I emphasize in my teaching: craft is nothing; sincerity is everything. I prefer "pious Aeneas" to "wily Odysseus." Virgil's hero did not squander his friends or take credit for the power of a golden bough.

p&w: "Craft is nothing; sincerity is everything." How do you teach this idea? Whom do you use, especially among contemporary writers, as your examples for your students?

DR: To teach sincerity. Hard. Hard. It involves respect for the material *as* spirit, as in truly knowing how to slice an onion. If I were in charge of admissions, I'd replace the Graduate Record Examinations (GRE) with a simple test: make a good bowl of soup. In my workshops, we work simply to cut out any lines or phrases that are not literally true. We ask the poem to stand by its words. We ask each other to stand by our words. We urge one another to be good, trusting the poems to follow suit. Only a good human can write a good poem. Good people can, of course, make terrible errors. But an error is not a lie. A poem can survive error (as in *The Cantos);* it cannot survive a lie. Classic example of this good news? Herbert's great "Jordan" poems. Of contemporary poets, I presently encourage my students to read Robin Blaser and Ronald Johnson with open hearts. They're terrific.

p&w: How has your relationship toward the reader changed since the publication of your first book?

DR: In my earlier work, I wanted to win an audience and an audience's approval, its admiration. And I did my circus tricks accordingly. Now, if and when I am any good, I seek only the poem's approval.

p&w: In the preface to *Arcady,* you write "I began to see poems: poems of mine, but hardly made."[2] Nearly all of the poems in the book are fourteen lines, and thus there is a formal precedent to each, a sense of inheritance based on form, as well as on vision. Is the sonnet, or at least the fourteen-line length, what appeared before you?

DR: What I see is not the sonnet, but the sonnet's world, its Arcadia. I see thus the poetry of a single "take," an instantaneous sighting (siting). No craft. No process. Only instances.

p&w: Are your poems behind you, then, when a book of them is published? What's next?

DR: What's next for me? I'm concerned with the governance of Heaven, which is mostly silence. Living in Utah and Nevada, I take my current instruction from snow and sand. They are heavenly forms—substantial and effortless. May poems be so.

Notes

1. Donald Revell, "Prefatory," *Arcady*, ix.
2. Ibid.

Work Cited

Revell, Donald. "Prefatory." *Arcady*. Wesleyan University Press, 2002, pp. ix.–x.

TOD MARSHALL

From "Celebrating Presence
Recasting the Poetry of Loss"

Few contemporary poets come close to the formal skill exhibited
in Donald Revell's work, and I'm not talking about sonnet making
but about fashioning a rhythm so propulsive and persuasive, so *ex-
actly right,* that a reader feels the music as deeply as she hears it. In
Revell's earlier work, the music seemed masterfully shaped, artfully
controlled. His obvious craftsmanship provided a sense of stability
to the surreal locutions of *Erasures* (1992), the lexical surprises of
Beautiful Shirt (1994), and the antinomian discord of *There Are Three*
(1998). His intelligence and exactitude were always in evidence but
without detracting from the poems' liveliness and immediacy.

On the other hand, *Arcady* is Revell's giving over to magic. Having
lost his sister a few years ago, the poet found himself suddenly dam-
aged; as his prefatory note points out, "It takes two (never fewer, rarely
more) to language. I was suddenly one. My native language lapsed.
Immediately, I lost my daily care for making poems."[1] But out of this
loss came the possibility of realizing that the "daily care" of composi-
tion may not always allow for the world's revelation; that is, whether
the poem is made or not, the poetry is there, immediately before the
attentive eye, always within the receptive ear. Great pain and loss can
sometimes shatter the structures through which the music routinely
flows, renewing language and, even more importantly, perception, so
that we see the art always before us. So renewed, we are free to let go
of the anxieties and worries and trivialities that made us fear that
pain—and even more, the letting go looses all holds, all barriers, all
blinders to the music and revelations around. The eyes that behold are
suddenly allowed vision; what do they see? As Revell puts it in his
prefatory note: "the Arcady all around."[2]

The magic of this book is glorious, and one of the primary
places in which the magic is present is in its evanescently contrary
music, ranging as it does from the harmonic notes of disjunctive
hymnals to the playful refrain of soulful echoes, from mantra and
childspeak to the plaintive strains of a bereaved brother. Consider
the poem "Light Lily Lily Light Light Lily Light":

Light lily lily light light lily light

Imagically
Lightli ly

Outline stones for the wind

All creatures come
To mind to oneness

Where I am formless   When I go back into
My breaking through   The ground the deep
Will be far greater   In me whence I came

Light lily lily light light lily light

Imagi
Cally
Lightli
Ly³

Revell's poetry has been rightly praised for its perceptive intelligence, its bold poetics, and its courageous politics, but not enough attention has been given to the musicality of his work. Ranging from exuberance at the syllabic level in pitch, tone, and duration (note the liquid roll of the "l" sound crisply finished by the dental driven "t" followed by a string of "l's" and long "e's"—part Bremondian "pure poetry," part piano notes tapped out on a keyboard) to interludes of discursive proposition ("All creatures come / To mind to oneness"), Revell's poem engages the ear at first reading and then, like the songs of Shakespeare's fools, invites the reader to engage more than the music. By combining the spell-like incantation of the opening with fragmented and ruptured attempts at discursive explanation and exuberant word play at the end of the poem (where magic and the image are bound together), Revell offers language both ritualistic and evocative.

There is another aspect of *Arcady* that is more difficult to describe, but that owes primarily to the disarming simplicity of the book's lexicon and the sparseness of its phrasing. The overall impression is one of great humility, sincerity, and integrity. Call it what you will, the music of this book is further complimented by a voice that rings true. Consider these lines from "Tooms 3":

> Our souls
> Almost the equals
> Of our bodies
> Love the world
> And stay there
> Sometimes crying[4]

Loving the world is staying in the world, accepting "The ground the deep," losses of home and beloved, whatever living might bring, and responding—"sometimes crying"—but always finding a way to "stay there," to remain present to the Arcadian bliss that surrounds.

There is much more to appreciate in *Arcady*, from the edifying ethos of many of the poems (especially "Tooms 4" and "All Summer Long") to the interpolation of Greek cosmologist thought ("Anaximander," "Democritus," and "Anaxagoras") to the powerful presence of Revell's guiding angels, Thoreau and Ives ("Arcady Ives" and "Conforming to the Fashions of Eternity"): the poetry maintains a fine balance between conveying a certain haphazard freedom (magic) and demonstrating that even the most powerful charm demands a shaping performance (craft). To put it another way, the book radiates a "found" quality—part automatic writing, part attentive engagement with the world—and this seeming arbitrariness is connected to the new liberty Revell discovered after contending with intense loss. As he phrases it in his preface, "I began to see poems; poems of mine, but hardly made. Sight has become my second language, native now. Sometimes I see a sky full of treetops. Sometimes I see my friend across the Pond. Sometimes I see poems from *Arcady* and I'm given to write them down."[5]

Notes

1. Donald Revell, "Prefatory," *Arcady*, ix. Note that this and all subsequent excerpts are from *Arcady*.
2. Ibid.
3. Revell, "Light Lily Lily Light Light Lily Light," 13.
4. Revell, "Tooms 3," 39–40.
5. Revell, "Prefatory," ix.

Work Cited

Revell, Donald. *Arcady*. Wesleyan University Press, 2002.

NATHAN HAUKE

"At My Soul's Edge"
Donald Revell's My Mojave

Donald Revell's *My Mojave* begins with "Arcady Again," a nod to his previous collection, *Arcady*, that links both works in an expansive motion of departure that rejects the possibility of doing anything again: "Gate into the rainy yard / Opens and even the little / Grass is very wide."[1] Leaving the isolating grief and intense coding of *Arcady*, *My Mojave* dilates an existence beside itself, torn by the jangling perception of an edge separating the visible and the invisible. The "my" in Revell's title registers the inescapable loneliness of subjectivity enlarged by the losses of *Arcady* with increasing urgency and cleaves to visionary force that asks no permission. *My Mojave* attends to the cataclysmic events of *Arcady* as a line in the sand that has twinned the poet's life. It is, thus, deftly divided into two parts, "Here" and "There," that live alone together, in suspension like Castor and Pollux, a dual meditation on the erasures and reversals that occur on both sides of death's creases.

"Here"

> *"The work of poetry is trust"*
> —"My Trip"[2]

In their humility, the poems in "Here" often find kinship with images that constitute reversals. "A perfect circle falls / Onto white imperfections,"[3] and "[a] silver fish head glistens beside a bottle cap" become a sign that "[p]lenty remains."[4] Excavated garbage becomes a treasured symbol of American life and process: "After a while the boys / Come up from the river / Hauling a tire into the sunlight."[5] This is one of the great accomplishments of *My Mojave*: the rich, generative attention of Revell's witness amplifies the fragility and transcendental potential of details. Reading, we *feel* that "[w]aters overplussed with pilgrim stutter" do indeed "[m]ake more wilderness."[6]

The joyful distractions of sound ("traffic noise") and experience in "My Trip"[7] anticipate the annihilation and afterlife of "Here," abandoned for the promise of "A tree is almost none."[8] Consensus is abolished and community is transmuted by visionary contact: "At a tree outside the city. We shall make / New sounds and leave our throats in that place."[9] Operating under Emerson's dictum that "particular natural facts are symbols of particular spiritual facts," these poems attempt to locate the sheer facts of salvation while they acknowledge that process erodes the possibility of reading by pointing outside of itself.[10] The fading of a speaker's "son's wet fingermark / From the warm stone" becomes a tender lesson in impermanence.[11] Elsewhere, contact can only constitute traces or echoes apprehended from the other side:

> The plane descending from an empty sky
> Onto numberless real stars
> Makes a change in heaven, a new
> Pattern for the ply of spirits on bodies.[12]

Heaven is a collaborative work-in-progress, amplified and degraded by the cultivation of presence. The promise of rest is simply being at peace with the rest of it, and the poems in "Here" "ache only for silence just one / With nothing to forgive."[13] If Revell's ability to break through the veil of hubbub is "effortless" in momentary ecstasies, he's careful to acknowledge that it's because his faith is immense. Acknowledging "nothing" and the emptiness of forms is to cleave to change as the only constant.

The temporality and peripheral impression of contact charges *My Mojave* with urgency and calls to good conduct. The poems of "Here" suggest that we should be careful to wonder at the world in the tradition of Heidegger, who tells us that "the painter . . . uses pigment but in such a way that color is not used up but rather only now comes to shine forth."[14] The care with which the speaker releases a bee that has gotten caught in the bottle of wine he shares with his lover in "Picnic" speaks to the exigency of being "Here" and doubles back on itself with gratitude to consider the way the intoxication of experience jams our ability to read news coming in from elsewhere: "I tapped him onto the ground, and he walked off / Untangling antennae from wings and wine. / We hurried to reach the car while there was still daylight."[15] Moments like these testify to Revell's humility and reveal its relation to the edge of the whole, as the meditative attention of *My Mojave* always recognizes the painful thrum of amendment as perception falls behind itself rending one into two.

"There"

"There" hinges on the imagination(s) of an afterlife across the threshold of "Here." The poems contemplate the act of dying and struggle to cleave to an understanding of death that's "[n]othing to do with pity / Everything to do with heaven."[16] "There" turns against the grain of the flashing dramas and upheaval of "Here" to posit Heaven as a place of agreement and infinite rest. In "For Andrew Marvell" Revell claims, "I remember because everything is all of its characteristics / Apart just once / Together for eternity in death's unlimited magic."[17] The depth and resonance of this assertion echoes through poems like "Banner":

> Say now aftermath
> And a new beginning
> One and the same
> Happy like a crocus.[18]

"Prolegomena" threads the needle, recognizing the similitude Revell anticipates as the resumption of old habits: "Before I was human / I worshipped everything."[19] Impatient for origins, souls shift, moving like mustangs from the schoolyard. Eternity haunts and eclipses time, and it's impossible not to feel the gratitude of the title "Given Days" splinter against the urgency of diagnosis.

The poems in "There" are aggrieved by their attachments and striated by impatience that leads to reversals, degrading the circumstances in relation to the remembered state of the afterlife:

> unable to bear
> The memory of Heaven a moment longer.
> Compared to Heaven,
> Music and peace are shit.[20]

Splashing color against disparate winter trees, a cardinal "[e]xposed to everything" registers as "a stab / Of the grotesque."[21] The desire for togetherness that will last eternity diminishes the want to keep worldly time and creates volatile tensions in the poet's life that become unbearably raw and terrifyingly real for the reader.

In *My Mojave,* presence is rent by attachment. The desire to cross the threshold of "Here" is torn by the desire to stay in appreciation, to receive more of the unfinished vision. The restless agitation of the world and its desensitizing flood of experience is slowly killing the poet's soul, drawing him into consensus that quarters spiritual vision. It's harder and harder "[t]o see what comes";[22] "the stream is frozen because it is cold."[23] "Counsel" enacts this conflict between attachment and fulfillment in a moment of estranged insistence:

> Redress my soul
> As in a mirror
> I can see myself
> Urging a friend
> To stay alive.[24]

Fault lines continue to expand, revealing further contradiction (and possibility), allowing *My Mojave* to recognize the way time shows seemingly antithetical emotions companion each other:

> True grief is endless
> As happiness
> Is unforgettable
> Every single time.[25]

Emotions exist at the knife's edge as the poems in "Here" and "There" foil and interpenetrate each other. It's Revell's tremendous grace to see through the suspensions that divide *My Mojave* as "love's doing," to be confounded and thankful:

> See
> How troubles twin us
> The white doe
> Afraid
> The National Bank
> Afraid
> Although the soul we have
> Is love's doing.[26]

"In Christmas" follows William Blake's assertion that "without contraries there is no progression"[27] to consider the possibility that unease rekindles innocence and informs a greater aptitude for belief: "And me who wants no comfort / Only to believe."[28] "Prolegomena," likewise, acknowledges the inevitability of transcendence (in no way related to effort): "And any way you look at it, you are, / Like a heron on one leg, halfway to Jehovah."[29]

Neither wholly "Here" nor "There," *My Mojave* catches Revell—and us with him—somewhere between, on the other side of the wild grief of *Arcady*. And while the precariousness of this position is certainly heartbreaking and rife for great doubt, Revell reveals that facing facts and embracing indeterminacy sets the stage for belief and tremendous possibility. The contraries that anchor *My Mojave*, ultimately, interpenetrate each other to mark a collaborative process of becoming that transcends agency and the logic of categorization. As the poems of "Here" yearn to "meet again / At a tree outside the city," the poems of "There" find themselves in a solitary place realizing community across the threshold of their humanity. "Prolegomena" claims that "[t]he little things of the woodland live unseen / At my soul's edge because the soul is alone."[30] The poems of "There" have begun to inhabit a new place, and, doing so, they have managed to recognize and carry the significance of their material experiences:

We are a protest
Raised against ourselves
And God comes now
And God is alone in a leaf
And we are snow in the desert
Making a new sound.[31]

This is Revell's achievement in *My Mojave*: the new sound that he anticipates in "Short Fantasia" ("Here") is being made in "A New Abelard" ("There"). The breadth of this accomplishment is remarkable because it solves and/or acknowledges the tension between the book's sections as articulated in "My Mojave," the title poem: while the earth is jealous, the soul of the poet "wants only to go."[32] As much "Here" as "There," Revell seems to realize that, for the time being, he is already home.

Notes

1. Donald Revell, "Arcady Again," *My Mojave*, 1. Note that this and all subsequent excerpts from Revell poems are from *My Mojave*.

2. Revell, "My Trip," 9.

3. Revell, "My Mojave," 13.

4. Revell, "My Trip," 8.

5. Revell, "Church and State," 15.

6. Revell, "The Government of Heaven," 24.

7. Revell, "My Trip," 9.

8. Revell, "Mechanics," 7.

9. Revell, "Short Fantasia," 16.

10. Ralph Waldo Emerson, "Language," *Nature,* https://ebooks.adelaide.edu.au/e/emerson/ralph_waldo/e53na/chapter4.html

11. Revell, "The Government of Heaven," 20.

12. Revell, "Short Fantasia," 16.

13. Revell, "The Government of Heaven." 21.

14. Martin Heidegger, "The Origin of the Work of Art," *Poetry, Language, Thought,* 47.

15. Revell, "Picnic," 27.

16. Revell, "Sermon," 31.

17. Revell, "For Andrew Marvell," 33.

18. Revell, "Banner," 34.

19. Revell, "Prolegomena," 36.

20. Ibid., 39.

21. Revell, "In Christmas," 46.

22. Revell, "Bacchae," 44.

23. Revell, "In Christmas," 48.

24. Revell, "Counsel," 41.

25. Ibid.

26. Revell, "A New Abelard," 51.

27. William Blake, The Marriage of Heaven and Hell, The Complete Poetry & Prose of William Blake, 34.

28. Revell, "In Christmas," 47.

29. Revell, "Prolegomena," 36.

30. Ibid., 39.

31. Revell, "A New Abelard," 56.

32. Revell, "My Mojave," 14.

Works Cited

Blake, William. *The Marriage of Heaven and Hell. The Complete Poetry & Prose of William Blake.* Revised ed. Edited by David V. Erdman. Anchor-Random House, 1988, pp. 33–45.

Emerson, Ralph Waldo. "Language." *Nature.* University of Adelaide, 2016. E-book, https://ebooks.adelaide.edu.au/e/emerson/ralph_waldo/e53na/chapter4.html

Heidegger, Martin. "Origin and the Work of Art." *Poetry, Language, Thought.* Translated by Albert Hofstadter. Harper, 2001.

Revell, Donald. *My Mojave.* Alice James, 2003.

ERIC WEINSTEIN

The Illuminations by Arthur Rimbaud, Translated by Donald Revell

It's not strictly rare to find a translation of poetry that is both faithful to the original work and a small masterpiece in its own right, but it's certainly uncommon. Donald Revell's translation of Arthur Rimbaud's *The Illuminations* is such a collection, a display of Revell's strength and considerable skill as both poet and translator, on par with David Young's translations of Rilke and Neruda or Seamus Heaney's translation of *Beowulf.*

Rimbaud's collection consists almost exclusively of prose poems, with the exception of "Marine" ("Seascape"), "Mouvement" ("Movement"), and parts of "Enfance" ("Childhood") and "Veillées" ("Vigils"), which are free verse. Although Revell rarely has to contend with line breaks or rhyme in his translation, he still manages to evoke a lyric quality reminiscent of the original French. From the first poem, "Après le déluge" ("After the Flood"):

> Aussitôt après que l'idée du Déluge se fut rassise, un lièvre s'arrêta dans les sainfoins et les clochettes mouvantes, et dit sa prière à l'arc-en-ciel à travers la toile de l'araignée.

> As soon as the mind of the Flood grew calm, a hare paused in the shivering bellflowers in holy clover, and he said his prayer to the rainbow through a spider's web.[1]

The final poem in the collection, "Solde"—which can be literally translated as "Balance"—Revell masterfully titles "Going Out of Business." Here, Rimbaud derides and satirizes the arbitrariness of the market, almost painfully opposing the notions of monetary and artistic value: "À vendre les corps sans prix, hors de toute race, de tout monde, de tout sexe, de toute descendance!"[2] The line literally reads, "To sell the bodies without price, outside of all races, of all the world, of all sex, of all descent"; Revell translates it as "On sale: priceless bodies, transcending race and world and sex and descent!"[3]

Revell is no newcomer to translation, particularly of late nineteenth-century French, and he has honed his abilities through translations of Guillaume Apollinaire *(The Self-Dismembered Man: Selected Later Poems* and *Alcools)* and other works by Rimbaud *(A Season in Hell).* To be concise: I have yet to come across a better living translator working in French today, and I wholeheartedly recommend Revell's translations to francophone and English-speaking readers alike.

Notes

1. Donald Revell, "After the Flood," *The Illuminations* [Rimbaud], 16–17. Note that this and all subsequent excerpts are from the bilingual edition of *The Illuminations.*
2. Rimbaud, "Solde," 108.
3. Revell, "Going Out of Business," 109.

Work Cited

Revell, Donald, trans. *The Illuminations.* By Arthur Rimbaud. Omnidawn, 2009.

ANDREW HALEY

Tantivy by Donald Revell

Over the last fifteen years, as a professor at the Universities of Utah and Nevada, Donald Revell has been writing poems that have evolved to match his surroundings. It is a true trajectory for a poet whose own manifesto is entitled *The Art of Attention*. There is little of the ivory tower in Salt Lake City and Las Vegas, and because of that, the attentive eye finds new contours and distinctions.

Revell's acclaimed earlier collections, represented best by *New Dark Ages* and *Erasures,* have seemed to wear away into essentials in the desert. The long lines and uniform stanzas gradually disappeared. Poems obsessed with the last European century and its ancient betrayals, and with the tropes of modernism Revell inherited from his native New York City—urban space, the crowd, chaos, and class—faded away. Imbued with an adaptive, transcendental, almost Cathar Christianity, the poems in *There Are Three, Arcady,* and *My Mojave* turn instead to the individual and the individuating landscape of the West. Revell found anew the mysteries of geology and climate, aridity, uplift, desiccation, the struggle of plants in the desert weather and the long suffering gardeners who grow them, as well as the idylls and isolation of first Salt Lake City and then the Las Vegas suburbs.

Revell's son, Benjamin, appears frequently in these poems in an idealized state of innocence that serves as the reliquary for Revell's lost innocence. His paeans to Jesus and God may stem from Thoreau but take on the desertstruck solitude of Saint Jerome, weaving together a conflux of transcendentalism, Albigensian mysticism, and pre-Socratic thought to create the songs and meditations of *Arcady* and *My Mojave:* a spare, free-form, personal but not confessionary lyric that surpasses his early work both in music and idea.

The Bitter Withy starts very much like a continuation of the style and sensibilities of *My Mojave* and *Arcady,* but with an unmistakable sorrow that is less present in his other desert books. "Longlegged Bird," the penultimate poem, captures the longlined clip and measure of poems in *Erasures* and the earlier books and brings to us again Revell's considerable anger and anxiety, his bitterness, though here it has nothing to do with the wars in Europe or the destruction of cities or peoples. Instead, his middle period is one of transcendence, wisdom, and religion. We have a poem tuned to the sound of Revell's mortality and the decline of his desert arcadia:

> I want to explain—tremolos
> And squealings and then a high sound
> Sweeten the little halfway house
> Forever. I mean it just goes on forever,
> As through the little portals children pour.[1]

Arcady has become a halfway house. The decline ordains Revell's own death with the transient and sacred essence that flits around and inside particulars but is apart from them, perhaps above them. It is a masterful poem, one of Revell's finest.

Tantivy carries this matured, sorrowful new music even further. In the previous decade, Revell translated Rimbaud, Apollinaire, and Laforgue. The French strain is strong here, more so than ever in his work, and the poems in this book provide the rare sensation of true originality, of a poet past caring, one who has not shed influence but has moved past concerns about it. The poems do not feel received but are new in the old way. *Tantivy* is one of those books that perfectly fits the occasion of its being, which is to say, it may well be a classic.

"The Last Men," the first of four sections, opens with a suite of poems, titled "Victorians (I)–(II)," which play with form and rhyme in a manner reminiscent of Revell's early work but in a completely unstudied way. There is nothing inherited in their formality. They give you the sense of how it must have been to hear the first rondel sung in torchlight 800 years ago: "Motherless goddamn modernity never grew. / Here we are again at Christmas / On fire escapes without a fire in view."[2]

The French poets have long provided their American counterparts an alternative approach to rhyme more suitable than that of the English Romantics. Though *Tantivy* is indebted to Alfred Tennyson, the play of rhyme in the book and the shaping of poems into resemblances of forms remind one less of that cardboard viceroy of old Britannia than of John Ashbery, whose poems Revell's early work sometimes resembles. Revell's poems have always been more somber, and that darkness is at its fullest in *Tantivy*. Consider the following lines from the first poem to follow the "Victorians" suite, "Homage to John Frederick Peto":

All in green we went out rioting.
Lute music demasked the commercial radio,
And girls knew everything.
[. . .]
Any ornaments for the poor man's store?
Any moments of leisure at the fishhouse door?
[. . .]
Time will come again to talk perfection,
A succession of creatures in midair.
I won't be there.[3]

Hardly Victorian, rhyme serves less as deep architecture here than ornament, like bells on a jongleur's hat. Tennyson serves as a kind of muse in *Tantivy*, but more as motif than as influence. True, there is a song-like quality to these poems that contrasts with the terse and incised modernist aesthetic Revell has long championed, but in its most self-conscious mock-medieval stylings, it is closer to Bertran de Born. Revell is married to poet Claudia Keelan, whose translations of the trobairitz, the female troubadours, was published by Omnidawn in 2015 under the title *Truth of my Songs: The Poems of the Trobairitz*. It seems that the music of 12th century Occitan poetry cross-pollinated *Tantivy*. The troubadours and the trobairitz faced the quintessential poetic problem: the inheritors of a vast, rich, but obsolete canon, they sought to make a new vernacular poetry that better matched the world at hand. Revell is on a like-minded quest in *Tantivy*—to make it new, even as Ezra Pound's dictum to that effect is now over a century old.

Tantivy's third section, "Tithon," is one of the most experimental poems in Revell's oeuvre. Only a few times has he stepped so far from uniform surface textures and standardized syntactical patterns. Revell's great short poem, "What Can Stop This," first published in *New American Writing* and later included in *Arcady* ("The sympathy of friends is pleasant VIOLINS / But it makes no difference anymore TROMBONES") indicates future directions.[4] But "Tithon" is big, filling the middle ten pages of the book. It is song-like and repetitive in passages but incorporates found materials (a letter reprinted in its entirety, quotes from Cézanne and Char, etc.) affixed to the poem with the logic of collage, so that the poem does not feel like a whole, smooth object, but rather a series of coincident, although not necessarily subsequent, parts. While the lines and phrases are highly melodic, their sequencing is discordant, giving "Tithon" almost a simultaneous rather than linear composition:

> Shadows of leaves
> Shadows of leaves
> *Je suis le prince*
> *D'un pays aboli*
>
> God counts only up to one
> His hands are small
> And in God's hands even
> Mountains are sparrow-sized
>
> Also the cloistered fountains, Lord,
> My dearest, my estranged,
> The fountains also
>
> Shadows of leaves
> Shadows of leaves[5]

This friction between lyric and discord is one source of "Tithon's" beauty, as is an overarching tension in the poem's mood. For all of its optimistic intent and homilies about unity, eternity, and transcendence, "Tithon" is ultimately about loss. Here, Revell follows most closely in Tennyson's footsteps, giving new light to the myth of Tithonus, who begged for immortality and was cursed with the perpetual attenuation of life, and whose anglicized name, Tithon, Tennyson first used in the 1833 version of his poem of the same name. Revell's "Tithon," like Tennyson's, is an elegy for lost time, a dirge not for the dead but for the remembrancers.

Tennyson may be the poem's kelson, but its language more closely resembles those other great elegies for the condemned, Ezra Pound's *The Pisan Cantos* and Dylan Thomas's *Fern Hill*. Like them, it is fixated on the disordered contents of memory—the flashes and fragments of a broken paradise illuminated and made otherworldly by the dawning of death.

> I lay my eyes upon the ground and see the ground
> I lay my eyes upon a cloud (clouds are France) and see the angel
>   there

I lay my eyes upon the slowly moving surface of the water
In a narrow pool between dragonfly and cruel acacia
And my eyes swim away from me finding my friends
Alive with skins made of diamonds (the poet Char) and high
    sounds (the poet Reverdy)
I lay my eyes upon the easternmost horizon just at dawn
And my only son Benjamin walks out of my eyes
Never to be seen by me[6]

In its closing, "Tithon" assumes most closely the music of elegy, which, like all lyric poetry, has the ego at its center. Tennyson's Tithonus is a stand-in for the bereaved for whom, abandoned by the dead, the world has lost its savor. Revell's Tithonus is himself the long practitioner of attentiveness, who mourns not his inability to die but the coming loss of the objects of his attention. His anxiety about this separation rings like a crisis of faith through the whole of *Tantivy* and seems to challenge the foundations of the mysticism Revell has built in the desert. Though deeply sad, Revell's work has never been finer.

Notes

1. Donald Revell, "Long-legged Bird," *The Bitter Withy*, 55–56.
2. Revell, "Victorians," *Tantivy*, 3.
3. Revell, "Homage to John Frederick Peto," *Tantivy*, 14–15.
4. Revell, "What Can Stop This," *Arcady*, 8.
5. Revell, "Tithon," *Tantivy*, 43.
6. Ibid. 52.

Works Cited

Revell, Donald. *Arcady*. Wesleyan University Press, 2002.
Revell, Donald. *The Bitter Withy*. Alice James, 2009.
Revell, Donald. *Tantivy*. Alice James, 2012.

DAN DISNEY

Songs without Words by Paul Verlaine, Translated by Donald Revell

Drunkard, ill-fated lover, silhouette amid shapes of the real, Paul
Verlaine pitched headlong across what he calls "a new oblivion."[1]
The Symbolist poet embarked on a series of famously doomed love
affairs, spent time abroad (including a couple of years in a Belgian
prison), and lived the last part of his life in an absinthe fog, wander-
ing the Paris slums. He died a relatively young man at the age of 51.
This book, *Songs without Words,* is poet and translator Donald Rev-
ell's sixth translated work of nineteenth-century French verse. These
English-language versions are (after Dryden) paraphrased echoes of
the poems Verlaine made while imprisoned after shooting at (and
slightly injuring) his young lover and proto-*arriviste,* Arthur Rim-
baud, in a jealous and drunken rage.

Verlaine lived a large but impoverished life, partied hard, then
expired; he leaves a considerable mythology, some of which is cap-
tured by the reverential tone in the translator's preface:

> Enchantment was the motive force of Paul Verlaine, man and
> poet. . . . In life, enchantment made for a series of fanatic devo-
> tions, erotic and spiritual, absolute in their addictedness and ab-
> solute also in their disaster. In poetry, it made for exquisite can-
> dor, a music whose purity, whether sounded on a lyre or barrel
> organ, remains matchless—almost hermetic, entirely its own.[2]

In his essay "The Task of the Translator," Walter Benjamin also
speculates on purity and avows that a pure language exists abstractly
and "no longer means or expresses anything but is, as expressionless
and creative Word, that which is meant in all languages."[3] This is
more than what Verlaine's contemporary and colleague Mallarmé
would designate as a function for poets (who, he felt, would purify
the dialect of the tribe); Benjamin posits a meta-language to con-
tain all possible expressions of nuance, gesture, and trope echoing
inside each living language. The task of the translator is to shift to-

ward trans-linguistic universalism: no poet and no language is hermetic, and all remain "interrelated in what they want to express."[4] What Verlaine expresses in these texts—so skillfully transferred by Revell—is an often-wrenching *cri de coeur* situating a continuum of affectivity from the mad swirl of reality:

> Round and go round! Ever so slowly
> The velvet of heaven is strewn with stars.
> The lovers drift away. The horses keep going
> In the bliss of abandonment, their song without words.[5]

to the lovelorn keening for a connection that has been lost:

> The waxy picturesque goes on forever.
> But you, you were real. Nothing else matters.[6]

These biographical sketches reaffirm the lore of an often out-of-control poet, hungry with desire for the satiation of authenticity; within the realm of appearances in which the poet gambols, carols, prances, and plays (he, at one point, suggests, "Let's be children, let's be little girls"), there are moments of weirdly ecstatic gloom:[7]

> Oh traveler, this fading picturesque
>   Mirrors death.
> And overhead, in the drowning branches,
>   All hope dies.[8]

In attempting to transmit pan-cultural affect into particular linguistic echoes, in his book *One Hundred and One Poems by Paul Verlaine,* Norman Shapiro locates the following language to express the Symbolist's same stanza:

> How often, traveler, have you seen your blear
>   Image reflected in life's drear,
> Bleak scene, while high above, midst bough and leaf,
>   Your drowned hopes, wailful, weep their grief![9]

If we can agree with Alexander Pope that sound and sense are inextricably connected, then what is happening to Verlaine's sense-making when it is transmuted elsewhere into

> How wan the face, O traveller, this wan
>   Gray landscape looked upon;

> And how forlornly in the high tree-tops
>   Lamented thy drowned hopes![10]

There are magnitudes of prosodic—and therein affective—difference here, and these three iterations exemplify the call poet-translators have made across the twentieth century: Bonnefoy, Valéry, Paz (among others) each avow that translations of poems are at best only ever variations; Scottish poet Don Paterson frames it as follows: "One can no more translate a poem than one can a piece of music."[11] In his essay, "The Preface to Ovid's Epistles," which essentially founds Translation Studies, John Dryden enumerates three modes of translation practice:

> First, that of metaphrase, or turning author word by word, and line by line . . . The second way is that of paraphrase, or translation with latitude . . . The Third way is that of Imitation, where the Translator (if now he has not lost that Name) assumes the liberty not only to vary from the words and sense, but to forsake them both as he sees occasion: and taking only some general hints from the Original, to run division on the ground-work, as he pleases.[12]

Revell's strength is that he shifts somewhere between Dryden's second and third principles, and his texts make interpretative, imitative sense of Verlaine's desperate, affective, ontological maneuvers. Rather than attempt (the impossible task of) equivalence, this translator's faithfulness is instead toward making poems that echo rather than closely resemble the syntax of the source. As a poet, one assumes Revell understands language can stretch and shift into musical investigation of those spaces where "[t]he air was screaming";[13] the same line is transmuted by Shapiro as, "That whir? / Like sistrum sounding."[14] While for some translators the relationship between source and target can best be framed as parasitic, the poems in Revell's *Songs without Words* are indeed poems in their own right: compressed, precise, wild propositions, which, as Seamus Heaney avows of all poems, successfully knock language—and therein accustomed modes of perception—sideward.

Notes

1. Donald Revell, "Forgotten Show Tunes," *Songs without Words* [Verlaine], 29. Note that this and all subsequent excerpts from Verlaine poems are from the bilingual edition of *Songs without Words*.
2. Revell, "Translator's Preface: A Prior Enchantment," 13.
3. Walter Benjamin, "The Task of the Translator," *Theories of Translation: An Anthology of Essays from Dryden to Derrida*, 80.
4. Ibid., 74.
5. Revell, "Brussels (wooden horses)," 55.
6. Revell, "Spleen," 79.
7. Revell, "Forgotten Show Tunes," 29.
8. Ibid., 41.
9. Norman B. Shapiro, *One Hundred and One Poems by Paul Verlaine*, 89.
10. Joseph M. Bernstein, "The Tree's Reflection," *Baudelaire, Rimbaud, Verlaine: Selected Verse and Prose Poems*, 276.
11. Don Paterson, *Orpheus: A Version of Rilke*, 77.
12. John Dryden, "On Translation," *Theories of Translation: An Anthology of Essays from Dryden to Derrida*, 17.
13. Revell, "Charleroi," 47.
14. Shapiro, *One Hundred and One Poems by Paul Verlaine*, 93.

Works Cited

Benjamin, Walter. "The Task of the Translator." *Theories of Translation: An Anthology of Essays from Dryden to Derrida*. Edited by Rainer Schulte and John Biguenet. University of Chicago Press, 1992, pp. 71–82.

Bernstein, Joseph. M. Baudelaire, Rimbaud, Verlaine: Selected Verse and Prose Poems. The Citadel Press, 1947.

Dryden, John. "On Translation." *Theories of Translation: An Anthology of Essays from Dryden to Derrida*. Edited by Rainer Schulte and John Biguenet. University of Chicago Press, 1992, pp. 17–31.

Paterson, Don. *Orpheus: A Version of Rilke*. Faber, 2006.

Pope, Alexander. "An Essay on Criticism: Part 2." *Poetry Foundation*, 24 May 2014, www.poetryfoundation.org/poem/174163

Revell, Donald, translator. *Songs without Words*. By Paul Verlaine. Omnidawn, 2013.

Shapiro, Norman B. *One Hundred and One Poems by Paul Verlaine*. University of Chicago Press, 1999.

DAN BEACHY-QUICK

On Donald Revell

There's a poem these days I keep turning back to, one recently dis-
covered, whose gentle prism minds and reminds me of what I love
most about Donald Revell's work. The poem is "Tools," and in it,
"the full moon / In its coin of rainbow / Called my name."[1] The
moon builds it rainbow in a circle around itself, unlike the sun, not
lighting up the falling rain, but spiriting visible the spectrum from
ice crystals floating in the air. The moon calls the poet's name, and
this warms him on a cold morning out walking his dog. The sun has
its innate heat, its self-sourced light, ancient symbol of reason and
self-sufficiency. The moon, like us, borrows what light illuminates it;
like us, the moon does not have the privilege of maintaining the
sphere of its own perfection, but varies, waxes and wanes, and so can
call out to us our names because, like us, it suffers that experience
we so gladly suffer—life.

Then come the lines I most love:

I have a name, and it isn't a problem.

I have a soul, and it's no problem
To feel it slipping away from me
Into a name the full moon
Shouts to the sun.[2]

Over-reaching, perhaps irresponsible to say, but it feels true none-
theless, that much of our poetry written in the last many decades
has occupied itself almost wholly with the trouble of having a name,
as if such trouble warranted the writing of a poem, as if the theo-
retical awkwardness of signification, the weightlessness of *différance*,
required that a poem look only inward, playing with its own wordy
parts, demonstrating again and again how the means of making
meaning mean nothing necessary, and that what realization we
come to, we construct ourselves. But "I have a name, and it isn't a
problem." In one line, Revell—as has so often been the case

throughout his writing life—trues us away from the ease of concept back to our more honest problems.

It might just be, I can hear him say, that our problem isn't a problem at all but a gift. The soul slips into the name, informs it just as it informs us—it's no problem. The moon shouts it back to the source of its own life, and the shout is praise-shout and shout-of-defiance, is faithfulness and doubt, is happy recognition that what is ours is ours on loan, as is the light of the moon, as is our name, as is our soul. Emerson reminds us, "Cause and effect are two sides of one fact."[3]

Revell reminds us of the same: the sun and the moon, the name and the soul, are each sides of the same fact. The poem may be no more than the rainbow that shines through the prism of that fact, beauty of no body, existent only by virtue of contingency—which is to say, I suppose, our best mirror.

Revell writes from a long and close acquaintanceship with time. It is his intimacy with the duration of life that makes his ear so attuned to those "tuneless numbers" that extend through time to reach past it.[4] Or maybe, thinking more dearly about Revell's project, I realize I've spoken the direction wrong: it is by the love he's found (and founded) within human life that allows him to be so companioned by the eternal when it pierces down into our temporal dwelling and beside us, within us, takes up its lodging.

Such attention is rare, maybe ever-rarer is this seeing past the problem of a name. It returns poetry to its oldest uses—dedication, and praise. When the soul slips into a name and the moon shouts it back to the sun, then any act of naming—that most basic function of poetry—affirms life far past the limits of life, offers itself to the dead as a small sacrifice, keeps intact the gods of the household and the heroes, keeps happy the ancestors upon whose lost lives our lives are built. For they are there in the names, all of them, and as Revell so rightly reminds, "You must breathe the dead to feel the dancing."[5] To my friend and mentor, I want to say, "See, I'm learning to dance." So he's taught me, as he's taught so many of us—as the worker bee returning to the hive—the dance that is our guide to the flower-field entire.

Notes

1. Donald Revell, "Tools," *The Bitter Withy*, 3.
2. Ibid.

3. Ralph Waldo Emerson, "Circles," *Essays: First and Second Series*, 165.

4. John Keats, "Ode to Psyche," *Poetry Foundation,* https://www.poetry-foundation.org/poems/44480/ode-to-psyche

5. Revell, "Long-legged Bird," *The Bitter Withy,* 55.

Works Cited

Emerson, Ralph Waldo. "Circles." *Essays: First and Second Series.* Edited by John Gabriel Hunt. Gramercy Books, 1993, pp. 158–70.

Keats, John. "Ode to Psyche." *Poetry Foundation,* 2019, https://www.poet-ryfoundation.org/poems/44480/ode-to-psyche

Revell, Donald. *The Bitter Withy.* Alice James, 2009.

RICHIE HOFMANN

"Shadows of Leaves"
Donald Revell

Donald Revell's poems are weird and beautiful. Weird because they seem, at times, to resist simple narratives, to create meaning out of disparate images and statements. Weird because they celebrate strange and obscure (sometimes archaic, sometimes contemporary) objects and places and people and quotations in poems that are sensuous and surreal. Beautiful because what these pastiches—playful and allusive—add up to are sumptuous and lyrical meditations on art, on the history of literature, on the erotic body, on the aging body, and on suffering and beauty itself.

The qualities I love in Revell's poems are on full display in "Tithon," the third section of *Tantivy*. "Tithon" is a name that evokes the Greek mythological character Tithonus—loved by Aurora, he is the once-mortal prince blessed/cursed with immortality by the gods, but without eternal youth—as well as the myriad works of art about him, including Tennyson's long dramatic monologue. It is also rendered, like so much of the book, through the windows of the gorgeous, sun-drenched world of French:

Shadows of leaves
Shadows of leaves
Je suis le prince
D'un pays aboil[1]

In the ten pages of "Tithon," we don't quite get a retelling of the myth; nor do we quite get a dramatic monologue or psychological portrait of a character. Instead, the poem intimates a story in simple, beautiful terms, in recurring images and landscapes. There is a prince. There was a prince. Though his country is lost, he seems to take solace in the sensuousness of the environment around him. Sometimes this is the Mediterranean world, with its Cézannesque flowers and mountains. Sometimes this is the world of art—the body rendered in paint, paint creating new bodies—which the speaker of the poem uses as touchstone for memory. The poem is an elegy; it is a song; it is a literary collage; it is both erotic and abstract, both grave and fanciful.

Revell's "Tithon" is a polyvocal text—filled with quotations from Cézanne, Traherne, Dylan Thomas, René Char, Conrad Aiken, and William Blake, with an interlude letter to Nathan from 2009—though even Revell's poetic musings feel swept and shaken up in a mistral of language. Central images and themes repeat: hands, mouths, sparrows, mountains, leaves, the presence of God, of Heaven, of artists, a blind girl, a fountain, an only son, a mirror. But each time they're invoked, they've been shifted into new patterns, into new landscapes of thought and feeling. First:

> God counts only up to one
> His hands are small
> And in God's hands even
> Mountains are sparrow-sized[2]

And later:

> My hands were as small as God's hands
> In heaven sparrows
> Became snows and cataracts around us
> Creation is the miniature of creation
> When God and I walked together we spoke paint[3]

And later yet, as the speaker reveals even more about himself—his loves (French poets), his losses (a son he will not know), his dreamy landscape ("clouds are France," the speaker says):

> The shadows of leaves are addressed to immortality
> Little birds give wings to the mountains and the mountains fly
> Underground streams find a fountain cloister in New York
> Nothing but one road in all this world there is nothing
> But God myself alone as a child and counting
> Up to one the garden number[4]

The poem is a difficult poem, but it would be inaccurate to call it dense. Its foliage is thick but familiar. And it's a pleasure—intellectual, aesthetic, erotic—to move through this terrain. In the end, as the speaker cycles through these images, I feel like I'm grasping for some story of loss, some consolation in the world of memory or in the world of art or in the natural world of sparrows and mountains. As Revell writes: "Who in his right mind would burden / This wonderful creation with a consciousness?"[5]

And in the end, we feel complicit with the estranged God of the poem, putting meaning into all these words and images, animating these allusions and illusions—unable to count up to one, and yet capable of doing nothing else: "And a prince beside himself with joy at the axle of sunlight / Knows that it is all hallucinations / And one of them is true."[6]

Notes

1. Donald Revell, "Tithon," *Tantivy,* 43.
2. Ibid.
3. Ibid., 44.
4. Ibid., 52.
5. Ibid., 53.
6. Ibid.

Work Cited

Revell, Donald. "Tithon," *Tantivy.* Alice James, 2012, pp. 43–53.

STEPHANIE BURT

Donald Revell

"The Northeast Corridor" Chronicle of a Poet's Rebirth in His Rust Belt Poems

William Butler Yeats insisted that artists become their own opposites, assimilate what seems most remote. Otherwise, he thought, happiness would escape them. Donald Revell has followed Yeats's prescription more than once, changing his style, his tone and his "mask," with each decade of his twenty-five years of published work; the changes chart a man moving from gloom to happiness by way of multiple rebirths.

Each change in his style and mood reflects a changed locale. His early poems reflected his grim memories of The Bronx, where he grew up, and of industrial decline in upstate New York, where he lived as a young man. Soon after the poet settled in Denver in the 1980s, he became opaque, abstract, and mystical, as if his new residence demanded a divorce from places he had once lived. His most recent style reflects a happy second marriage, a newly confident Christian faith, and—not least—a move to the desert Southwest: his clear lines and joyful prospects match its stark, vivid colors and open skies. To read Revell's best poems in the order in which he wrote them is to partake of the pleasure of self-reinvention, and to watch a man's outlook rotate 180 degrees, from lost and disappointed to unlikely joy.

Most of Revell's new book of prose, *The Art of Attention*, describes the style and the beliefs he holds now. *The Art of Attention* does, however, mention his early poems of the 1980s: Revell calls them, slightingly, works of "dogged precision," cast in "dour iambics." He also writes in that same essay that "Location's inescapable."[1] Indeed, the 1980s poems reveal a man who often seems depressed because he cannot escape his locale: the poems are durable versions of a particularly Northeastern discontent.

One of his best, and last, poems in this early style is "The Northeast Corridor," a two-page poem from *New Dark Ages*. Revell has written that this poem began in a bar called the Iron Horse within the old, grimy, unrenovated Grand Central Station, but it's important to the poem that we don't know exactly where we are: "the bar in the commuter station" could be any of a dozen-odd uneasy spaces to drink while awaiting Amtrak or MARC or Metro-North. It looks, to Revell, like a theater showing a failed play:

> The bar in the commuter station steams
> like a ruin, its fourth wall open
> to the crowd and the fluttering timetables.
> In the farthest corner, the television
> crackles a torch song and a beaded gown.
> She is my favorite singer, dead when I was born.
> And I have been waiting for hours for a train,
> exhausted between connections to small cities,
> awake only in my eyes finding shelter
> in the fluttering ribbon of shadow
> around the dead woman singing on the screen.[2]

The "fourth wall"—the invisible partition between audience and actors, which protects the suspension of disbelief—has failed; the stage is "open / to the crowd" and to the timetables. The drinkers are here not to have fun but to kill time. Once, this Northeast held genuine pleasures—the pleasures of pre-rock popular song, preserved in frustrating imperfection by a "crackling" television— but such pleasures are not part of the speaker's life; they could never have been: "my favorite singer" was "dead before I was born." In such a place, the succession of hours, days, years, the forward movement of time, can bring nothing but trouble:

> Exhaustion is a last line of defense
> where time either stops dead or kills you.
> It teaches you to see what your eyes see
> without questions, without the politics
> of living in one city, dying in another.[3]

Suppressing questions, imposing a Lethean forgetfulness, this bar in New York City or Stamford or Baltimore becomes a kind of failed afterlife (as in Eugene O'Neill's *The Iceman Cometh*): commuters are shades, paying homage to "exhaustion," too tired even to ask questions, certainly too tired to understand "the politics" (that is, the social and ethical causes) behind what looks, right now, like a meaningless life.

Few page-long poems have sounded more so. That first stanza contains few full stops at line endings (five in sixteen lines), few places to pause and catch your breath, and even fewer suspenseful enjambments. Instead, Revell's music is an intentionally grinding plod, ending line after line at the end of a phrase, and ending eight of sixteen lines on unstressed syllables ("open," "cities," "politics," "another"): nothing seems ready to move.

While waiting for this train, in this decrepit environment, a tired-out Revell dwells on that time before his birth when life in Northeastern cities felt authentic and hopeful:

> How badly I would like to sleep now
> in the shadows beside real things or beside
> things that were real once, like the beaded gown
> on the television, like the debut
> of a song in New York in black and white
> when my parents were there. I feel sometimes
> my life was used up before I was born.
> My eyes sear backwards into my head
> to the makeshift of what I have already seen
> or heard described or dreamed about, too weary
> not to envy the world its useless outlines.[4]

He is the shade in Acheron, presenting a nostalgia for "things that were real once." He feels "too weary / not to envy the world its useless outlines," viewing the present as a collection of line drawings, all black and white. By the end of this second verse-paragraph, Revell seems to have boarded a train (perhaps during the stanza break), but though he is bone tired, he cannot sleep: instead, he feels as if he had already died, his eyes rolling backward into his head as his consciousness turns, with searing inevitability, toward the past. However fast his train moves forward, he cannot escape the feeling that he is moving backward, through urban history and through his own life: he seems to see, as the stanza continues,

> Books of photographs of New York in the forties.
> The dark rhombus of a window of a train
> rushing past my train. The dark halo
> around the body of a woman I love
> from something much farther than a distance.[5]

What is "farther than a distance," more remote than a physical remove? It must be either the separation imposed by death, or else the psychological separation imposed when a woman says to a man "I never want to see you again." The "woman I love" exists at a more than physical remove either because she has died (as Eurydice dies to the backward-looking Orpheus) or, more likely, because she is "dead to him."

We are reading a breakup poem, a poem of nearly metaphysical despair, and a poem of appalled reaction to a used-up, rusted-out, exhausted regional landscape: a poem similar to, but much more intellectually ambitious than, Richard Hugo's "Degrees of Gray in Philipsburg." Revell avoids Hugo's local consolations, avoids Hugo's moderately happy ending, and pursues instead a hallucinatory escape from any landscape or cityscape we could actually see. As the train seems to leave its underground station and chugs toward its challenging end, it also moves away from literal description toward general claims, such as the line with which the last stanza begins:

> The world is insatiable. It takes your legs off,
> it takes your arms and parades in front of you
> such wonderful things, such pictures of warm houses
> trellised along the sides with green so deep
> it is like black air, only transparent,
> of women singing, of trains of lithium
> on the awakening body of a landscape
> or across the backdrop of an old city
> steaming and high-shouldered as the nineteen-forties.[6]

The world as seen from a Northeastern train makes your legs hurt ("The world is insatiable. It takes your legs off"). The seats are cramped, provoking heavy drinking (getting "legless"), making Revell hunger for things and people and experiences he can no longer have. The attractive houses seen from a train must be only "pictures of warm houses," as remote from the present as dead singers in pearled gowns. The world in which they fit, the world in which Revell may find himself satisfied, is an impossible and hallucinatory past, a druggy "black air." Revell could have ended the poem in a moment of gloomy, smoky nostalgia. Instead, it ends this way:

> The world exhausts everything except my eyes
> because it is a long walk to the world
> begun before I was born. In the far corner
> the dead woman bows off stage. The television

crumples into a white dot as the last
train of the evening, my train, is announced.
I lived in one place. I want to die in another.[7]

The poet never reaches that place of "black air": he hasn't even caught his train! Though the poem has already portrayed a journey (and though it participates in a tradition of good poems about bad train rides—see Philip Larkin's "Dockery and Son," for instance), it has been stuck in the bleak bar all this time. As his train finally pulls in (or at least "is announced"), his last links to an imagined past disappear. Rather than conclude with the same harshly piled anti-climaxes that have characterized the poem thus far, Revell ends with an isolated, quotable line: "I lived in one place. I want to die in another."

Notes

1. Donald Revell, *The Art of Attention,* 102.
2. Revell, "The Northeast Corridor," *New Dark Ages,* 12.
3. Ibid.
4. Ibid.
5. Ibid.
6. Ibid., 12–13.
7. Ibid., 13.

Works Cited

Revell, Donald. *The Art of Attention: A Poet's Eye.* Graywolf, 2007.
Revell, Donald. *New Dark Ages.* Wesleyan University Press, 1990. Kindle edition.

Contributors

Geoffrey Babbitt currently teaches at Hobart and William Smith Colleges and holds a PhD from the University of Utah. His nonfiction has appeared or is forthcoming in *Pleiades, DIAGRAM, The Collagist, Drunken Boat, Confrontation,* and elsewhere, and his poetry has appeared or is forthcoming in *Notre Dame Review, CutBank, Colorado Review, Free Verse, TYPO, Witness,* and elsewhere.

Dan Beachy-Quick is a poet and essayist, author most recently of a study on John Keats, *A Brighter Word than Bright,* and a book of poems, *gentlessness.* His work has been supported by the Lannan and Guggenheim Foundations, and he teaches in the Master of Fine Arts (MFA) Writing Program at Colorado State University.

Bruce Bond is the author of twenty books, including *Blackout Starlight: New and Selected Poems 1997–2015* (E. Phillabaum Award, Louisiana State University Press, 2017), *Sacrum* (Four Way Books, 2017), *Gold Bee* (Helen C. Smith Award, Crab Orchard Award, Southern Illinois University Press, 2016), and *Immanent Distance: Poetry and the Metaphysics of the Near at Hand* (University of Michigan Press, 2015). Presently, he is a Regents' Professor of English at the University of North Texas.

Stephanie Burt is a professor of English at Harvard and the author of several books of poetry and criticism, among them *Belmont* (2013); *The Art of the Sonnet,* with David Mikics (2010); and *Close Calls with Nonsense* (2009). Essays and reviews appear regularly in several journals in Britain and America, including *ALH, Boston Review,* and the *New York Times Book Review.*

Peter Covino is an associate professor of English and creative writing at the University of Rhode Island. He is author of the poetry collections *The Right Place to Jump* (2012) and *Cut Off the Ears of Winter* (2005), both from New Issues Poetry & Prose, and he is co-editor of the collection *Essays on Italian American Literature and Culture* (Bordighera, 2012). His poems, translations, and essays have been widely published in the United States and in Italy, including in such places as *American Poetry Review; The Paris Review; The Yale Review;* the Modern Language Association textbook *Teaching Italian American Literature, Film, and Popular Culture;* and *The Penguin Anthology of Italian-American Writing.* He is one of the founding editors of the journal *Barrow Street* and of Barrow Street Press.

Kathryn Cowles's first book of poems, *Eleanor, Eleanor, not your real name,* won the Brunsman Poetry Book Prize. She has had recent poems and poem-photograph hybrids in the 2014 *Best American Experimental Writing Anthology* (Omnidawn), *DIAGRAM, Free Verse, Witness, The Offending Adam, Drunken Boat, Colorado Review,* and the Academy of American Poets Poem-a-Day. She earned her doctorate in poetry from the University of Utah and teaches at Hobart and William Smith Colleges in the Finger Lakes region of New York.

Dan Disney is an award-winning poet, academic writer, occasional translator, and book reviewer. His books include *Report from a Border* (Light-Trap, 2016) and *either, Orpheus* (University of Western Australia Publishing, 2016). He currently teaches in the English Literature Program at Sogang University in Seoul.

Norman Finkelstein is a poet and a literary critic who has written extensively about modern American poetry and Jewish American literature. His books of poetry include *The Ratio of Reason to Magic: New and Selected Poems* (Dos Madres, 2016) and the serial poem *Track* (Shearsman, 2012). His most recent book of criticism is *On Mount Vision: Forms of the Sacred in Contemporary American Poetry* (University of Iowa Press, 2010). He is a professor of English at Xavier University, where he has taught since 1980.

Eryn Green holds a PhD from the University of Denver and an MFA from the University of Utah. His first book, *Eruv* (Yale University Press, 2014), won the 2013 Yale Series of Younger Poets Prize, judged by Carl Phillips.

Andrew Haley is the author of *Good Eurydice* (Otis Nebula, 2011). His translation of Leopold Lugones's *Metamusic* appeared in *La*

Cinta Transportadora by Ulises Conti (Mansalva, 2015). His essays, poems, stories, and translations have appeared in *Color Pastel Poesía, BlazeVOX, Kill Author, Fanzine, Stop Smiling,* and other places.

Nathan Hauke is the author of *Every Living One* (Horse Less, 2015), *In the Marble of Your Animal Eyes* (Publication Studio, 2013), and five chapbooks, including most recently *Tinder Is a Hatchet Job* (LRL Textile Series). His poems have been anthologized in *Hick Poetics* (Lost Roads, 2015) and *The Arcadia Project: North American Postmodern Pastoral* (Ahsahta, 2012).

Richie Hofmann's debut collection of poems, *Second Empire* (Alice James, 2015), won the Beatrice Hawley Award. His honors include the Ruth Lilly Poetry Fellowship and the Academy of American Poets Prize.

Mark Irwin is the author of nine collections of poetry, including *A Passion According to Green* (New Issues Poetry & Prose, 2017). Other recent collections include *American Urn: Selected Poems 1987–2014* (Ashland Poetry, 2015) and *Large White House Speaking* (New Issues Poetry & Prose, 2013). His collection of essays, *Monster: Distortion, Abstraction, & Originality in Contemporary American Poetry,* was published by Peter Lang in 2017. He teaches in the PhD in Creative Writing & Literature Program at the University of Southern California.

Rebecca Lindenberg is the author of *The Logan Notebooks* (Center for Literary Publishing, 2014) and *Love, an Index* (McSweeney's, 2012). She is the recipient of an Amy Lowell Fellowship, a National Endowment for the Arts Literature Grant, and residencies from the Fine Arts Work Center at Provincetown and the MacDowell Arts Colony. She holds a PhD in literature and creative writing from the University of Utah. More information can be found at: www.rebecca-lindenberg.squarespace.com

Jacqueline Lyons is author of the poetry books *Earthquake Daily* (New Michigan Press, 2017), *Lost Colony* (Dancing Girl, 2009), and *The Way They Say Yes Here* (Hanging Loose, 2004), which won a Peace Corps Writers Best Poetry Book Award. She has received a National Endowment for the Arts Poetry Fellowship, the *Indiana Review* Poetry Prize, Utah Arts Council Awards in both poetry and nonfiction, and a Nevada Arts Council Fellowship in nonfiction. She is currently an assistant professor of English-Creative Writing at California Lutheran University.

Tod Marshall earned an MFA from Eastern Washington University, and graduated with his PhD from the University of Kansas. He directs the Writing Concentration and coordinates the Visiting Writers Series at Gonzaga University, where he is the Robert K. and Ann J. Powers Endowed Professor in the Humanities. He served as the Washington State Poet Laureate from 2016–18.

Michelle Mitchell Foust is the author of *Circassian Girl* (2008) and *Imago Mundi* (2005), both from Elixir Press. An anthology she edited with Tony Barnstone, *Poems Dead and Undead,* was released by Everyman Press in 2014. Their second anthology, *Monster Verse: Poems Human and Inhuman,* followed from Everyman in 2015.

Andrew S. Nicholson is an assistant professor-in-residence at the University of Nevada, Las Vegas, where he was a Schaeffer Fellow in poetry. His first book of poetry, *A Lamp Brighter than Foxfire,* was published by the Center for Literary Publishing in 2015.

Marjorie Perloff teaches courses and writes on twentieth and twenty-first century poetry and poetics, both Anglo-American and from a comparatist perspective, as well as on intermedia and the visual arts. She is Professor Emerita of English at Stanford University and Florence R. Scott Professor of English Emerita at the University of Southern California. She is an elected fellow of the American Academy of Arts and Sciences and the American Philosophical Society and is the former president of the Modern Language Association.

Derek Pollard is co-author with Derek Henderson of the book *Inconsequentia* (BlazeVOX, 2010). His poetry, criticism, and translations have appeared in *Best of the Net, Colorado Review, Drunken Boat, Edgar Allan Poe Review, Six-Word Memoirs on Love & Heartbreak,* and *They Said: A Multi-Genre Anthology of Contemporary Collaborative Writing,* among numerous other anthologies and journals. He holds a PhD in English from the University of Nevada, Las Vegas, where he was a Beverly Rogers, Carol C. Harter Black Mountain Institute Fellow in poetry and served as associate editor at *Interim: A Journal* *of Poetry and Poetics.* More information can be found at http://dpol-lard.squarespace.com.

Mary Ann Samyn is the author of six collections of poetry, most recently *Air, Light, Dust, Shadow, Distance,* winner of the 2017 42 Miles Press Prize; and *My Life in Heaven,* winner of the 2012 *FIELD* Prize (Oberlin College Press). She is a professor of English at West Virginia University, where she teaches in the MFA program.

Susan M. Schultz is author of several books of poetry and poetic prose, including *Dementia Blog, "She's Welcome to Her Disease": Dementia Blog, Vol. 2* (Singing Horse, 2013), and several volumes of an ongoing project, *Memory Cards,* most recently from Talisman House (2016). She also wrote *A Poetics of Impasse in Modern and Contemporary American Poetry* (University of Alabama Press, 2005). She is editor and publisher of Tinfish Press out of her home office in Kāne'ohe, Hawai'i. She teaches at the University of Hawai'i at Mānoa.

Nick Twemlow's first book of poems, *Palm Trees,* received the Norma Farber First Book Award from the Poetry Society of America. New poems have recently appeared in *Lana Turner, Jubilat, Court Green,* and *The Paris Review.* He coedits Canarium Books and teaches at Emory University. His second book, *Attributed to the Harrow Painter,* was published by the University of Iowa Press in 2017 as part of the Kuhl House Poets Series.

Eric Weinstein's poems have appeared or are forthcoming in *AGNI, AQR, Barrow Street, The Believer, Court Green, Crazyhorse, The Iowa Review, The New Yorker, Ploughshares, The Southern Review, The Yale Review,* and others. He lives in Los Angeles.